Peak Performance Table Tennis

CHURCHIB

To my beautiful wife

KEVIN FINN

PEAK PERFORMANCE TABLE TENNIS

UNLOCK YOUR POTENTIAL
AND PLAY LIKE THE PROS

MEYER & MEYER SPORT

British Library of Cataloguing in Publication Data
A catalogue record for this book is available from the British Library

Peak Performance Table Tennis
Maidenhead: Meyer & Meyer Sport (UK) Ltd., 2022
ISBN: 978-1-78255-228-4

Aachen, Auckland, Beirut, Dubai, Hägendorf, Hong Kong, Indianapolis, Cairo, Cape Town, Manila, Maidenhead, New Delhi, Singapore, Sydney, Tehran, Vienna

Member of the World Sport Publishers' Association (WSPA), www.w-s-p-a.org
Printed by Versa Press, East Peoria, IL, USA
Printed in the United States of America

ISBN: 978-1-78255-228-4
Email: info@m-m-sports.com
www.thesportspublisher.com

CONTENTS

A NEW ERA

"The balls are bigger and you need to be much more fit—it takes a lot of power when you play. You cannot practice like before."

—Jan Ove Waldner on the plastic ball

As a rule, table tennis players are not too fond of change. We love our sport. We love spin. We love speed. Pips players, such as myself, love the challenge of changing and manipulating the spin in a disruptive way. We spend inordinate amounts of time obsessing over our equipment until we get things just right. . . and then, the ITTF comes along and throws a wrench in things with a major change to the rules.

I've spent over ten years frequenting the most popular online table tennis forums, and I can confidently report to you these changes are usually met with horror, shock, doom, and gloom. To many of us, it feels like rather than attempting to enlighten the public on the intricacies of table tennis through better education, coverage, and analysis that the ITTF chooses to "dumb down" the sport by making it slower and less spinny—the very things that make our sport so unique! Still, we begrudgingly accept the changes, and once the dust settles, we adapt and press onwards. But there is a clear pattern at play here.

Over the past 20 years, nearly all the major changes implemented by the ITTF can be explained by two driving forces:

1. The desire to make the sport more spectator-friendly to boost viewership and worldwide appeal.

2. The desire to increase the safety of our sport by reducing exposure to volatile organic compounds and ending the mass production of celluloid (which is highly flammable).

Major Changes to the Game in the Past 20 Years

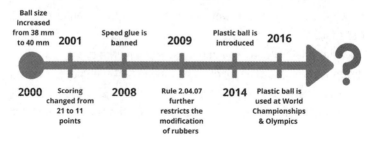

Interestingly, regardless of the rationale, each change ends up reducing both the speed *and* spin athletes can impart on the ball. The latest switch to plastic balls exemplifies this perfectly. It was done out of safety concerns but included a sneaky change to the size of the ball as well, making it slightly larger on average. Unsurprisingly, both anecdotal reports from players and scientific research show the new plastic balls have less speed and spin compared with celluloid balls. [1]

With no speed glue or boosting allowed, attempting to compensate for the loss in spin and speed with faster and faster equipment is, at best, a Band-Aid solution—and with some of the newest generation of rubbers costing nearly $100 apiece, it's an expensive one at that. This leaves us with one viable option: upgrade the *player*.

In the research phase of this book, I read dozens of studies about the physical and nutritional demands of table tennis. In these studies, when coaches and players were surveyed, one common thread was a decided lack of focus on both physical training [2] and nutrition and supplementation [3] when compared with skills training and tactics. This is the old paradigm. It's time for table tennis to advance and adopt a more integrated view of training that views physical, nutritional, psychological, social, and emotional skills as vital parts of the yearly plan.

The game has changed. Will you?

THE ORIGINS OF THIS BOOK

The amount of quality information available to table tennis players today is astounding. As a young adolescent, I remember searching fruitlessly for table tennis books at my local bookstore and library.

Every once in a while, I was lucky enough to find one, but that was a rare occurrence. Now, between books, blogs, magazines, and social media platforms, such as YouTube, the average player has easy access to a nearly endless supply of content right at their fingertips.

And yet, as I survey the landscape of table tennis-related content, I have not found a truly comprehensive look into the realms of physical training and nutrition. There are a few books floating around that appear to do so, but closer inspection reveals them to be nothing more than shoddy, "copy/paste" jobs where half the book contains generic recipes and the rest is recycled content used for a dozen different sports. Needless to say, I think the table tennis community deserves better!

I first noticed this need back in 2016, so I published a free, internet eBook titled *The Table Tennis Player's Guide to Health and Fitness*. My goal for the guide was to provide the typical club player with some evidence-based guidelines for improving their health and fitness without needing to quit their day job to make it happen. It outlined a "minimum effective dose" approach that I felt would be ideal for casual and amateur players. Thousands of downloads later, the same questions kept cropping up from my readers:

> *What if I'm not after the 'minimum,' but instead seek optimal? What's the next step? How can I more directly apply this information to improve my table tennis performance?*

I decided to answer those questions with a second edition, so I took a deep dive into the literature regarding sports psychology, motor learning, advanced periodization strategies, recovery protocols, injury prevention, and other novel ways to improve performance and athleticism. I also read every study I could find that was performed directly on table tennis players. This whole process opened a can of worms that resulted in well over a year of research and over a hundred pages of notes, references, and ideas.

What started as a revision turned into a complete rewrite. I have kept the skeleton of certain sections of the eBook, but what you hold in your hands now is another beast entirely. This is a fully referenced book chocked full of the latest sports science aimed solely at improving your table tennis performance. It is both a toolkit and a blueprint for the advancement of your athletic development. Whether you're a coach, a professional, or just a passionate club player, this book will uncover paths to improvement you didn't know existed. The journey will not be an easy one, but worthwhile things rarely are.

WHAT IS PEAK PERFORMANCE?

I've titled this book, *Peak Performance Table Tennis*, but what does that mean exactly? What does it mean to achieve peak performance? Rest assured, I will be going into the exact details of this at great length in this book, but for now, a quick analogy will suffice: think of a Swiss watch. On its face, it appears quite simple. Three hands—two relatively motionless, while a third moves gracefully and reliably around the track. Peek inside, however, and the truth is revealed: behind the scenes, there is an intricate series of cogs functioning seamlessly in concert.

Likewise, an athlete who has achieved peak performance plays in a way that looks effortless on the surface, but hidden underneath is a vast network of machinery that has been carefully calibrated, oiled, and designed for one purpose—to win!

The Components of Peak Performance

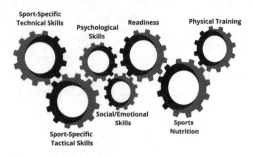

Let's briefly look at each component in turn:

→ **Sport-specific technical skills:** Your ability to execute the strokes required with good form.
→ **Sport-specific tactical skills:** The strategic decisions and actions you take to gain an advantage.
→ **Psychological skills:** Your ability to focus and think clearly under pressure.
→ **Social/emotional skills:** Your ability to maintain a confident and positive emotional state during play, and, more broadly, your ability to maintain and develop positive relationships with those around you and lead a balanced life.
→ **Readiness:** The state of being physically, mentally, and emotionally recovered so you can bring your full abilities to bear.
→ **Sports nutrition:** Dietary manipulations that ensure performance is fueled maximally and body composition stays optimal.
→ **Physical training:** Supplemental training to make your body stronger, faster, more enduring, and more resilient.

In this book, I comprehensively cover these seven domains and provide actionable steps for you to take to ensure you are putting yourself in the best possible position to play your best when it matters most. After all, in the end, it doesn't matter how good of a player you are on paper, it matters how good you are when it counts.

WHAT YOU WILL GET FROM THIS BOOK

Cutting edge sports science, curated specifically for table tennis athletes—a deep dive into sports nutrition, supplementation, training methodologies, holistic periodization, advanced recovery tactics, injury prevention, psychological and emotional skills training, motor learning, and more. I will shed light on the intangible elements that separate a good athlete from a great one.

WHAT YOU WON'T GET FROM THIS BOOK

This book is *not* designed to teach you the game of table tennis.

As a strength and conditioning specialist and speed and agility coach, I'm confident in putting out information on how to improve athletic performance. In the world of table tennis, however, I'm nothing more than a scrub, middle-of-the-pack player who happens to be passionate about promoting our sport. My areas of expertise are in teaching, coaching, researching, and experimenting. As an athlete, I'm nothing special!

So, there will be no discussion of how to perform basic strokes, the rules of the game, equipment, or in-depth analysis of top players. But let's be real; tactics aside, you're not going to learn how to play table tennis from reading a book. That's done best in person with an experienced coach.

For the sake of completeness, I do have a section touching on the technical and tactical sides of peak performance, but the purpose of those chapters is to show how those cogs fit into the rest of the machinery rather than providing specific instructions regarding technique or tactics. It's a big picture view that focuses more on the *how* than the *what.*

HOW TO USE THIS BOOK

I did not design this book to be read front-to-back one time. In fact, I encourage you to skip around to the sections that interest you the most first. Think of this book more as a reference to be returned to many times, depending on the stage of your athletic development and your individual needs. As you read, I recommend jotting down notes, highlighting, underlining, and annotating as you go. There are dozens upon dozens of performance-enhancing strategies revealed in this book. To attempt to apply them all at once would be overwhelming. Instead, pick a handful of items and start making changes until they become second nature. You can slowly start incorporating other elements as time goes on. The key thing to avoid is trying to overhaul everything, becoming overwhelmed, and ending up doing nothing as a result. Some of these changes may seem trivial or insignificant when viewed in isolation, but taken together, they will have a dramatic impact.

"I'm not saying that if you eat good you will be 20% better, but maybe you will be 1% or 2% better, and maybe if you do some physical training you will be 3% or 5% better, or maybe if you improve your sleep you will get 1% better. I mean, it's not one part where you can say this is very important, if you do that you will be immediately 20% better. You have to think about many things." [4]

—*Michael Maze on the importance of attending to tiny details (Lightly edited for clarity).*

Dave Brailsford, the former performance director of British Cycling, calls this attention to detail the "aggregation of marginal gains." This is the philosophy that tiny improvements in several areas will result in significant change. This book is essentially a collection of hundreds of tiny improvements that you can make to your training and lifestyle. You may never be able to compete with certain players based on raw talent alone, but if you're willing to put in the work—to attend to those tiny details that most overlook—you may just find yourself on the champion's podium. Hard work beats talent when talent doesn't work hard.

Are you ready to get to work?

GET AN EDGE OVER YOUR COMPETITION WITH PERSONALIZED ONLINE PERFORMANCE COACHING

The information found in this book is more than enough to get your feet wet, but the real magic happens when these principles are applied and expertly tailored to your exact needs by an experienced coach.

If you are a professional player or dedicated enthusiast who is determined to leave no stone unturned in your development as an athlete, apply today to join my team!

To apply to become a PPTT Athlete, use the QR Code below or go to https://peakperformancetabletennis.com/coaching

SECTION I

TECHNICAL AND TACTICAL SKILLS

SECTION OVERVIEW

In this section, we will cover the technical and tactical domains of peak performance. As I stated in the introduction, I'm not going to be focusing on teaching the specifics of correct form or diving into detailed tactical plays against various styles. Instead, I'll be focusing on the *how*:

→ How can you arrange a practice session to best promote rapid learning?
→ How do various coaching cues and methods impact learning?
→ How can one begin to develop a personal strategy?
→ How are tactics developed and honed?

First up, we have a chapter on rapid learning techniques to help improve your technical skills through more efficient practice. After that, a chapter on tactical skills introduces the "Vitruvian Man" exercise as well as my philosophy regarding tactics.

TAPPING INTO THE MATRIX: IMPROVE YOUR TABLE TENNIS WITH RAPID LEARNING

"Be stubborn about your goals and flexible about your methods."

—Unknown

Remember that scene from *The Matrix* where Neo is hooked up to a computer and they upload black-belt level mastery of dozens of martial arts disciplines directly into his brain? In minutes, he was able to learn what would have taken many lifetimes to learn in the real world. Imagine if you could do the same for table tennis...

Jan-Ove Waldner's ball control and artistry, Ryu Seung-min's footwork, Wang Liqin's raw power, Xu Xin's spin. . . I suppose you'd end up with a player who looks a lot like Ma Long. Perhaps that's how he's been so dominant? Someone check the footage to see if he has those Matrix-style "port holes" in the back of his head!

On a more serious note, ever since I saw that scene from *The Matrix*, I've always been fascinated with the concept of learning. Is it actually possible to "hack" the learning process? How do different methods of practice impact learning? In search of answers, I took a deep dive into the literature regarding motor learning and how it relates to optimizing sports performance. This chapter is a distillation of the most relevant and useful learning tactics I came come across—most of which can be neatly dropped right into your existing practice schedule. To set your expectations accurately, don't expect anything revolutionary. This isn't science fiction, and unlike *The Matrix*, there are no quick fixes that can substitute for good, old-fashioned hard work.

Instead, I will provide some suggestions to help you better utilize the time you *already have* so you can eke out a little more progress. I have intentionally chosen some strategies that seem relatively novel and counterintuitive because, in doing so, I hope to offer you some untrodden paths you may have never considered. Don't feel like you need to try to implement everything from this chapter all at once; instead, pick a strategy or two and simply give them a try. If you notice a positive difference, great! If not, try another or simply go back to what you were doing.

FUN FACT:

Hugo Calderano, the first player from Latin America to reach the Top 10 of the ITTF World Rankings, likes to use a Rubik's Cube to train himself to both think and *move* quickly at the same time. He can solve it in under 20 seconds!

WHAT DOES THE RESEARCH SAY REGARDING MOTOR LEARNING?

Motor learning is the process of acquiring and mastering simple and complex movement patterns through practice or experience. Although the data regarding motor learning is somewhat messy, I've done my best to make recommendations based on where I felt the weight of the evidence lies. I came across one integrative review by Nicholas Soderstrom and Robert Bjork titled "Learning Versus Performance: An Integrative Review" [1] that I found particularly enlightening and will be drawing from heavily in this chapter. It matches both my own reading of the literature as well as my personal experience teaching and coaching individuals over the past 10 years. Before diving into the review, we should first examine the terms *performance* and *learning* in the way they define them:

PERFORMANCE

"The temporary fluctuations in behavior or knowledge that can be observed and measured during or immediately after the acquisition process."

In other words, how well can you execute the task *right now*?

Example:
After practicing your forehand push in a given session, you are able to execute the movement consistently and with good form at the session's end. That reflects good performance.

LEARNING

"The relatively permanent changes in behavior or knowledge that support long-term retention and transfer."

Example:
How well can you perform that same forehand push a couple of days later? The extent to which you can reproduce your previous performance reflects your learning.

The reason this distinction matters is that there is a counterintuitive relationship between these two terms, as Soderstrom and Bjork describe here:

> *The distinction between learning and performance is crucial because there now exists overwhelming empirical evidence showing that considerable learning can occur in the absence of any performance gains and, conversely, that substantial changes in performance often fail to translate into corresponding changes in learning. Perhaps even more compelling, certain experimental manipulations have been shown to confer opposite effects on learning and performance, such that the conditions that produce the most error during acquisition are often the very conditions that produce the most learning.*

This means the practice protocol that produces the most substantial gains in performance within a session may not necessarily translate into the best performance gains *long term*. This distinction is useful on two fronts.

First, knowing this fact should bolster your resolve during a training session where many errors are being made. In this situation, it's easy to feel like you're not improving or are even *regressing* due to your poor performance. The studies outlined in this review, however, demonstrate that learning can occur even in the absence of performance. This should be a rallying cry for you in the thick of training and allow you to maintain a level of enthusiasm and clear-headedness that you may not have had otherwise. Secondly, it also opens the door to alternative methods of training that you might have otherwise discounted due to a high number of initial errors. So, with this in mind, let's look at a few of the key concepts found within this review.

CONCEPT ONE: LATENT LEARNING, FATIGUE, AND OVERLEARNING

Imagine performing a basic drill where you're working on your forehand loop against a block. As mental and physical fatigue sets in and you begin to make more mistakes, does continuing the drill beyond that point only serve to reinforce those mistakes? Should you terminate the drill as soon as your performance begins to decline in order to maintain "perfect practice"? Not necessarily. Soderstrom and Bjork identify three interacting concepts that explain how you may still be benefiting from practicing a drill, even though performance has stagnated or declined:

> The learning versus performance distinction can be traced back decades when researchers of latent learning, overlearning, and fatigue demonstrated that long-lasting learning could occur while training or acquisition performance provided no indication that learning was actually taking place.

For example, Soderstrom and Bjork cite one study [2] where trainees from the Air Force performed a rotary pursuit task where they manually tracked a target with a wand. The researchers manipulated the rest intervals between trials in a way that caused some of the trials to be performed in a fatigued state. Unsurprisingly, the subjects' performance suffered on the individual trials performed while fatigued, but when they were retested (after fatigue had dissipated), their performance *improved despite the earlier decline*. So, learning can indeed occur even when short-term performance is masked by fatigue.

This doesn't mean fatigue has *no* consequences on learning, however. There is research that shows motor learning occurs at a slower rate when the task is performed in a fatigued state [2a]. Furthermore, the negative effects seem to persist even in subsequent sessions when fatigue has dissipated. Thus, you should take steps to minimize fatigue as much as possible when learning (the "distribution of practice" method outlined in the next section is good for this), but at the same time, don't lose hope and abandon training simply because you are making mistakes while learning. It's a balancing act!

Soderstrom and Bjork also identify *overlearning* as a critical part of improving long-term retention of a skill. As a musician, this is a concept with which I am intimately familiar. If you plan on performing a piece in front of a group of people, it is not enough to simply practice until you can perform it with no errors. To reliably perform it well, you must practice until you can perform the piece perfectly, many times in a row under a variety of conditions. This is overlearning. It's performing repetition after repetition even *after* mastery seems to have been achieved. This is the reason dedicating enough "table time" is so important to developing your skills as a table tennis player. You may be able to learn how to perform a forehand loop in relatively short order, but how reliably will you be able to implement that stroke within the context of a competitive match?

Learning isn't enough, you must *overlearn* your strokes if you want to be truly consistent.

THE LESSON

I'm probably not alone in feeling frustrated when I make a large number of errors during a drill or practice session. The poor performance causes a feeling of wasted potential—like I'm not benefiting from the time spent training. Consequently, this can cause a loss of focus and drive, ultimately reducing the quality of the session. I also tend to brush off strokes that feel too easy (pushes, I'm looking at you), when perhaps a bit of overlearning is precisely what is needed to increase my consistency of these basic strokes during tight matches.

Being aware of the concepts of latent learning, fatigue, and overlearning can be a useful way to shift your mindset. Remember, if you are making a large number of errors and performance seems to be declining or simply stagnating in a given session, you are still "planting the seeds" of long-term learning deep below the surface. Improvements are being made. Don't give up! It's perhaps a tad cliché to say "learn from your mistakes," but the research indicates that we indeed do just that!

CONCEPT TWO: DISTRIBUTION OF PRACTICE— MAKING YOUR STROKES "STICKY"

Now that we've established that learning and performance do not always directly correlate, let's explore some ways in which that may impact your training. Suppose you have 30 minutes to perform drills with your partner and you have three strokes you'd like to work on—a backhand counter, a forehand push, and a forehand loop. Which approach would you suspect to be superior?

→ 10 minutes devoted to each stroke before moving on to the next one.
→ 5 minutes devoted to each stroke before moving on (allowing each stroke to be revisited one additional time).

The first option, typically referred to in the literature as "blocked" or "massed" practice, allows you to really dig in and learn each stroke in depth. Research shows this would likely result in better performance of each stroke by the end of that session. The latter, "distributed practice" option, however, would likely result in better long-term retention of the strokes.

Think of the difference between cramming for a test the night before (only to forget everything immediately after taking the test), and distributing that same amount of studying over a period of days. Most would clearly recognize the second option as the superior choice for long-term learning, but we don't typically carry this concept over to individual sessions. The authors of this review point to research by Shea and Morgan, [3] which shows that the "interleaving" approach to distributing practice seems to promote long-term retention of skills. They also found that participants who had practiced the skills in a more random fashion rather than in a completely fixed manner were better able to execute *new* response patterns, allowing the athlete to utilize that skill more effectively under a wider variety of contexts.

The benefits of a distributed practice schedule are particularly apparent when attempting to master complex motor skills. [4] Since many of the strokes performed in table tennis are complex in nature, the table tennis player should strongly consider utilizing a distributed practice schedule when training. This is supported by at least one study [5] where researchers studied table tennis players and found a distributed practice schedule resulted in better performance in topspin forehands compared to a massed practice schedule.

This is not to say that one should *always* default to distributed practice when training. If a player has not had enough of an opportunity to grasp the fundamentals of a stroke, jumping right into a highly distributed practice schedule may be too overwhelming. In a 2012 study, [6] Asif Ali and colleagues point out that practice schedules that cause high levels of contextual interference (as distributed practice does) may present too great a challenge for learners, and they cite several studies that support this notion. Thus, it may be best to follow a massed practice schedule when first learning a brand-new stroke and then to hone that skill through distributed practice. There's both an art and a science here, so you may need to experiment a little to find the balance best for you.

THE LESSON

Ever practice a stroke during training and seem to have it down pat, only to find you're back to square one once you try to implement it in a game? I know I have! To help make your strokes more "sticky," try distributing your practice on two fronts:

→ *Within* sessions: Use the "interleaving" approach described in the beginning of this section to allow each skill to be revisited additional times within a single session.
  • So rather than devoting three 10-minute blocks for three separate skills, try six 5-minute blocks.

→ *Between* sessions: Up the frequency of your training when possible, even if the total time spent training per week remains the same.

- Rather than devoting 8 hours per week spread over two sessions, try four sessions at 2 hours each.
- Consider "two-a-days" to further break down your training. So, rather than training for 3 hours in the evening, perform a 1.5-hour morning session and a 1.5-hour evening session.

Seo Hyo-won, the 2013 winner of the Korean Open is a prime example of the latter method of distributing practice, as she reportedly splits her training into four daily sessions: "I work out for an hour at sunrise, 2 hours in the morning, 2 and a half hours in the afternoon, and another hour at nighttime. Altogether about 6.5 hours each day." [7]

Remember, this style of training may result in a greater total number of errors made on a session-to-session basis, but will ultimately lead to better retention of the skills practiced. Soderstrom and Bjork point to the "reloading hypothesis" to explain why this occurs:

> *Distributed practice encourages learners to reload or reproduce the to-be-learned motor skills during acquisition, which is a potent learning event, despite appearing not to be during acquisition. . . the spacing inserted between practice sessions results in a temporary loss of access to the relevant motor commands. The effortful processing required to reload the commands during distributed practice appears to facilitate learning but impede short-term performance, compared with blocked (massed) practice in which skills are performed over and over again.*

So, while you may feel like you've taken a step backward at first, you'll be taking two steps *forward* once it's time to put your skills to the test!

CONCEPT THREE: PRACTICE VARIABILITY

One of the things I stress a lot in this book is the law of specificity. One's main focus when attempting to improve a skill should be to devote more quality practice time to performing the exact skill you're trying to improve. There is some evidence, however, that a certain amount of variability—that is, an introduction of related *but different* skills, and/or the manipulation of the conditions of practicing the target skill—may lead to better long-term learning and transfer of said skill.

This is where the concept of *practice variability* comes in. For example, let's say you're a player who likes to stay very close to the table and play aggressive topspins, common sense would dictate that you should practice nearly all your shots from close to the table to mimic match conditions. Specificity, right? Well, interestingly, there may be a benefit to introducing some mid-range topspins into your drills and practice sessions. Not to merely cover your bases in case you get pushed back and happen to have a rally from that distance, but to actually improve your shots at the table as well!

The review cites two studies to support this notion: one in basketball players [8] and one in tennis players. [9] In both these studies, the participants were grouped in either fixed practice conditions (such as practicing free throws exclusively from the free throw line), or variable practice conditions (practicing free throws from multiple distances in addition to the regulation 12-foot distance). And in both studies, the variable practice group outperformed the fixed practice group. Soderstrom and Bjork point to the *schema theory* as a possible explanation for why variable practice seems to promote long-term learning:

> *The schema theory of motor control claims that variable practice—that is, practicing iterations of a skill that are related to but different from the target skill—fosters long-term learning because it sensitizes one to the general motor program, or schema, underlying a skill.*

This has been demonstrated in a study involving table tennis players as well. In a study titled, "The effect of consistent and varied follow-through practice schedules on learning a table tennis backhand," the researchers asked players to practice their backhand stroke in a fixed or variable manner. They found practicing the follow-through in a random-variable fashion "enhanced learning of the preceding shot compared with blocked-variable practice or no follow-through instructions." [10]

Even something as seemingly innocuous as a change in venue when practicing may positively impact your learning! The authors point to several studies that show studying material in various locations results in superior retention when compared with studying the same material in one location. [11–12] I'm sure you've experienced how playing in an unfamiliar club can have a detrimental effect on your performance—particularly if you are not used to doing so. And, since tournaments are often in unfamiliar locations, it makes sense to vary the location of your practice sessions as well, to help train your ability to perform in unfamiliar venues.

So, if you have multiple clubs in your area, but happen to strongly prefer one due to superior playing conditions, you might want to consider rotating in other clubs from time to time to ensure you're able to transfer your skills to other venues and recreate your performance under a variety of conditions.

THE LESSON

Experiment with varying the distance and location from which you perform certain strokes in order to better grasp the movement parameters and underlying motor skills required to play the stroke. When possible, try to train in a variety of venues to both increase learning and to mitigate the reduction in performance that can occur when playing in unfamiliar environments.

CONCEPT FOUR: WHEN LESS IS MORE—"HANDS OFF" COACHING AND NONLINEAR PEDAGOGY

As a teacher, trainer, and father, I know how tempting it is to explain things thoroughly and take a "hands on" approach to teaching a skill. I go through this daily when trying to get my three-year-old son to dress himself! This also happens to be when the potential drawbacks of this approach become painfully apparent. At the end of the day, who is *really* putting on those pajamas? Me (through gritted teeth) or my son (whose body resembles something approximating Jell-O). At some point, my "helping" him is really just a means of expediting the process while delaying his ability to perform the task independently.

Anyone with kids can relate to the above, but what about when the learner is a motivated athlete? Physically guiding the athlete through an unfamiliar movement pattern seems like a commonsense approach to teaching, but is it effective? Soderstrom and Bjork reviewed the literature and concluded that it may not be. Although physically guiding learners through the desired motions seems to improve initial performance and reduce errors, it can actually *harm* long-term learning. Instead, having the athlete observe the stroke first and then "testing" the athlete without further guidance may be a superior starting place. From there, the instructor can begin to identify which errors need to be specifically addressed and which are simply due to random variation and natural inconsistencies in the stroke. By cueing too early, you may overburden the learner and "short circuit" some of the *positive* aspects of the learner's movement they would have otherwise intuitively performed. As Nick Winkelman, the head of Athletic Performance & Science for Irish rugby would say, "Coach the *signal* not the noise."

One effective way of teaching a stroke without excessive explicit instructions is to use an analogy. In a study performed on novice table tennis players, [13] researchers compared explicit instruction versus instruction by analogy. The explicit learning group was given a set of instructions that detailed exactly how to hit a forehand topspin. The analogy group was simply told to imagine a right-angled triangle and to swing his or her racket up along its hypotenuse while hitting the ball. At the end of the trial, they found that novice table tennis players who learned the forehand topspin stroke by analogy performed better, had a better *implicit* grasp of the stroke, and their skills held up better under pressure compared with the explicit learning group. The authors state that the effectiveness of an analogy hinges on its ability to "integrate the complex rule structure of the to-be-learned skill in a simple biomechanical metaphor that can be reproduced by the learner" and that "Most importantly, the essential rules needed to impart topspin do not need to be explicated; they remain disguised in the right-angled triangle analogy."

Another study, performed by Fatemeh Valeh and colleagues, had similar findings [14]. In this study, 22 novice level girls aged 9–11 years old were randomly split into two different learning groups:

→ **Linear Pedagogy (LP):** A "traditional" approach to teaching where all participants were taught to perform the forehand stroke the same way with careful supervision on proper form, lots of repetition, and prescriptive instructions.
  • **Example:** Textbook form is taught via internal focus cues (feet shoulder width apart, rotate at the waist, etc.) with hand-over-hand instruction and lots of repetition through drilling.
→ **Nonlinear Pedagogy (NP):** A student-centered approach that manipulates the constraints of tasks so the learner can explore functional movement solutions. Less emphasis is placed on explicit instruction and more autonomy is given to the learner.
  • **Example:** Students see a demonstration of a good forehand stroke and then are encouraged to recreate the stroke in their own way. Cues are external and outcome based such as "hit the ball to make a rainbow arc above the net." Things like ball size and net height may be manipulated as well.

The study included five stages: pretest, acquisition, immediate retention, delayed retention, and transfer stages (four weeks later). The accuracy of the strokes performed on the tests was recorded by cameras and scored by an examiner. In the end, both groups improved their scores, but the NP group had *slightly better* results— although the differences did not reach statistical significance.

THE LESSON

As I've become more experienced as a trainer, I've found that when it comes to cueing form and technique, oftentimes, less is more. If you are attempting to coach another table tennis player and teach him or her how to perform a stroke, resist the urge to jump right into hand-over-hand guidance and lots of detailed instructions. Instead, try a more minimalist approach: go with the "test first" method and allow them to feel out the stroke for themselves first. Use analogies when possible and don't overburden the player with multiple cues. Keep it simple.

Furthermore, utilizing nonlinear pedagogy techniques when teaching new skills may result in equal (or slightly superior) learning compared with linear pedagogy. NP also has the added benefit of potentially improving decision making and creativity in players as they are given more freedom to explore solutions autonomously. I'm not saying there is no place for LP. A good coach should flexibly utilize both approaches to meet the unique needs of each learner. NP is just another tool in the belt!

WRAPPING UP

This concludes my summarization of the findings from "Learning versus Performance: An Integrative Review." Taken together, many of these tips can be grouped under what Soderstrom and Bjork refer to as "desirable difficulties"—interventions that make learning more difficult and induce more errors, but result in superior long-term learning. I'll leave you with this quote which sums it up nicely:

Expediting acquisition performance today does not necessarily translate into the type of learning that will be evident tomorrow. On the contrary, conditions that slow or induce more errors during instruction often lead to better long-term learning outcomes, and thus instructors and students, however disinclined to do so, should consider abandoning the path of least resistance with respect to their own teaching and study strategies.

In the next section, I will outline a few more learning strategies I picked up while perusing the literature.

A Note to Coaches: Research demonstrates that even a sham, "placebo" intervention can measurably improve learning provided the learner *expects* it to work [15]. The more "buy in" you can get from your athletes regarding the training techniques you employ, the more effective your sessions will be. Framing the strategies discussed in this chapter as evidence-based "learning hacks," can be an ethical way to further enhance learning by adding a placebo effect on top of the already demonstrated benefits shown by science.

ACCLIMATIZATION TRAINING

If you're the type of player who plays great during practice matches and drills but falls apart during an actual tournament, you should specifically look to include some training that mimics the high-pressure situations that occur during a tournament match. In the literature, this is referred to as *acclimatization training*, and it's been identified as one of the most effective methods of reducing instances of choking. [16]

The idea is to deliberately introduce some elements of self-consciousness, pressure, and/or anxiety into your practice matches. This will give you more exposure to playing under those conditions and will provide an opportunity for you to learn how to regulate those feelings. One simple way to accomplish this is to record yourself while playing a match. This will also provide you with some invaluable feedback on your form and gameplay tactics. If you aren't used to being recorded, you'll feel a level of scrutiny that you didn't before. Want to up the ante? Livestream your match on social media for all your friends and family to see.

Having some footage of yourself playing under pressure is also a great way to tailor your positive mantras (see the chapter on meditation for more info on this) to more accurately describe what you need to do to correct your stroke. For example, one study did a close analysis and comparison of table tennis players' forehand topspin shots while relaxed versus under pressure and found that players tended to adopt a more stunted, lower-speed stroke when pressured. [17] This risk-averse strategy tended to result in a reduction in performance. Video analysis will allow you to see if this bears out for you as well. If it does, you could tailor your mantra and your mental imagery to counter this tendency. You could choose the words "full swing" and imagine yourself performing an assertive and snappy forehand loop.

Another approach you could take is to play a practice match with punishment contingencies (loser must break down all the tables at the end of the session), and/or reward contingencies (winner gets a free lunch). Create some stakes and watch yourself rise to the occasion!

ACCLIMATIZATION TRAINING WITH LOWER-LEVEL PLAYERS

If you are the type of player who struggles with maintaining intensity once you've fallen behind on points, I recommend deliberately practicing winning from behind so you can build up that mental resilience. It's so easy to give up at 6–10 when you know it's just a casual game, but if you continually do this, what are you teaching yourself? You're missing an incredible opportunity to practice applying the focus and strength of will needed to snatch victory from the jaws of defeat!

One way to intentionally practice this is to use a point handicap when playing against a lower-level player. Don't be obnoxious about it. You don't want to come off as arrogant. Instead, frame it this way: "Hey, do you mind if I spot you a four point lead this game? I've noticed I'm weak mentally when I'm behind in points and I'd like to practice making a comeback."

This is effective on multiple fronts. Instead of making the lower-level player feel like you are trying to show off, you are presenting it as a way for them to help you improve. Plus, since many clubs utilize a sign-up system that allows the winner to get to play again first, by making the games closer in this way, you give them an opportunity to get more playing time, further increasing the stakes!

USE TIME-OUTS IN PRACTICE MATCHES

Research on table tennis players has shown that taking a time-out in a negative momentum situation is an effective way to recover psychologically and may help turn the tides back in your favor. [18] It's incredibly rare, however, for players to take advantage of using a time-out during non-tournament matches—at least in the clubs in which I play. But if you wait until you're at a tournament to start using time-outs, how will you know how to best implement them? Like I mentioned above, it can be incredibly difficult to have the resolve to not give up when a game seems hopeless. You should proactively put yourself into these tough spots and take advantage of every tool at your disposal to increase your chances of victory.

Deliberately practice using time-outs, even during casual matches. When you find yourself in a tough spot in a tournament, you'll be happy you did!

SET CHALLENGING GOALS

Did you know that simply setting challenging (but realistic) goals has been shown to independently improve performance? A study that examined the rate of serving success among table tennis players compared a group of players who set moderately difficult goals during training with a group who set no goals or easy goals. [19] Crucially, both groups spent the same amount of time practicing and had the same instructor. The key difference was the group who set moderately challenging goals had specific goals relating to the accuracy and successful serving rate of their sessions and were given ongoing feedback regarding their progress toward said goals. In the end, the group who set moderately difficult goals during training had significantly better outcomes compared to the other groups.

It's easy to fall into the habit of merely going through the motions when training—of putting in the time but not really extracting the most benefit from it. Setting challenging goals that keep you oriented toward continual improvement is key.

One popular way to set a goal is to follow the SMART acronym:

→ SPECIFIC
→ MEASURABLE
→ ATTAINABLE
→ RELEVANT
→ TIMELY

Rather than setting a vague goal such as "I'd like to loop better," you should instead try something like, "I will be able to consistently loop 10 balls in a row against a variable backspin serve by the end of the month." Once you meet your goal, set a new one that's even more challenging.

METHOD OF AMPLIFICATION OF ERROR

Do you have a persistent error in form that you seem totally blind to? You perform the stroke with what you feel is sound technique, but upon review (whether on video or through feedback from your coach), you find your technique is off? Conventional thinking leads us to identify the error and then try again while intentionally taking steps to redress that specific flaw in your form. But what if you did the *opposite* first?

In one study on Olympic lifting, [20] the authors tested two different correction strategies for improving technique on the snatch, a highly technical lift. They compared the traditional method of error correction (point out the error in technique and then tell the athlete how to correct the error) with a method called "method of amplification of error" (MAE).

In the MAE technique, rather than attempting to avoid the mistake in technique, one modifies the technique to *amplify* the error. This is only done temporarily so you obtain a better awareness for what the improper technique feels like. Interestingly, this study found the MAE technique produced superior results to the traditional model of error correction after only a single coaching session. Furthermore, the improved technique was still evident a week later.

This falls in line with much of the literature cited by Soderstrom and Bjork that I mentioned earlier in the chapter; particularly, the *schema theory* of learning that the concept of variability of practice is built upon. It's important to note, the aim of the MAE technique is *not* to practice repeatedly with poor form. You are simply "leaning into" your error for a few strokes so your brain can learn to better identify the error and then recalibrate.

Here's how you might implement the MAE for table tennis:

→ Have a coach/partner identify an error in your technique.
→ Modify your technique to exaggerate the error and perform a few strokes to get a feel for it.
→ "Reset" and attempt to hit the ball with proper technique once more.
→ Alternate between the above as needed to build awareness and understand the difference between the two extremes.

Personally, I have found this technique particularly useful for those who are past the beginner stage and have a solid grasp of the fundamentals but still reliably exhibit a particular technical error in their form. I would not recommend using this as your "go to" method for teaching novice players a brand-new stroke.

WANT TO GET BETTER? DREAM ON!

There's a reason we often advise people to "sleep on" an important decision before taking action. A study titled, "How to become an expert: A new perspective on the role of sleep in the mastery of procedural skills," [21] found sleep is "uniquely involved in memory consolidation over the course of the mastery of a new cognitively complex skill." Much like restarting a computer will help it run better, sleep helps us process and internalize things we learn.

Another study [22] found that a 60- to 90-minute nap was just as effective as a full 8 hours of sleep for invoking what they describe as "sleep-dependent learning." So, if sleep is a crucial ingredient to learning and task mastery, *and* it doesn't require a full eight hours to tap into those benefits, a potential strategy emerges:

→ Work on a new skill in a morning session.
→ Eat lunch.
→ Take a nap.
→ Return to the same skill in the afternoon/evening.
→ Sleep.

In doing this you double the number of learn-sleep cycles. I realize it's a rare individual who has time for both two-a-day training sessions *and* a 60- to 90-minute nap on a daily basis, but it remains a possible short-term strategy for rapid improvement. It is also possible, although this is mostly speculation, that you can still receive some of the same sleep-dependent learning benefits from a shorter, 20- to 30-minute nap.

ROBOT TRAINING

Training with a table tennis robot can be an extremely effective way to develop your technical skills—especially if it means your total practice time goes up. If you're the rare individual who has the luxury of having an experienced multi-ball feeder available at your beck and call, perhaps there is less of a need. For most players, however, a robot allows them to get some effective training in at home. This increase in training frequency and volume is very valuable from a learning perspective.

There are three main concerns I hear talked about on the forums regarding using a robot to train:

→ Unrealistic spin.
→ Might unknowingly reinforce bad form.
→ Doesn't translate well against real players.

With the older, single-wheel style robots, you could make a case for there being an issue with the spin. With these robots, the spin and speed are tied together—a faster ball always has more spin, and a slower ball always has less spin. Robots in general can also produce some unnaturally strong spins, at least for us mortal players who aren't playing against Timo Boll regularly. Modern robots with multiple wheels have largely fixed this issue, however. Even so, I've spent the bulk of my robot training time with my trusty Newgy Robo-Pong 1040 (a single-wheel model) and still have found it to be very beneficial.

As for the latter two concerns, a robot only reinforces bad form if you let it. You could just as easily reinforce bad form while training against other players. Trust me, I did it for years! The key to using a robot effectively is to use video analysis to get frequent feedback on your form, and to have a coach help you choose the proper drills to perform. Finally, you can't expect to seamlessly incorporate a stroke you've just learned on the robot in a match situation right away. Just because you've grooved the motor patterns against the robot does

43

not mean you've learned how to utilize that stroke correctly within the context of a match. This is no different than playing great against your coach—who is feeding you specific balls within a learning environment—and then struggling to reproduce those strokes in a match against a much lower ranked player.

Despite their limitations, robots have some strengths as well. I have found them to be particularly useful for the following:

→ Drilling fundamentals and learning new strokes.
→ Reprogramming the timing of your stroke (like learning to hit the ball right off the bounce when pushing).
→ Footwork drills.
→ Overspeed training (training at a faster than usual pace).
→ Sport-specific conditioning.
→ Serve practice (the ball collection net makes cleanup a lot easier).

Robot training should be used in conjunction with practice against real players. It's not a replacement. It's just another tool in the belt. Some of my best periods of development came about because I was able to use a robot to train when I would have had no one to play against otherwise. If you also find yourself struggling to get reliable training partners, a robot is something you might want to consider!

A NOTE ON NOTE-TAKING

Serious table tennis players should carry a notebook in their table tennis bag. You should take notes on your game, tactics that you find effective against certain opponents, and any coaching advice you happen to receive. Taking notes in this way has several benefits: First, just the fact that you are aware you have a notebook and should be writing something down may cause you to reflect on your game more than you would have otherwise. This will help you build a better understanding of your needs as a player and can inform your training. Second, the act of note-taking itself will help you better retain the insights you gain from the session. [23] I recommend a physical pen and paper notebook for this—don't use your phone. There is something uniquely beneficial to learning that occurs when you physically write something out. [24–25]. And finally, the notebook provides a valuable record for later review. This will serve to chronicle your growth as a player. It's fairly common for players to have a bit of downtime between matches at a typical club. Why not utilize that time to jot down a few notes? Your game will thank you for it.

BEAT FAILURES IN CONCENTRATION

Here's a simple tip to help you get in the zone before training: Put some headphones on and listen to a "binaural beats" track! Binaural auditory beats are a perceptual phenomenon that occur when you hear a slightly different tone in each ear and a perception of a phantom *third* tone appears. You can listen to binaural beats in isolation or disguised within music. Headphones must be used for the beats to have the desired effect. Why binaural beats?

A 2019 meta-analysis examined 22 studies and found that binaural beats improved cognition, reduced anxiety levels, and reduced the perception of pain. [26] The effect seemed to increase with exposure and was persistent across various beat frequencies. You can easily pull up some binaural beats for free on Spotify or YouTube if you'd like to hear them for yourself. Personally, I like to listen to them while I meditate and during my warm-up/serve practice. I find it helps me get calm, focused, and in the zone!

CHAPTER SUMMARY:

→ Research on motor learning indicates that the conditions that produce the most errors during the acquisition of a skill are often the same conditions that produce the most learning.

→ The *reloading hypothesis* suggests that following a more distributed practice schedule, both within and between sessions, can speed up the learning process and result in greater long-term retention.

→ The *schema theory* explains why introducing a degree of variability when learning a stroke can promote long-term learning by allowing the learner to gain a better understanding of the movement parameters and underlying motor skills necessary to play the stroke.

→ Don't put all your eggs in one basket; training in more than one venue may help improve learning and make your performance more consistent.

→ When coaching a player, *less is more*—avoid over-cueing and excessive hand-over-hand instruction in the initial stages of learning.

→ Use analogies when describing a stroke to promote *implicit* learning.

→ Acclimatization training (training that mimics the high-pressure situations that occur during a tournament match) is an effective means of reducing instances of choking.

→ Acclimatization training can be accomplished by recording yourself during practice, creating higher stakes with punishment/reward contingencies, and using point handicaps against lower ranked players.

→ You should practice using time outs during casual matches as well as important ones.

→ Setting challenging SMART goals can independently improve performance.

→ The MAE technique can be used to recalibrate a stroke in which you consistently exhibit an error in form.

→ Sleep can be used strategically to consolidate memory and enhance learning; a 60–90-minute nap can be just as effective as a full 8 hours when attempting to take advantage of sleep-dependent learning.

→ Robot training can be an effective tool for learning if used properly.

→ Keep a notebook in your bag and hand write notes in between matches.

→ Binaural beats can be used as a tool to help you focus and get in the zone.

TACTICAL SKILLS: CREATING YOUR "VITRUVIAN MAN" AND BUILDING A TACTICAL PLAYBOOK

"However beautiful the strategy, you should occasionally look at the results."

—Winston Churchill

When I first sat down to write this chapter, I unironically explored the possibility of simply making it one sentence long: "Go buy *Table Tennis Tactics for Thinkers* by Larry Hodges." If you are at all interested in improving your game via tactics, that book is your one-stop shop! As I mentioned in the introduction, I don't have the experience or the skills as a table tennis player to weigh in on providing specific tactics for you as a player. Instead, much like I did with the technical skills chapter, I will provide you with a framework into which you can neatly drop the much *better* advice you will receive from experienced coaches and players whom you encounter.

STRATEGY VERSUS TACTICS

Before we get started, I'd like to make a brief distinction between the terms *strategy* and *tactics*. They are often used interchangeably, but there is a technical difference between them that's worth pointing out:

→ **Strategy:** Your "big picture" plan on how to win the game.
→ **Tactics:** The specific steps you take in order to accomplish your objectives.

Put another way, your strategy is the *what* and your tactics are the *how*.

"Strategy is buying a bottle of fine wine when you take a lady out for dinner. Tactics is getting her to drink it."

—Frank Muir

CREATING YOUR "VITRUVIAN MAN"

Leonardo da Vinci's famous, "Vitruvian man" was meant to demonstrate the ideal human body proportions. Much like table tennis, it's a brilliant blend of art and science. This balance of art and science is important to understand as an athlete because both are required to achieve peak performance. You must lean on science to inform your training, develop your technique, and devise an overall strategy for your game. But if you truly want to perform at your peak, you must surrender to "art" so you can enter a flow state where performance is automatic and expressive.

I mention this because in any discussion of strategy and tactics, you want to avoid the pitfall of overburdening yourself with complex tactics *while in a match*. There are simply too many variables involved once a rally extends past the third or fourth ball, and to think you will be able to anticipate these variables is a fallacy of control. To prove my point, even though Larry Hodges's book is chocked full of tactics, here is what he put on the back cover:

> *Tactics isn't about finding complex strategies to defeat an opponent. Tactics is about sifting through all the zillions of possible tactics and finding a few simple ones that work.*

So, we'll keep things simple, but perhaps not so simple that you become simple-minded! You should still think deeply about your game and your best path toward victory. To assist with this, I have created the "Vitruvian Man" exercise. As you might have picked up from the previous chapter, I'm a big believer in the benefits of physically writing things out. Writing has a unique effect on the brain—the focus and introspection required in the act of writing are valuable in and of themselves. In the previous chapter, I recommended buying yourself a notebook for table tennis. Now we're going to put it to use.

The "Vitruvian Man" exercise (VME)[1] is a way for you to create a strategic profile for yourself as a player. What is your style of play? What are your signature strengths? The answers to these questions

---

1   To download a free template of this exercise, head to peakperformancetabletennis. com/resources.

The "Vitruvian Man" Exercise

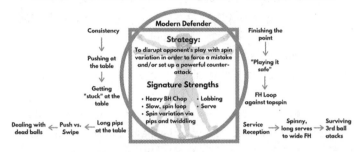

go within the "inner chamber" of the circle-square matrix. These are the things that are currently within your reach and solid parts of your game. On the outside, you should list some of your current weaknesses—things you feel are currently holding you back. As these items fall outside the circle-square matrix, they are just slightly out of reach and represent areas of growth.

The actual format you use here is arbitrary. You don't have to copy exactly what I've done above. You can use a simple word web or even just write it out in paragraph form. The important thing is to conceptualize your central strategy and take account of your current strengths and weaknesses. Ideally, this is something you should do with your coach. At the very least, consult with a few other experienced players to gain an outside perspective. They may be able to point out weaknesses you weren't aware of, or help you formulate a basic strategy if you don't have one. Once you've completed this exercise, you can begin to work on some tactics that you can employ.

GETTING STARTED WITH TACTICS

As I've stated many times at this point, this book is not about explicitly teaching you the sport of table tennis, so I will be staying true to my word and avoid going into depth regarding specific tactics against various styles of play. Get a coach or pick up Larry Hodges's book if you'd like more information about that sort of thing. Instead, I will briefly touch on a few ways in which you can start to identify and implement some basic tactical training into your practice sessions.

At the heart of it, tactics are really about problem solving. And the simple answer to the problem you may be facing could very well be "get better at table tennis." We'll get a bit more nuanced than that, but the point is this—*tactics should start with practice*. You could tell a beginner to "hit to your opponent's playing elbow," but does that beginner even have the ability to place his shot with that much accuracy? Probably not! Tactics are only as useful as your ability to reliably implement them. Thus, the place to start with tactics is in the training hall.

Having completed your VME, you should have a good idea of a few of your basic strengths and weaknesses. A good place to start with tactical training is to look at each of your strengths and weaknesses in turn and ask yourself the following questions:

→ *What shots will put me in a good position to utilize my strengths?*
→ *What shots can I play to decrease the likelihood of my weaknesses becoming exposed?*

Okay, these questions are not exactly rocket science, but if you've never thought these things through before, then you might be surprised at some of the insights you can gain from this. I'll use myself as an example. If you haven't guessed already, the VME exercise pictured earlier is one I completed for myself. An area of frustration I identified was my tendency to get "stuck" at the table pushing the ball around and making unforced errors with my long pips.

After consulting with a coach, I made the following adjustments to my training to address this:

→ Develop a consistent, *deep* push to the corners of the table from both wings.
→ Master a consistent "pips push" at the table.
→ Incorporate step-around looping drills from the backhand corner.

But are these things really tactics? Aren't they just normal training designed to increase my consistency and correct weaknesses in my game? The answer to both questions is *yes*. The two are intrinsically linked. The first "tactic" that my coach and I identified was to push *deep and heavy* more often. This would force two likely responses: Either a weaker attack, which I could start chopping (which is a strength), or a deep push return, which I could use my slow spinny loop against (another strength). This is an effective tactic for my game *at my level*.

Upon reflection, however, I realized that nearly all my pushes were actually half-long. This allowed my opponents to easily push back short, flick, or open up with a loop. So even though we identified the proper tactic, I had to take a step back and put in some work before I could implement it properly. I also had to buckle down and do the boring work of mastering a long-pips push at the table. At the end of the day, fancy tactics won't make up for skimping on basic, fundamental strokes. Finally, to preemptively eliminate the common strategy of pinning down a pips player on the backhand, we included some step-around footwork drills.

A careful analysis of this approach reveals three steps:

1. **Identify and address the root issue:** In my case, it was my consistency and control with pushing—particularly with the long pips.

2. **Create a tactic to address the situation:** Push deep and heavy to the corners.

3. **Pave a path to your strength:** Chop the weak attack and get into a defensive flow, or attack the long push with a forehand loop.

If you follow this approach, you'll quickly find that tactics are like rabbits. They breed quickly! You know how to make a deep push even more effective? Occasionally throw in a short push. Can you do that consistently? Now that's another thing to add to the list.

BUILDING A TACTICAL PLAYBOOK

Tactics do not exist in a vacuum. They must always take the opponent into consideration. Once you've got a few basic tactics built around your strengths and weaknesses, you'll want to start paying more attention to how those tactics interact with various opponents and styles of play. As you do this, new problems will emerge and these problems will lead to additional tactics. This is where some judicious note-taking is useful. When you make an observation or get a good piece of advice, jot it down! This will help to tuck it away more securely in your subconscious, and it will serve as a reminder to apply it to your training later.

Table tennis is not like football where you may have complicated plays written out and rehearsed ahead of time. It's much more like poker—your "hand" is your personal strategy, skills, and tactics, but once the point is underway and additional "cards" are revealed, the value of individual elements of your hand may change dramatically. If your bread-and-butter serve is a short, heavy side/underspin ball to your opponent's backhand and you play an OX long pips hitter, you might quickly discover this serve is no longer effective. The pips player will gladly take all that spin, reverse it, and send it back to you at an awkward angle. Your tactic happened to play right into their strength! So, make a note:

Avoid serving short side/under serves to Johnny Pips' backhand—and maybe against long pips users in general.

Congratulations, you just wrote the first few lines of code for a tactical "program" against this particular player and long pips players more generally. Over time, as you gain more experience and collect more data, this code will morph into a complex algorithm that operates quietly in the background as you play, without much need for conscious monitoring.

TRIGGERED SEQUENCES AND MODIFIED MATCHES

Occasionally, you may find a certain technique or tactic is too overwhelming to use within a match at first. If you have a lot of indecision or uncertainty around a technique, you will hesitate when attempting to implement it and it will fail. This is normal. It just means this particular technique isn't "match ready" just yet. A "triggered sequence" is one way you can help bridge the divide between a rehearsed drill and an actual game. To explain how it works, I'll use my own experience in learning how to twiddle[2] as an example.

When I first learned how to twiddle, my primary struggle was not *how* to twiddle or even how to hit an inverted backhand, it was *when* to twiddle. The option to twiddle was always lurking in the background during a rally. The "open-endedness" of it was distracting. I found myself twiddling for the sake of twiddling with no real purpose and often getting stuck having the wrong rubber on the wrong side at the wrong time.

To fix this, I simplified things by deciding to only twiddle in the following instances:

→ During my serve.
→ During my opponent's serve.
→ After I performed a heavy, low chop.

Service was a natural place to start because it's predictable and predetermined. The natural time between points gave me a window to decide ahead of time whether I would twiddle or not. But why after a heavy chop? That one requires a bit of explanation.

I noticed that nearly every time I'd get a really good chop in, my opponent would do one of the following—push the chop back (requiring me to run back to the table), or slow loop the chop to lift it safely over the net. Knowing this, I realized that if I twiddled after

---

2   Twiddling is the strategic turning of a combination racket during a rally in order to introduce spin variation and/or overcome some of the physical limitations of playing surfaces, such as pips or antispin.

a heavy chop, it would put me in a good place to either push back heavy with the inverted rubber, *or* go for a quick inverted block off the high-arcing loop. Often, the startling change in pace after the latter tactic was enough for me to win the point outright.

This is something I call a *triggered sequence.* You identify a common pattern and decide on a tactical response—for example, if *x* happens, then *y*. Notably, I like to start the sequence with a trigger that *I* control rather than the opponent. Don't let your opponent be the one with their finger on the trigger! So rather than deciding to twiddle when my opponent pushes short, I decided to twiddle after my *own* shot, based on the responses I knew were most likely.

By simplifying and "confining" my twiddling in this way, it became a lot more manageable. Consequently, I was able to use it more judiciously during matches. This helped me build enough confidence with it to eventually incorporate it more fluidly. I now twiddle a lot more instinctively during games—sometimes without even realizing I've done so. I have shed the "training wheels" of the triggered sequence.

MODIFIED MATCHES

A modified match is another way to help introduce a new skill or tactic into the arena of actual gameplay. Modified matches can take many forms, but most will have some artificially imposed rules agreed upon by each player. They may also include some element of free play where the point is "played out." Since many players find drills to be repetitive and boring, playing a modified match is a good way to "gamify" the learning process. If you find yourself just going through the motions when performing a drill, a modified match is a good way to reignite your engagement and enthusiasm.

Here are a few examples:

→ **Service reception**: Only your opponent gets to serve for the whole match.

→ **Serve/third ball**: You have to follow-up every serve with a third ball attack.

→ **Pushing**: Play a "push only" match. No attacks, no flicks.

→ **Pushing low**: play a "push only" match where you can only win points if your ball skims the net as it goes over.

→ **Placement**: Block out certain "dead zones" on each side of the table with a towel. If you hit the towel, you lose the point.

→ **Footwork**: Play a "forehand only" match where you must hit every ball with your forehand, even from the backhand side.

These are just a few examples. With a little creativity, you can come up with all sorts of interesting modifications. These types of games work especially well if you and your training partner have complimentary skills you'd like to work on. So, if your partner is working on a new serve, and you'd like to work on your service reception, having a game where your partner does all the serving kills two birds with one stone.

CONCLUDING THOUGHTS

Good tactics can be communicated in a few simple words or even a gesture. Tactics spring from your personal strengths and weaknesses, but must morph and change as they bump up against opponents who have tactics of their own. Be wary of the sometimes-blurry line between "good tactics" and "bad table tennis." If you're a pips player like myself, is covering the entire table with your long pips backhand an effective tactic? Perhaps in the short term. But if you use this tactic as an excuse to skimp on training your forehand, then you might be winning the battle but losing the war.

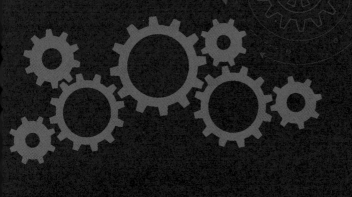

SECTION II

PSYCHOLOGICAL AND SOCIAL/EMOTIONAL SKILLS

SECTION OVERVIEW

Now that we've covered the technical and tactical domains, we will move into the realms of psychological, social, and emotional skills. You could easily make a case for combining these into one category— and as you read, you'll see there is quite a bit of overlap between them—but I wanted to separate them because I feel the social and emotional aspects of being an athlete are often overlooked and warrant special attention.

In the following chapters, we will focus on the optimal mental states associated with peak performance in table tennis and also consider the "bigger picture" where I challenge the idea that the path to peak performance must involve narrow-mindedly sacrificing everything for your sport. Finally, there is a chapter on the myth of motivation and what it really takes to successfully implement the behavior changes necessary for achieving your goals.

MASTERING THE MENTAL GAME

"Concentration and mental toughness are the margins of victory."

—*Bill Russell*

It is abundantly clear that table tennis players are smarter than the average bear, but is there any truth to the claim that table tennis is the number one "brain sport" on the planet? Turns out, there is! In one study, they found elite and sub-elite table tennis players are "characterized by above-average scores on several higher-level cognitive functions." [1] And another study found that table tennis players display superior conscious and unconscious response inhibition when compared with non-athletes. [2]

But what is driving this higher cognitive functioning? Is it that smarter people tend to excel in the sport and thus end up disproportionately populating the elite levels? Or is it the exposure to table tennis itself that is improving cognitive functioning? Either way, my recommendation is to attack the problem from both ends: play more table tennis, *and* find ways to optimize your cognitive functioning.

In this chapter, we will be focusing on the latter. A study on elite table tennis players [3] identified five optimal mental states associated with peak performance in table tennis:

→ Concentration.
→ Self-Confidence.
→ Positive Thinking.
→ Emotion Management.
→ Motivation.

With deliberate practice, these mental states can be *trained*. A 2020 systematic review that examined the efficacy of mental training programs in racket sports such as table tennis found mental training programs result in positive outcomes on performance. [4] You work on your technical skills, right? You exercise to get stronger and faster. Why not dedicate a little time to strengthening your mental game as well? If you keep an open mind, you will find it's not as difficult to do as you might think! I'll help get you started by outlining a simple method of improving your focus and concentration.

THE BENEFITS OF MEDITATION

Table tennis is as much a mental struggle as it is a physical one. You can be physically fit, well-rested, and brimming with explosive energy, but if your head's not right, your game is going right down the drain. You can't perform at your best physically if you're not firing on all cylinders mentally. This fact is reflected in a study on elite table tennis players where they concluded that to reach optimal performance, psychological training programs should be integrated into the daily training routine. [5]

One way to accomplish this is to start a daily meditation habit. If you're anything like me, when you hear the words *meditation* or *mindfulness* you have a knee-jerk reaction to it—it seems a little too "woo-woo," for lack of a better term. But don't worry, we're not going to be talking about "cosmic energy" or any of the other mystical elements that are so often linked to the practice of meditation. Instead, we will focus on the empirical, scientifically proven benefits of this simple practice. I made the mistake of casually dismissing meditation for years before I finally started taking it seriously. Since then, I've noticed a significant improvement in my mental resilience during match play. It remains one of the most impactful changes I've made to my daily life, so I strongly encourage you to at least give it a shot for a couple months.

Meditation has benefits that will affect your game in both indirect and direct ways. It has been shown to potentially help reduce physiological markers of stress, [6] improve sleep quality for those who suffer from insomnia, [7] improve the quality of relationships, [8] reduce chronic pain and symptoms of depression, [9] and even aid weight loss efforts. [10] All of these things can contribute indirectly toward making you a better player, but here's something interesting I found:

When looking at the research on the *direct* benefits of meditation on sports performance, four things stuck out:

1. Meditation seems to have an outsized benefit for athletes in sports that require a *high degree of precision* where both

physiological and psychological markers are directly improved, resulting in better performance outcomes. [11]

2. Meditation can specifically relieve pre-competition stress, allowing you to perform your best when it counts the most. [12]

3. Mindfulness can improve an athlete's mental resilience, attention, and mood state. [13]

4. There is an interesting, although somewhat tenuous, link between the much coveted "flow state" and high levels of mindfulness. Although direct causality has not been established, there is a tight correlation between high levels of mindfulness and the ability to achieve a flow state. [14–16] Thus, developing one may help foster the other.

For all the above reasons, the strategic use of meditation should be seriously considered by the table tennis athlete. Fortunately, it is extremely easy to get started with meditation. Apps such as Headspace, Insight Timer, and Calm can be downloaded in minutes and have free beginner courses to guide you through the process. Just 3–10 minutes per day is all that's needed to get started.[3]

If you've tried meditation before and were frustrated because your mind wandered too much, don't worry. The fact that your mind wanders is not a sign that meditation is not working; it's a sign that you're getting a good workout! The harder you find meditation, and the more distracted you feel, the better the workout. Tony

---

3   I have created a free guided meditation session specifically designed for table tennis players available at peakperformancetabletennis.com/resources.

Stubblebine, the founder and CEO of Coach.me, likens this to doing "mental pushups":

> *With meditation, you're practicing a two-step process that you will use outside of the meditation. The first step is becoming aware of where your mind wandered, acknowledging the thought and then putting the thought down. Call that Awareness. The second step is bringing your focus back to your point of focus (usually your breath). Call that Focus.*
>
> *This Awareness-Focus loop is what you are practicing during a meditation session. A lot of people feel bad if their mind wanders during meditation. But you should actually feel good. The more often your mind wanders, the more times you get to practice this Awareness-Focus loop. I tell people what they are doing is mental pushups. The more wandering they do, the more pushups they get in.*

USING MEDITATION TO ENHANCE PERFORMANCE AND PREVENT CHOKING

In addition to the benefits listed in the previous section, I have found meditation to be particularly useful in perfecting and "supercharging" one's *pre-performance routine* (PPR). A PPR is a "sequence of task relevant thoughts and actions which an athlete engages in systematically prior to his or her performance of a specific sport skill." [17] For the table tennis athlete, the perfect time to engage in a PPR is right before you serve. The intermittent nature of table tennis provides many opportunities for you to "reset" both mentally and physically during a game. Take advantage of this!

If you carefully observe the pros when they play, you'll quickly start to pick up on a few of these ritualistic routines—they may touch the table up near the net with the palm of their hand, they may bounce the ball a certain number of times before serving, etc. These routines are more than just random tics or superstitious quirks. They are done deliberately as a means of centering oneself, gathering one's thoughts, and preparing for the next point. But is there any value in such routines?

Well, in a 2017 systematic review of the literature, PPRs were identified as one of the most effective interventions for reducing the instances of choking under pressure. [18] One theory for why PPRs are effective is because your working memory is limited, if you "flood" your brain with the performance of these ritualized behaviors, you can effectively suppress thoughts that are detrimental to performance (fears, doubts, overthinking, etc.). You're essentially "crowding out" the bad thoughts with good ones.

Common elements of an effective PPR include the following:

→ Deep breathing
→ Relaxing
→ Cue words
→ Envisioning success via mental imagery
→ Discrete physical actions (bouncing the ball a certain number of times, touching the table, etc.)

Conveniently, most of these elements are also core pieces of an effective meditation session. This is the hidden benefit of meditation to your success as an athlete! It provides the opportunity to practice the individual components of your PPR under focused and calm conditions. Rather than attempting to get your emotions and thoughts under control on the fly, meditating allows one to perfect those skills ahead of time so they're there for you in the heat of a match. Let's take a moment to examine how you might develop and enhance your PPR through meditation by taking a look at each of the above-mentioned elements in turn.

Deep breathing and relaxation are already major parts of most types of meditation; when meditating, you learn to become aware of your breathing and how to control it to a greater extent. By practicing this daily, you enhance your ability to engage the *right* kind of breathing—those deep, belly breaths that engage the diaphragm and activate the parasympathetic nervous system to help you better control your emotional state. [19] This skill is extremely important for those times in a match when you need to regulate your arousal and think with clarity.

Cue words also exist in meditation under a different name—mantras. An athlete, knowing his or her own personal weaknesses, will utilize certain cue words and positive self-talk in between points. A player who overcommits on his shots and is frequently caught out of position might use the phrase "ready position" as a reminder to return to the ready position. Or players who tends to be a little tentative and choppy when playing might use the phrase "follow through" to help them swing with more confidence. These types of words and phrases are quite similar to a positive mantra that one might repeat while meditating. As silly and inconsequential as it may sound, having a positive mantra is a scientifically validated way to improve performance! When linked with meditation, a positive mantra becomes a verbal trigger—a shortcut to a state of peak performance.

Visualization can also be incorporated seamlessly within a meditation session. Visualization, or mental imagery, is the practice of mentally rehearsing your performance before play. It can be done in the heat of a match, right before a rally, or it can be performed in a separate session of its own. There are guided meditation sessions that focus specifically on visualization available within the apps previously mentioned, but one easy technique I like to employ is to visualize a single table tennis ball in the mind's eye while meditating. I've found this simple visualization helps tremendously with obtaining a focused "quiet eye" during a match. It's deceptively simple, but learning to obtain a quiet eye—a "visual fixation toward a relevant target prior to the execution of a movement"—is yet another research-backed method of improving performance and preventing choking. [18] We've all heard the phrase "keep your eye on the ball," but there's a difference between casually looking at something and *really* looking at something. Think about the difference between someone watching TV with eyes glazed over, and how a tiger looks at its prey. Now ask yourself, do you want the eye of the couch potato, or the eye of the tiger?

As you gain experience, you can begin to engage in more elaborate mental rehearsals and visualizations of successful table tennis rallies—both of which have also been shown specifically to improve performance for table tennis players. [20–21].

Think of how much overlap there is between the optimal mental states associated with peak performance (concentration, self-confidence, positive thinking, emotion management, motivation) and the skills you will develop through meditation and the consistent implementation of a PPR. This is powerful stuff. Ignore it at your peril.

CREATING A PERSONALIZED PRE-PERFORMANCE ROUTINE

You likely already engage in one or more ritualistic behaviors while playing already. Perhaps you are aware of these actions, perhaps not. The next time you play, pay attention to how you act between points and jot down some notes in between games. Better yet, film yourself or get a training partner observe you while you play so you can gain an outside perspective. Note both the positive actions (deep breaths, positive affirmations, consistency between points, etc.) and the negative actions (displays of anger, negative self-talk, distractedness).

The next step is to actively create a PPR based on what you found. Keep and refine the positive and shed the negative. Physically write out step-by-step what you will do after each point and in various situations.

Here's one possible example:

→ If I win the point, I will celebrate. (Harimoto: "Check. Got that one down!")
→ If I lose the point, I will acknowledge my opponent's skill, attempt to identify any errors in technique or tactics I may have made, and quickly visualize correcting said mistakes.
→ I will use pre-determined cue words and/or positive mantras to empower myself while the ball is being retrieved in between rallies.

Before serving:

→ I will take a deep, belly breath to help regulate my emotions.
→ I will bounce the ball three times on the table.

→ I will envision a successful serve.
→ I will begin service.

Before receiving:

→ I will take a deep, belly breath to help regulate my emotions.
→ I will tap the table with my non-playing hand.
→ I will crouch down into the ready position.
→ I will obtain a "quiet eye" and focus intently on the ball.

By deliberately mapping out a PPR, you can be more consistent in practicing it. You could even jot it down on an index card and bring it to the table with you during training! This consistent practice and repetition will ingrain your PPR so that it becomes automatic. Ever drive home and realize you were on "autopilot" and have no idea how you actually got there? Your brain can automate *incredibly* complex behaviors! That's what we're after with a PPR. You want to initiate a series of familiar behaviors that culminate in automatic performance.

CHAPTER SUMMARY:

→ The five mental states associated with peak performance in elite table tennis players are concentration, self-confidence, positive thinking, emotion management, and motivation.
→ Mental toughness and the ability to focus under pressure are extremely important skills to foster for table tennis athletes.
→ Research demonstrates that meditation can improve your table tennis through both indirect and direct means.
→ Apps such as Headspace, Insight Timer, and Calm offer free guided meditations that you can perform yourself in as little as 3–10 minutes per day.

➔ PPRs are an effective way to prevent choking during critical points.

➔ The breathing techniques, visualization, and positive mantras utilized during meditation sessions can dovetail seamlessly into your PPR.

➔ Take the time to create a personalized PPR and use meditation to supercharge it.

SOCIAL AND EMOTIONAL SKILLS

"Learn to control your emotions or they will control you."

—*Edgar Martinez*

To reach your top level of performance in a way that is sustainable and healthy, you will need to address the larger context of your life first. This veers into the area of metaphysics, which is beyond the scope of this book. Nonetheless, let's briefly look at the bigger picture. The sad examples of top athletes who excelled in their sport but failed at life are too many to list. We witness stellar performance, yet a string of broken relationships, financial failure, legal problems, even preventable collapse of physical health. We also witness other athletes who seem to fit their achievements into a larger framework of a healthy and happy life. Performance aside, it is clear you would want to be in that second group.

Very likely you already have resources around you that address issues of ultimate meaning, purpose, and the inherent value of human life. It may be within your extended family or your faith tradition. In the East this is addressed as "balance"; in the West, most frequently as "priorities." Your ability to focus is what enables you to perform at top levels. But undue focus on performance and technique can be counterproductive. Think of the legs of a chair. Its stability comes from having multiple legs. Table tennis can be a point of focus that turns you into a chair with one leg. Pretty wobbly! But what if, in addition to that leg, you had the additional stabilizing, balancing supports of family, faith, and friends? That would not only lead to a better life, but also resilience and an ability to recover and come back stronger when you face the inevitable setbacks and slumps that all athletes face.

Those campy old martial arts films flash an occasional nugget of wisdom. In *Enter the Dragon*, Bruce Lee was advising one of his students that the development of his martial arts skills was like a finger pointing at the beautiful moon. If you get too caught up in technique and performance, your focus on "the finger" will cause you "to miss all that heavenly glory." What that glory is, you will have to find out for yourself. Don't make it overly complicated. There are already pathways and clues, all around you that you can pick up and pursue. The main point is you will need a larger framework, a life into which your sport fits. That will make things better, not only for you but the people who live around you that you care about.

FOSTERING THE REMAINING MENTAL STATES FOR PEAK PERFORMANCE

With the above firmly in mind, we can now dive into the specifics of how to utilize social/emotional skills in the context of sport performance. In the last chapter, I revealed the five optimal mental states associated with peak performance in elite table tennis players:

→ Concentration
→ Self-Confidence
→ Positive Thinking
→ Emotion Management
→ Motivation

In that chapter, the primary focus was on building your concentration, but those same strategies can bolster the other mental states as well. A 2017 systematic review, for example, found meditation can improve positive prosocial emotions and behaviors in addition to its other benefits. [1] Still, there are additional steps one can take to address the remaining mental states in a more direct way, which we will now explore.

EFFECTIVE WAYS TO DEVELOP AND SELF-CONFIDENCE AND POSITIVE THINKING

There's no magic switch for you to flip that's going to dramatically change your personality and turn you from a timid pessimist to a confident optimist overnight. But there are lots of little things you can do—seeds you can plant—that will have a small but meaningful effect on your general outlook. Some of those seeds may turn out to be slow-growing. Others may shoot up like bamboo if given a little time. The most important thing to do is to be proactive and take action *now*.

I have found that many of the strategies used to develop self-confidence also work to make you a more positive thinker. They are two sides of the same coin. This means you can kill two birds with one stone if you take some time to work on this area. A 2014 study [2] published in the *Journal of Applied Sport Psychology* interviewed ten different sport psychology consultants regarding how to best develop and maintain robust sport-confidence. From these interviews, they distilled the expert advice into ten effective strategies:

STEPS TO BUILDING CONFIDENCE[4]

1. DEVELOP UNDERSTANDING AND AWARENESS OF CONFIDENCE

The first step to becoming more confident is learning what confidence really is. Being a confident individual does *not* mean you

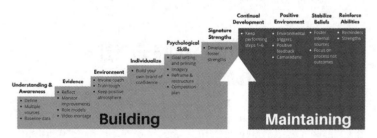

Achieving Robust Sport Confidence

---

4   I have conceptualized these strategies as "steps" but they do not need to be focused on sequentially. The first six strategies are all areas of focus that can be attended to from day one.

never experience fear or doubt. Confident people experience these emotions but press on anyway! It is in *overcoming* your fears that confidence is forged.

Another important step toward attaining robust confidence is to identify *multiple sources* of confidence so you have a more stable foundation. Remember the chair I alluded to in the introduction? You can't place your entire self-worth on any one sport—even a sport as great as table tennis! This is the reason you'll see such a strong focus on a holistic approach in this book. Take time to tend to your relationships. Lead a balanced life with other interests and pursuits.

Even something as superficial as your appearance can be a source of confidence. Don't dismiss attending to your appearance as mere vanity. Dress well. Take care of your skin. Dial in your nutrition and physical training protocols. A hidden benefit to building some muscle and getting stronger is what coaches refer to as the "tight jersey effect." A player who has transformed their body will play with a level of confidence they didn't have before. This is something the 2016 Summer Paralympics Games gold medalist Will Bayley noticed firsthand when he took his physical training more seriously: "I feel fitter and better about myself, so it's psychological as well." [3]

Finally, it's a good idea to get some baseline data on your sources and levels of confidence so you can develop more effective interventions. Based on research by Kate Hays and colleagues, [4] I have developed a table tennis-specific confidence profile that is available for free download so you can easily accomplish that.[5]

---

5   Head to peakperformancetabletennis.com/resources to download the confidence profile.

2. LOG EVIDENCE

Are you tired of me harping on about the importance of journaling yet? If so, too bad. We press onwards! An incredibly effective way to build confidence in yourself is to track your progress. To feel confident, you must provide yourself with plenty of evidence that you are *deserving* of confidence. This means crossing your t's and dotting your i's when it comes to your training. If you haven't put in the work, you're not going to be able to trick yourself into believing otherwise.

Wayne Goldsmith, an Olympic level swimming coach, contends that the "critical confidence equation" is *self-confidence = self-belief x evidence.* In order to provide yourself with plenty of evidence, you should keep both qualitative and quantitative data on your progress. This can take the form of journaling—noting things you're feeling good about—and monitoring your improvements in a more quantitative way, such as keeping a gym log so you can see your performance improvements over time. Another form of evidence is to find a role model—ideally someone who was once in your shoes but is now a few levels ahead. Talking to these "trail blazers" can be an inspirational way to see the path more clearly to your *own* improvement.

CREATE A PERSONAL HIGHLIGHT REEL

An extremely effective way to show yourself "proof" that you've got what it takes is to make a highlight reel of your best points. I first heard of this idea from Brett Clarke, the former National Head Coach of the Australian team, but the expert consultants from the study I referenced also mentioned this as an effective strategy. It takes a bit of work on the front-end to do this, but it's well worth it. I like this idea because it necessitates recording yourself playing quite a bit so you can accumulate enough footage for a highlight reel. That alone will be beneficial if you aren't in the habit of doing so already!

Once you've got a nice collection of clips, edit it together into a montage[6] with one of your favorite high-energy, "pump-up" songs. Save the video on your phone and/or put it up on YouTube as an unlisted/private video so you have easy access to it. Once you have your video, watch it a couple times per week and make it a part of your pre-game ritual before important matches.

Humans naturally tend to remember the negative over the positive. Winning an outstanding point feels great but the feeling is fleeting. *Lose* a critical point, however, and the experience seems to tattoo itself onto your subconscious. Watching your highlight reel will help to counterbalance this. You need to remind yourself of how capable you really are!

3. MANIPULATE THE COACHING ENVIRONMENT

A good coach can do wonders for your self-confidence. A bad one can leave you with scars that last a lifetime. One key area identified by the sport psychology consultants in this study is the importance of training in a positive environment. I've spent my entire adult career teaching and coaching kids and young adults from ages ranging from 6–21 years of age, and I can tell you one thing for certain, frequent positive praise *works*. And it works well. The next few paragraphs will apply mostly to coaches, but if you're a player, it pays to know this as well.

---

6   If video editing seems like an absolute nightmare to you, you can utilize services like Fiverr.com to hire someone to do it for you. Most gigs for this type of service run in the $10-30 range.

Behavioral scientists have found that a ratio of approximately five phrases of praise for every one reprimand is the "magic" number and seems to result in better outcomes. [5] If you are a coach, don't mistake this level of praise for being soft on your players. You can still be extremely tough and demanding while maintaining a positive atmosphere along the way. One of the best compliments I've ever received as a teacher was that I am "strict but nice."

Praise is not merely a means of helping someone feel better. You aren't just padding their self-esteem (although that's a side benefit). It's a *tool* for shaping behavior. Praise is positive reinforcement. Behaviors that are reinforced tend to increase in frequency. Knowing this, you can target specific behaviors and reinforce them with plenty of praise in order to increase their likelihood of occurring again. This is called "behavior-specific praise" and it's like a beefed-up version of normal praise. If a player performs a drill well, rather than praising them with pat phrases such as "good job," try mentioning specifically the things they did well: "Hey, I really like how you stayed loose and relaxed during those forehand loops. Nice work!"

Of course, there are times when you must correct, criticize, and reprimand. This is unavoidable. The key is to maintain that 5:1 ratio as best you can along the way. There is *always* something positive to find if you are vigilant. Find those things your player is doing well and praise them. One effective strategy I like to employ is the "criticism sandwich." If you find a mistake that you'd like to correct, first mention something they did well, then offer the criticism, and follow that up with another piece of behavior-specific praise.

Another important part of creating an environment that will build confidence is to train under pressure. You might recall from the motor learning chapter that acclimatization training is an effective way to prevent choking during a match. As it turns out, it was also identified by the expert sport psychology consultants as a good strategy for building confidence. Clearly the two are related! Want to get stronger mentally? Well, a 2011 study found that a harsh physical training environment plus a positive mental environment is an effective one-two punch for achieving mental toughness in athletes. [6]

4. TAILOR FOR THE INDIVIDUAL

You need to find your own brand of confidence. It may be the quiet self-assurance of Timo Boll, or perhaps you play with a bit of swagger like Xu Xin. Either way, it's important to figure out what behaviors, postures, and mental states make up your own personal brand of confidence. Record your matches for clues here. Analyze those matches in which you felt confident and mentally strong. Look carefully at your body language and note any trends. Some research indicates your physical posture can influence your level of confidence, [7] so find your own "power postures" and use them proactively before games to boost your confidence. Fake it till you make it, as they say.

A SNEAKY WAY TO BOOST CONFIDENCE BEFORE A MATCH

To be fair, the research regarding power postures is a bit mixed. It's certainly not going to have a *huge* effect, but I'm a big fan of things that are easy to implement with few or no downsides. Of course, one tangible downside of using power postures is the fact that you may feel ridiculous doing them. Some of the more popular power postures such as the hands-on-hips, "Wonder Woman" pose, or the arms outstretched "V for victory pose" might feel a little conspicuous to perform right before a match.

A sneaky way around this is to incorporate the power poses into your pre-match warm-up routine. The "crucifix stretch," for example, not only feels great, it's also an iconic power pose. To the outside observer, it looks like you're just limbering up, but in your head, you're already standing on the champion's podium with arms outstretched in victory!

5. USE PSYCHOLOGICAL SKILLS

Some of the most effective psychological skills identified by the sport psychology consultants were goal setting, imagery, reframing/ restructuring, and having a psychological competition plan. We've already discussed goal setting and imagery in previous chapters, so we won't go into depth with them again here—although it's nice to know they can also help with confidence in addition to performance! Reframing/restructuring is a psychological tactic where you think rationally about the negative emotions you are experiencing and put them into perspective using evidence and hard data. This is yet another reason to collect evidence of your successes and keep them cataloged: performance statistics, personal bests, trophies, encouraging notes, etc.

Finally, simply having a specific psychological performance plan ready to go for competitions can help you feel more confident. This will give you a feeling of control as you can check items of the list and know you've done everything you should to prepare. In the "Game Day Protocols" chapter, I outline a step-by-step method for getting yourself psychologically ready on the day of your competition, so feel free to skip ahead if you'd like to get a feel for what a performance plan might look like.

CAN YOU BOOST CONFIDENCE WITH UNCONSCIOUS GOAL PRIMING AND SUBLIMINAL MESSAGING?

There are some interesting lines of research indicating how subliminal messaging or "priming" can impact behavior. [8] This has been studied at great length by advertisers in hopes of influencing consumer choices, but it also has been studied in the realm of sport science for the purpose of performance enhancement. Interestingly, there *is* evidence that subliminal priming can improve both confidence [9] and performance [10] during athletic pursuits.

Notably, unlike popular fictional portrayals of subliminal messaging, there is no loss of free will here. For it to work, you need to be receptive and *willing*. Studies on subliminally priming beverage choice, for example, only work if the participants are actually thirsty. [11] Fortunately, for our purposes here, there should be no conflict between the subliminal priming messages and your own goals. No nefarious intent, just a desire to succeed. If you *want* it to work, it will be much more likely to do so.

In the study mentioned above, where subliminal messaging was used to improve sport confidence, the "priming protocol" involved the subjects participating in a "semantic categorization task" where they sorted vocabulary words that appeared on a screen as either *sport-related* or *not sport-related*. As they completed the task, positive vocabulary words related to confidence were paired with sport-related vocabulary words and were flashed on the screen for 20 milliseconds (faster than the eye can consciously register). This was performed biweekly for just six minutes. After one month, they found that multi-unconscious goal priming was effective at increasing both explicit self-confidence *and* implicit self-confidence in athletes. They even performed multiple experiments with different groups of athletes in different sports to see if the effect replicated. It did.

Interesting stuff!

6. DEVELOP YOUR SIGNATURE STRENGTHS

What are you most proud of in your game? If you can answer that question quickly and easily, you have a good chance of being more confident as well. As players, we often focus on our weaknesses in training. This has some merit because it only takes one or two significant weaknesses for an experienced player to be able to exploit them and shut you down. But from the standpoint of building confidence, it also pays to spend a little time fostering your signature strengths. Plus, as Larry Hodges is fond of saying, if you don't have at least one overpowering strength, you won't be able to threaten those stronger players in the first place! This doesn't mean you spend all your training time doing things you are already good at. It simply means you should find your personal strengths as an athlete and figure out ways to use those strengths to gain a competitive advantage.

STEPS TO MAINTAINING CONFIDENCE

The four remaining strategies focus on *maintaining* confidence. They are continual development, positive environment, stabilize beliefs, and reinforce abilities. I will condense the steps in this section because they are somewhat repetitive with what was discussed before. The real key is this: whatever you did to build up your confidence, you must *continue* doing in order to maintain it.

In terms of the physical training environment, one of the things the sport psychology consultants touched upon was the use of environmental cues or triggers—things like the colors of the room, lighting, posters on the wall, music, etc. This is something a person like me totally overlooks. Case in point, when my family came to visit me in college, my brother remarked that my dorm room looked like a prison cell. Bare walls. No decorations of any kind. It simply never occurred to me to try to brighten up my room. But little details like that can actually make a difference! So, pay attention to the *atmosphere* of your training environment and put some inspirational words and/or images up on the walls. It's simple to do and can help you get into the right mindset faster.

Another important thing that will help you maintain your confidence is developing a sense of camaraderie with your training partners. Simply being around other people who are striving for a goal can trigger automatic goal pursuit in *you*—this is something researchers call "goal contagion." [8] The flip side of this is that you need to be aware of your own responsibility to be a positive contagion for your teammates.

ON GIVING AND RECEIVING COMPLIMENTS

One of the best ways to build camaraderie is to go out of your way to give sincere and *specific* compliments to your teammates and training partners. As you build others up, you'll find you get pulled along too. Making others feel good about themselves will make *you* feel better! When you receive compliments, make sure you do it graciously. I have the bad habit of downplaying or explaining away compliments when I receive them. Don't do this. A simple *thank you* is all that's needed.

By not accepting compliments, what you're really teaching yourself is that you are not worthy of compliments. And while you may think you need to be tough on yourself to reach the highest levels, research shows that self-compassion may be an effective approach to treating psychological distress among athletes, even at the highest levels of competition. [12] Not accepting compliments graciously also has the unintended effect of training others to give you fewer compliments. Eventually, the well will dry up and you won't get compliments any more. How do you think that will affect your confidence?

You can stabilize and reinforce your beliefs in self-confidence by fostering internal sources of confidence. This is achieved by taking a multi-dimensional approach and making sure you are leading a balanced and stable life. You are more than just an athlete. Look to the bigger picture. Focus on *processes* rather than outcomes. You can control your processes; you can't control outcomes. Perhaps you lost a game. Did you play well? Did you do everything you needed to prepare? Focusing on the things you can control puts the power back in your own hands.

Finally, you should reinforce your confidence through continual awareness of your achievements and strengths. Think of yourself as a lawyer presenting evidence to a skeptical jury. Can you prove beyond a reasonable doubt that you are a good player? If you're going to do so, you'll need some hard evidence! I already mentioned the personal highlight reel, but another tactic one of the sport psychology consultants used to help with this was a deck of flashcards with reminders of an athlete's strengths, victories, and growth as a player. As you gain experience, you can keep adding cards to the deck.

EMOTION MANAGEMENT

The next mental state we must cover is emotion management. A student who consistently "acts out" in school will very often have an unstable or troubled home life. There are exceptions, of course, but it's very common. Despite the safety and security of the school environment, these troubles can't help but bubble to the surface—often despite the student's best efforts to suppress them. Likewise, an athlete who might have his or her training completely on point, but doesn't have their house in order, may find that troubles at home easily become troubles on the court. I mention this because even though "emotion management" is something you will specifically need to attend to during a match, it should *start* long before the match begins. This means putting in the time practicing your psychological skills, but it also means attending to the "bigger picture" I alluded to in the introduction.

One of the first things you should work on when attempting to manage your emotional state is eliminating negative self-talk—especially during training and matches. Easier said than done, I know, but don't write this off. It's easy to conflate negative self-talk with intensity and passion, but allowing anger to take control of your emotions is not a path you want to go down. Anger and negative self-talk have been shown to be detrimental to sport performance—particularly in sports that require high degrees of selective attention and fine motor control, such as table tennis. [13] Furthermore, research shows that a negative emotional state can make you physically *slower*. [14] Both factors are supported by direct research on table tennis players that shows positive emotions during matches enhances the win rate of a competition, while a nervous or anxious emotional state negatively affects your results. [15] Thus, it's extremely important that you find a way to get a handle on your emotions during a match. Fortunately, this is an ability that can be trained.

In one study, [16] researchers had a group of table tennis players undergo cognitive behavioral therapy with the purpose of anger intervention. They utilized a multi-faceted approach that integrated cognitive-relaxation skills as well as social problem-solving skills. The program was deemed effective and resulted in anger reductions in table tennis players. Of particular note, is the fact that the results were still present a *year later* when they performed a 12-month follow-up!

In a video on mental strength in table tennis, Timo Boll discusses the importance of not complaining or lamenting after losing a point. [17]. He wisely reminds us that this only serves to build up your opponent's confidence! Instead, you should practice keeping a table tennis "poker face" when playing. This is an effective way to wage psychological warfare on your opponent. Become unflappable (or at least *appear* to be). I know all too well how difficult this is; I tend to engage in negative emotional displays during match play and have found it very difficult to break the habit. Two things have helped me in this regard: First, I focus on *progress* not perfection. If you get upset over the fact that you're getting upset, you've only created a vicious cycle! Give yourself a little grace and understand you'll slip up and shout out something negative from time to time. Second, I like to balance any negative self-talk with a positive mantra or affirmation on the occasions in which I do falter. This helps to get me back into the right frame of mind before the next point. Every time I say something negative, I follow it up with a positive statement.

CONCLUSION

So far, we've covered strategies for improving your concentration, self-confidence, positive thinking, and how to manage your emotions. Entire books could be written about each of those items alone, but I hope I've given you enough to chew on for now. The last mental state we will cover is motivation, but I will be taking a slightly different approach with that one, as you will see in the next chapter.

CHAPTER SUMMARY:

→ An athlete who attends to the "bigger picture" of his or her life will ultimately be able to perform better.

→ Many of the techniques used to achieve the five optimal mental states are synergistic and have overlapping benefits.

→ Self-confidence and positive thinking can be improved by things such as a personal highlight reel, monitoring improvements, goal setting, and developing signature strengths.

→ To achieve mental toughness, you should train hard but maintain a positive environment.

→ Negative emotions can physically slow you down, so learning how to manage them is key.

→ Try to keep a "poker face" when you've lost the point or made an unforced error.

→ Replace negative self-talk during a match with positive mantras.

THE MOTIVATION MYTH: ACHIEVING SUCCESS THROUGH HABITS, GOAL SETTING, SYSTEMS, AND STRUCTURE

If you aim to achieve your goals by relying on motivation, you are like the foolish man who built his house upon the sand. A wise man builds his house on a foundation of stone: simple habits that can be adopted now and repeated daily.

Motivation is overrated. It's a false fuel—a fleeting feeling. Relying on motivation to achieve your goals is like hoping the "puppy love" infatuation stage of a relationship will get you through a 50-year marriage. Romantic feelings of love may come and go, but true love is a *choice*. It's something you make sacrifices for day in and day out.

Likewise, a dedicated athlete should not rely on feeling motivated to accomplish their goals. Instead, they must focus on relentlessly implementing daily habits and creating a structured, systematized life. We know that motivation is a key mental state for peak performance, but it's not something you can simply conjure with a snap of the fingers. My best tip for feeling motivated on game day is to *put in the work beforehand*. Humans are naturally loss averse. If you do everything possible to prepare for an event, you will be much more motivated to see a return on your investment. You will not want all that work to go to waste!

For this reason, my approach to helping you achieve a motivated mental state during competition is to attack the problem from a different angle. Instead of a rah-rah speech about how you're a "warrior" entering the field of battle, I'm going to give you my best strategies and tactics for adopting and sustaining new habits. I will then help you to create systems and structure so you can successfully incorporate these habits into your life in a balanced way. I've worked with many people in my time, as a coach and trainer, and it is almost never a failure of information that causes bottlenecks in performance—it is typically a failure of *adherence* to the plan. All the best sport science in the world can't save you if you don't know how to change your daily behavior!

THE WILLPOWER MYTH

We've tackled the myth of motivation, but it's time to take on another myth—willpower. Most people think that behavior change is a brute force endeavor, an epic arm-wrestling match between your willpower and temptation. Except your opponent is Hafþór Júlíus Björnsson— the Icelandic strongman famous for portraying "The Mountain" on HBO's *Game of Thrones* and the winner of 2018's World Strongest Man competition. The truth is, successfully adopting new habits and resisting temptation is less about willpower and more about tactics. Research shows that people who *appear* to have high levels of self-control and willpower often just arrange their life in a way that minimizes temptations by relying on beneficial habits. [1] So it's not that these people have superhuman levels of willpower, it's that they structure their lives in a way that doesn't require as much use of willpower in the first place! There is no need to resist the donut if there is no donut there to begin with, right?

Furthermore, the idea that willpower is a limited resource that is "used up" during the day has also come under scrutiny. After performing a series of meta-analytic tests, one study found little evidence for willpower depletion and found the results of their analysis to "strongly challenge the idea that self-control functions as if it relies on a limited psychological or physical resource." [2] Interestingly, it seems that one of the major factors that affect self-control performance is your *beliefs* about willpower: if you believe your willpower is being used up throughout the day, you are more likely to give in to temptations. [3]

This information is valuable because it puts the power of behavior change back in your hands. You are not at the mercy of some inborn trait. With the right habits and systems in place, you can absolutely adopt and sustain the key habits needed to take your performance to the next level. To return to the arm-wrestling analogy, even an opponent as formidable as Hafþór can be defeated by someone nearly half his size with the proper technique.[7]

Now that you understand the role willpower plays in your life, we'll move onto goal setting.

---

7   If you don't believe me, search "Thor arm wrestle" on YouTube to see Hafþór face off
     against the much smaller arm-wrestling champ, Devon Larratt.

GOAL SETTING

One of the most powerful things you can do to increase your chances of sticking to new habits is to take some time to create goals and then to think carefully about the kind of future you want for yourself. One of the ways in which your mind justifies your current behavior is by disconnecting your present self with your future self. So, in order to really understand the consequences of your present actions, you need to feel like your future self is *real* and connected to you. This isn't just some feel-good mumbo jumbo; there's some real evidence demonstrating that people who feel more connected to their future selves tend to be more likely to make better choices regarding things that will impact them in the long term—things such as healthy eating, exercising, and saving for retirement. [4]

With that in mind, I'd like you to take part in a series of writing exercises[8] where you will take some time to think about the future and set some goals. I've found this to be an extremely powerful exercise, but it's one that takes some time and careful thought. Feel free to break this up into multiple sessions over a period of days rather than completing it all in one sitting.

SPEAKING YOUR FUTURE INTO EXISTENCE: THE PROMISE OF HEAVEN

Grab your table tennis journal and spend 5–10 minutes imagining your ideal future as it relates to you as an athlete.

→ What kind of lifestyle do you want to have?
→ What physical feats would you like to be able to accomplish?

---

8   This exercise is inspired by and based upon the "Self Authoring" online writing program available at selfauthoring.com.

→ What are some table tennis-related accomplishments you'd like to achieve?

→ How would that feel?

→ Why do you want these things?

→ How will you achieve all of this while maintaining balance?

Now I want you to write about this future you've just imagined. Make this as close to a stream-of-consciousness response as you can manage. Just keep writing with no filter.

Try to keep going for at least 10–15 minutes.

THE GHOST OF YOUR FUTURE: THE FEAR OF HELL

We will now engage in the opposite exercise: an exploration of a future you would like to *avoid*. You will move quickest toward your goals when you have both something to run toward and something to run from.

What will your life be like if you failed to pursue the life you described above? What would happen if you allowed bad habits and laziness to spiral out of control? What would that look like? To you? To your family and friends?

Think about times in the past when you've failed to live up to your own expectations of yourself. How did that feel? Tap into those feelings when you write this. Write until this vision of your potential future is as clear as you can bear.

Like before, make this as close to a stream-of-consciousness response as you can manage. Just keep writing with no filter and try to keep going for at least 10–15 minutes.

YOUR "BIG THREE" GOALS

"If you have more than three priorities, you don't have any."

—Jim Collins

Now that you've imagined both your ideal future and a future you'd like to avoid, it's time to drill down and get a little more specific about how you can start moving toward that vision you have for yourself. In the introduction to this book, I urged you to take notes as you read. You may want to skip this section for now until after you've had a chance to read through this book in its entirety. Once you've done so, you can review your notes and pick three "high priority" goals you'd like to adopt to help improve your health and performance as an athlete.

Remember, a good goal is SMART:

→ Specific
→ Measurable
→ Attainable
→ Relevant
→ Timely

So rather than setting a vague goal such as "I'd like to get leaner," you should instead say something like, "I'd like to lose 10 lb. in the next 60 days." Instead of "I want to be stronger," you could say, "I'd like to be able to perform five pull-ups by the end of this year." Instead of saying you'd like to "have more focus," you should aim to meditate for 5 minutes each morning.

Once you've identified your big three goals, you should rank them in order of importance. Go ahead and jot those down in your journal.

Next, you should examine each of your three goals in greater detail with the following in mind:

→ What are your motives?
→ What specific steps will you take to achieve this goal?
→ What are some potential obstacles and how will you deal with them?
→ How will you measure progress?

Research shows that thinking your goals over in this manner increases your chances of accomplishing them. One study [5] performed on 256 women, aged 30–50 years old, compared a "health information" only intervention with an information plus cognitive-behavioral, "self-regulation" intervention (similar to the one outlined here). The purpose of the study was to see which would have a better effect on the women's amount of physical activity per week.

At the end of this four-month study, they found that the women in the "self-regulation" group—the ones who recognized the possibilities of setbacks/failures ahead of time and planned accordingly— were twice as active as the women who did not. As it turns out, understanding that you will face obstacles and planning accordingly makes you better prepared to overcome said obstacles down the road.

Hope for the best, but plan for the worst.

THE FOUR LAWS OF BEHAVIOR CHANGE

Now that you have some goals in mind, we can get into the nitty gritty on specific strategies you can employ to make adopting these new habits as easy as possible. In his New York Times bestselling book, *Atomic Habits*, James Clear identifies four laws of behavior change[9]:

1. Make it obvious.

2. Make it attractive.

3. Make it easy.

4. Make it satisfying.

These laws are based on the cue, craving, response, reward sequence that behavioral scientists have identified as the underpinnings of why we do the things we do. Take out your notebook—it's time to do some more writing.

LAW #1: MAKE IT OBVIOUS.

First, we need to get specific about when and where you will complete each of your habits. This may seem arbitrary, but it's extremely important. For each of your three habits write down the following:

I will [BEHAVIOR] AT [TIME] in [LOCATION].

---

9   Many of the tips and terminology in this section are borrowed from his book. I highly recommend picking up a copy and giving it a read—it's the best I've read on the subject.

Examples:
I will meditate for 3 minutes at 6:30 a.m. in my living room.

I will work out for 30 minutes at 3:00 p.m. at the gym.

Next, we will use a technique called "habit stacking" to help pair your new habit to an already existing one. This will allow you to "piggyback" off a habit you already have so that you have a built-in cue for this new habit. Add the following sentence for each habit:

After [CURRENT HABIT], I will [NEW HABIT].

Examples:
After I start the coffee in the morning, I will meditate for 3 minutes in my living room.

After I clock out from work, I will drive straight to the gym.

Finally, we will design your environment to enhance the visual cues for your new habit. These cues should be "front and center" and easily accessible in the location you have designated the habit to occur.

Examples:
→ A note on the coffee machine that says MEDITATE.
→ Place your gym bag in the driver's seat of your car, so that when you go to leave from work you must move it out of the way to sit down.
→ Have a fruit bowl with at least two different types of fruit displayed prominently in the kitchen.
→ Have a recurring calendar event logged in your phone that sends you a push notification when it's time to perform your habit.

Return to your notebook and write down three ideas of how you will manipulate your environment to make the cues to your habits obvious and visible.

LAW #2: MAKE IT ATTRACTIVE

One of the best ways to make a new habit more attractive and desirable is to utilize a concept called "temptation bundling." Temptation bundling involves pairing a habit you need to do with a habit you want to do. So, if you need to go outside and do yard work, you could save a favorite podcast to listen to for the duration of the task.

If your new habit is the medicine, this is the spoonful of sugar.

Here's the formula:

After [HABIT I NEED], I will [HABIT I WANT].

This pairs well with the habit-stacking formula mentioned above. If you were focused on building a morning meditation habit, the two formulas might look like this:

→ **Habit Stack:** After I make the coffee, I will meditate for 3 minutes.
→ **Temptation Bundling:** After I meditate, I will check social media.

In your journal, think of good temptations you can bundle along with the habit you're attempting to build. You may have to experiment a little to find something that works best.

The next step in making your habit more attractive is to join (or create) a culture around it. We are social creatures and are influenced easily by our peers. Use this strategically to your advantage to help build your new habit.

Here's a few examples:

→ Get a friend or training partner on board as an accountability partner.
→ Join or start a club at work where you take turns bringing healthy lunches.
→ Join a Facebook group or online forum and interact with the existing community of people who are already enthusiastic about your habit.

Jot down a few ideas for how you might join or build a community around your new habit.

You can tap into the power of ritual to help increase the attractiveness of your habit further still. This motivational ritual should be something simple and repeatable that you can use as a powerful cue to signal to your brain, "It's game time."

For me, I've carefully curated a workout playlist on Spotify that I put on whenever it's time to train. It's music that I enjoy but don't typically listen to anywhere else. I put it on during my warm-up, and within minutes, I feel my energy levels rising in expectation of the hard work to come.

When I need to perform some deep, focused work, I always put headphones on and listen to a particular binaural beats song as background noise. I've done this so much I automatically become more productive and focused as soon as I put my headphones on.

In your journal, list a couple ideas for a ritual of your own that you can use to lead into your new habit.

Other ideas:

→ Create a positive mantra.
→ Have a special preworkout drink you enjoy before training.
→ Use a favorite outfit as a type of "uniform" each time you will perform the habit.

LAW #3: MAKE IT EASY

"The perfect is the enemy of the good."

—*Voltaire*

Humans are hard-wired toward dichotomous thinking:

→ *I don't have enough time to perform my full workout, so I can't go to the gym today.*
→ *I already had a donut this morning, so I'll just start fresh on my diet tomorrow.*

All too often, we want to do it perfectly or not at all. Here is an embarrassing example. . .

I've struggled for years with flossing consistently every day. By the time I put the kids down at night, I'm so tired I just want to lie in bed and watch Netflix. I'd manage to get my teeth brushed, but the flossing never seemed to happen. I tried all sorts of things to help me floss at night: getting a bunch of those disposable "one time" flossing sticks and putting them beside my bed. Setting a special alarm in my phone. . .

Nothing worked. The only thing that was "sticking" was more and more plaque to my teeth as I went another day without flossing! Then I made ONE little change and now I floss every day effortlessly. What was it?

Flossing in the morning.

Yep. That's it. It seems trivial but it's been a game changer. At night, the flossing was just one more thing keeping me from my warm, cozy bed. But in the morning, as I'm listening to a podcast and getting ready for the day, the flossing is a natural fit. If anything, it allows me to put off starting work for another minute or so.

I had never tried to floss in the morning because I always thought flossing at night is best. Obviously, it's better to floss at night so you don't have any food in between your teeth overnight, right?

But like I said above, the perfect is the enemy of the good— *zero* nightly flossing is certainly not better than daily adherence to flossing in the morning! By allowing myself to change the parameters and timing of my goal, I was able to seamlessly accomplish it without feeling like I needed any additional willpower.

I made it easy.

And that's what this third law is all about.

The first step toward making your new habit easy is to set yourself up for success ahead of time. When the time comes to perform your new habit, everything should be easily accessible and ready to go. Take *preemptive action*. You could. . .

→ Pack your gym bag the night before and leave it by the door.
→ Take an hour to prep some food each weekend so healthy foods are pre-portioned and "grab and go."
→ Keep a big water bottle at your desk so you can drink more water.

You need to off-load that "in the moment" struggle of getting your habit started. Return to your journal and write down a couple ideas for how you can make your new habit as easy as possible to begin.

The next step is to master the art of "showing up." One of the most important things you can do to develop a habit is consistent repetition. It's the frequent, reliable implementation of the habit that is key—not your actual performance!

One way to ease into a new habit is to follow what James Clear calls the "two-minute rule." What this means is that you should scale your habit down until you can complete it in two minutes or less. You want to make it so easy it would feel ridiculous to say no.

Examples:

→ If you had an ultimate goal of meditating for 20 minutes each morning, you should start with 2 minutes.
→ If you want to write three pages per day, instead start with writing one sentence.
→ If you'd like to run a mile each morning, instead start with jogging to the end of your block and back.

This may seem like a waste of time, but it's far from that. It's vital you learn to break that "all or nothing" mindset. In your journal, write down how you can scale your habits down so they fit the "two-minute rule."

Another sneaky way of making your new habit easy to do is to make *not* doing it difficult. We can achieve this by using a commitment device such as a Ulysses pact. A Ulysses pact is a decision you make in the present that controls your actions in the future.

Here's one my wife uses:

Typically, when she drops the kids off at daycare, she leaves the car seat there so I'll have it when I pick them up in the afternoon. On days when she wants to work out, however, she takes the car seat with her. This means I'll be unable to get the kids unless she meets me at the gym and gives me the car seat. And once she's there, she might as well work out!

If you get creative, you can think of all sorts of little hassles you can create for yourself that will force you to make better decisions. In your journal, think of at least one solid Ulysses pact you can make for each of your habits.

LAW #4: MAKE IT SATISFYING

One of the most reliable ways to increase a behavior is by rewarding it. Just think about how you train a dog to do tricks. We reward them with a treat. If you think you're any different from a dog rolling over for a little piece of cut up hot dog, think again! All our current habits, good or otherwise, have some element of reward built into them.

Open your journal and come up with a couple ideas for how you might reward yourself for completing your new habits. Make sure you don't reward yourself in a counterproductive way, however. If your goal is to go to the gym more regularly, "rewarding" yourself with a Big Mac and fries afterwards is probably not the best idea! Instead, you might reward yourself with a healthy meal that you really enjoy.

The more immediate the reward, the more effective it will be. A simple way you can reliably provide an immediately satisfying reward for completing a habit is to track it. This allows you to visibly "check it off" and create a nice streak of consecutive successful days.

Since we want this reinforcer to occur immediately after completing the habit, I recommend using a free habit tracking app. This will allow you to quickly and easily "check it off" and also to see your past successes. There are several free habit tracking apps available for both android and iOS, download one and input your new habits so you can begin tracking them.

THE "NEVER MISS TWICE" RULE

Sooner or later, you *will* miss a day and break your streak. Here's James Clear on the matter:

> *The first mistake is never the one that ruins you. It is the spiral of repeated mistakes that follows. Missing once is an accident. Missing twice is the start of a new habit.*

We all fall off the wagon from time to time. This is no big deal as long as you hop back on and get going right after. Make it a hard rule to never miss twice.

DO NOT BEAT YOURSELF UP OVER FAILURES

This may seem counterintuitive; after all, you don't want to "go easy" on yourself, right? Isn't that just letting yourself off the hook and allowing for future failures? Interestingly, studies have shown that if you treat yourself kindly and with compassion after a failure, you are actually more likely to take responsibility for your failure and seek to do better next time. [6-7]

Beating yourself up emotionally may *increase* the chances you'll repeat the behavior again because once we "punish" ourselves, we are more likely to seek comfort afterwards—and that comfort may be the very thing we were trying to avoid in the first place!

Instead, this should be your thought process after a failure:

→ First, be mindful of your thoughts and feelings after failing. Don't try to hide from your feelings!
→ Next, realize you're not alone. We all mess up. This is a normal part of the process.
→ Finally, use encouragement over criticism: Think about what you would say to your son or daughter if he or she was discouraged and say that to yourself.

It's so easy to let a little hang-up derail the rest of the day. And once the day is "ruined," might as well blow the whole weekend, right? This inevitably leads to the snowball effect—we let that small little failure keep rolling, and it turns into something a lot bigger.

So, remember the "never miss twice" rule and use the strategy outlined above to acknowledge your mistake, encourage yourself rather than criticizing, and move on.

CREATING STRUCTURE AND ROUTINE: BUILDING YOUR "PERFECT WEEK"

Your ability to create, adopt, and maintain habits will be critical in your success, not just as an athlete but in your broader life goals as well. And if you truly want to adopt these habits and change your lifestyle, you need to sit down and figure out the best way to make them fit into your schedule.

These new habits are not simply going to "happen." You have to make them a priority by creating dedicated spaces for them within your schedule each week. Remember, being disciplined is not about monumental feats of willpower, it's about creating habits.

The way we will build these habits is by creating structure and routine.

You might think this will restrict and suffocate you, but it will do the opposite. It will FREE you. Eventually, you'll fall into a pattern where you won't have to rely upon a bunch of willpower to haphazardly shoot down tasks, you'll simply follow the path you've already laid out for yourself. It will take some effort at first, but once you've blazed the trail, it's there for you. Just keep walking it.

The following is something I developed based on Jon Goodman's Dream Week exercise. It will help you take proactive control over your time and will make you a more focused, productive, and fulfilled person.

A QUICK NOTE ON WHAT I REALLY MEAN BY *PERFECT*:

In taking the time to create your "perfect" week, what you're doing is creating an ideal—a target to shoot for. It needs to be the type of week you'd actually *want* to experience, so don't try to cram so much in there that your schedule becomes a tyrant. Be reasonable and include breaks and fun activities in addition to productive tasks.

Ironically, I do not want you to worry about following your perfect week, *perfectly*. In fact, whether or not you stick to the schedule day-to-day is not what's most important.

The important thing is knowing that each time you choose to do something, you are choosing to *not do* something else. You should know what you are saying *no* to when you decide to say *yes* to something.

Having a schedule means you will be forever aware of that.

STEP ONE: YOUR LIFE IN A LIST

Create a list of categories for how you spend your time. Include obligations and responsibilities, such as work and household chores, but also include your training, hobbies, family time, and the **three habits** you'd like to develop.

Your time is a precious thing. We're going to split it up in a purposeful and visible way; in doing so, you will have to make some hard choices as to what will stay and what must go.

Remember, structure = freedom.

Here are some possible categories you might have:

→ Morning routine
→ Table tennis sessions
→ Meals (breakfast, lunch, dinner)
→ Sleep/wake times
→ Work schedule
→ Reading
→ Journaling
→ Workouts
→ Food shopping
→ Meal prep
→ Walks
→ Date nights
→ Church/worship
→ Pay bills
→ Clean house

→ Meditation/mindfulness
→ Netflix and chill
→ Evening ritual

Only choose the things relevant to you and feel free to add categories that I may have left out.

STEP TWO: CREATING YOUR PERFECT WEEK

Now that you have a master list of activities, you'll need a digital calendar. Choose a calendar that you can set up on your desktop that will also sync with your phone—I like Google Calendar or iCal.

Now that you have a calendar, you're going to schedule your entire day.

That's right, you're going to book your calendar with "appointments" such as...

Go for a walk.

Or *go food shopping.*

My day is typically scheduled from 5:00 a.m. when I wake up until 6:00 p.m. Save for rare exceptions, I do not work past 6:00 p.m. as this is my time to spend with family, and to relax and unwind for the night. Put in your concrete, "set in stone" responsibilities first, and sprinkle the rest in as you see fit. Remember, this is just a template for your hypothetically "perfect week." This isn't something you're creating from scratch every day.

By taking the time to plot out the things you'd like to accomplish on a daily, weekly, and monthly basis, you are creating a system you can fall back. This will prevent situations where you simply feel you have too much to do, get overwhelmed, and end up doing nothing.

If you have a fairly static work schedule, creating this calendar is mostly a "one and done" kind of deal. If you do shift work where your work days and hours change from week to week, you may need to shift to a more flexible template for tracking your activities, or simply forgo this activity all together.

If you find this activity to be extremely difficult to do, consider it a red flag. This means there is a high level of chaos and unpredictability in your life. You may or may not have much control over that, but seek to add regularity and structure as much as you are able.

STEP THREE: A MORNING ROUTINE

A perfect week is built from perfect days. And a perfect day springs from a perfect morning. In this step, we're going to find a simple morning routine you can stick to, and we'll make it a part of your new lifestyle.

Here's mine:

→ Wake up 5 a.m.
→ Use the bathroom and weigh myself.
→ Go downstairs, start the coffee, and drink one large glass of water.

→ While the coffee brews, I go for a short 5-minute walk (weather permitting), and/or do some light stretching.
→ Next is appx. 5 minutes of mindfulness and quiet meditation. As the coffee percolates, so does my mind.
→ I then pour myself a mug of coffee and sit down for about five minutes and create a prioritized list of tasks for the day, and enter them into Asana.
→ Finally, I turn on a 10,000 lux, full spectrum light and spend a minimum of 30 focused minutes working on my number one priority. This is deep work and I devote my full, undivided attention to it.

By starting my day in this way, I have ensured that even if *nothing* else gets accomplished, I have at least identified what is most important to me that day and have dedicated some time and focus toward that goal. The light is to help set my circadian rhythm and signal to my brain it's time to wake up (I'm up early, often before the sun has risen).

Your routine might end up looking a little different, but I highly suggest incorporating some form of the following:

→ Movement
→ Mindfulness
→ Purpose
→ Light

You want to have positive triggers for both your body and mind that it is time to start the "booting up" cycle. Movement and mindfulness will accomplish that. Once you're firing on all cylinders, you need to decide upon a *purpose* for the day.

Each day, you will have several unique tasks that must be completed. These are things that may be impossible to anticipate but are important nonetheless. Your job is to figure out what is *most* important for each day.

What is your "deep work" for the day? What are the most pressing tasks that must be done?

Narrow it down to a list of 3–5 actionable things.

You can keep it old fashioned and write them down on paper, or you can go digital and use apps like Asana or Google Tasks to keep your daily list. Either way, it's important to have a specific focus for each day.

STEP FOUR: AN EVENING RITUAL

A perfect morning won't just happen, it is preceded by a perfect night's sleep and a perfect evening. All of this connects. The first step of a good evening ritual is to figure out what you need to prepare the night before in order to have time for your morning routine the next day. For me, this boils down to getting my work clothes, workout clothes, and my first two meals prepped for the next day, each evening.

Since I wake up quite a bit earlier than the rest of my family, I have to creep around in the dark each morning like a ninja. In the past, I would struggle to pick out my clothes in the dark—just try picking out the *right* type of black socks, from a drawer full of black socks, in a pitch-black room . . . madness!

The whole thing was a ridiculous waste of time.

Now my mornings go smoothly and I have time to organize my thoughts and prepare for the day. What a difference!

Maybe for you it's getting the kitchen cleaned after dinner. Maybe it's straightening up your office so your work area is clean and free from clutter. The important thing is to ask yourself, *"what will it take for me to have peace of mind when I wake in the morning."* Answer that question for yourself and use that to guide you.

One last critical step is getting to bed at the same time each night. Your body works very well with consistent sleep/wake cycles, so set an alarm on your phone for your bedtime. It may sound backward, but this alarm is the trigger that lets you know it's time to start your bedtime sequence.

Here's an example of one possible sequence for a 10:00 p.m. bedtime:

→ 9:35 p.m: Bedtime alarm goes off.
→ 9:35–9:40 p.m: Use the bathroom/brush teeth.
→ 9:40–10:00 p.m: Spend 20 minutes reading fiction (something not related to work or real life preferably), or listen to a book on Audible.
→ 10:00 p.m: Go to sleep.

Reading before bed is a habit that *many* very successful people seem to adopt. I highly recommend it.

CLOSING THOUGHTS

You don't set out to build a wall. You don't say 'I'm going to build the biggest, baddest, greatest wall that's ever been built.' You don't start there. You say, 'I'm going to lay this brick as perfectly as a brick can be laid.' You do that every single day. And soon you have a wall.

—*Will Smith*

I realize this chapter is a somewhat odd take on the concept of motivation. But if we define motivation as the *reason* you have for doing the things you do, it starts to make a little more sense. Find your "reason" and then create the habits and structure necessary to pursue it in the most efficient way possible. Your goals may change over time. That's a natural part of the process. The only way to gain the perspective and wisdom necessary to truly refine your goals and reach that vision you have for yourself is by learning to take imperfect action *now*.

SECTION III

READINESS

SECTION OVERVIEW

Do you know what an athlete's most important ability is? It's *availability*. You can be the best player in the world, but what good is it if you're injured from your training, mentally run down, and sick as a dog? There is a reason the readiness cog is positioned near the center of the peak performance graphic. All your training and preparation hinge upon you actually being healthy and vital enough to bring those abilities to bear on the day of competition.

Readiness is the state of being physically, mentally, and emotionally recovered. In this section, we will cover a wide range of topics to ensure you can achieve that. Here are a few of them:

➔ Sleep (and how it can be used to actually *enhance* performance).
➔ How much training is too much (overreaching versus overtraining)?
➔ How to properly warm-up.
➔ Injury prevention.
➔ Advanced recovery protocols.
➔ Reducing illness.

The first chapter is devoted completely to one of my all-time favorite things—sleep.

SLEEP: THE DARK HORSE OF PERFORMANCE ENHANCERS

"I love sleep. My life has the tendency to fall apart when I'm awake, you know?"

—*Ernest Hemingway*

What if I told you there was a way to improve your reaction time, boost your serving accuracy, decrease fatigue levels, and increase your mood state? Would you be interested? What if I *also* told you this could all be accomplished without any special equipment or extra training on your part? Moreover, it's so easy to implement it can be done with your eyes closed (literally). Sounds too good to be true, no?

Amazingly, all this can be achieved with just a little extra sleep.

Depending on the statistics you look at, the average adult gets around seven hours of sleep per night. And it's fairly common to hear seven-plus hours per night recommended as the minimum amount of sleep needed by adults for general health and wellbeing. [1] But what if you're after more than just general health? As it turns out, there is a difference between what's sufficient for general health and what's needed for optimizing athletic performance. Two studies come to mind that demonstrate this quite well.[10]

The first was conducted on basketball players. In this study, [2] the players increased their nightly time in bed from an average of appx. 7 hours to 10+ hours for a period of 5–7 weeks. Actual sleep time went up by around 2 hours for each participant—from a mean of 6.6 hours to 8.4 hours.

Here's a quick rundown of what happened:

→ Subjective fatigue levels down by 80% on average.
→ Subjective ratings of mood state improved significantly.
→ Timed sprint speeds improved (16.2 seconds to 15.5 seconds).
→ Free throw and three-point shooting accuracy improved by 9–9.2%.
→ Reaction time decreased significantly (remember a decrease here is a *good* thing).

Not too shabby, but we're not done yet!

A 2015 study [3] followed a similar protocol and had tennis players increase their time asleep by roughly 2 hours per night (from 7.14

10 Credit to Greg Nuckols for assisting with the analysis of these two studies via his excellent research review, *Monthly Applications in Strength Sport.*

hours to 8.85 hours) for one week. Again, predictably, subjective ratings of sleepiness decreased, but they also observed a 14.3% average increase in serving accuracy.

What's notable about this second study is that the improvement came after a mere *week* of sleep extension. This means even if your schedule does not typically allow for 8+ hours of sleep per night, you can still implement a sleep-extension protocol around important tournaments and reap the benefits, at least in part.

So how much sleep do I actually need?

Based on these studies, it is clear athletes can potentially benefit from getting more sleep than the typical adult. Because sleep is linked so tightly with performance and recovery, it's only natural that as one pushes their physiology to achieve higher and higher levels of performance, the need for sleep increases. Put another way, there's a difference between just pushing pencils and pushing a serve in preparation for an all-out loop battle!

General recommendations for sleep tend to converge on around 7–8 hours, but I like to see athletes aim for a *minimum* of 8 hours per night and experiment with periods of 8–10 hours per night around important events. I know this may seem high, but it's almost impossible to overstate the importance of sleep. This is something most people will pay lip service to, but continually fail to prioritize in daily living. If the two studies mentioned above weren't enough to convince you, consider this:

A 2018 systematic review of the literature sought to get to the bottom of the competitive advantages of sleep. After reviewing 19 studies representing 12 sports, they found that sleep manipulations seem to disproportionately impact sports requiring speed, tactical strategy, and technical skill. [4] Speed, tactical strategy, and technical skill. . . what sport does that sound like? Sleep deficiency has also been demonstrated to worsen reaction times, [5] increase the risk for injury by a whopping 60%, [6–8] and reduce your ability to recover from training. [9]

As for the consequences to your health, in an amazing overview of the literature regarding sleep, Michael Grandner sifted through well over 100 studies to conclude the following:

> *Sleep has been shown to be a key predictor of shorter lifespan, as well as weight gain and obesity, hypertension, hypercholesterolemia, atherosclerosis risk, diabetes, poor mental health, smoking, alcohol misuse, unhealthy diet, and sedentary activity. In addition, sleep is an important factor in brain functions that are important for the workplace, including sleepiness, attention, and decision-making. [10]*

So clearly, for a host of both health and performance reasons, it's worth spending some time to get your sleep in order.

HOW TO IMPROVE YOUR SLEEP

I will now provide an evidence-based list of my top tips for improving your sleep quality. I will first list what I believe are the most important and impactful tips and then create a secondary list with some other things to consider.

Top Tips:

→ Establish a bedtime routine and maintain a consistent sleep/ wake cycle [11]—try setting an alarm for your *bedtime* not just for when you need to wake up.

→ Get room-darkening shades (or use a sleep mask) and ensure that your bedroom is as dark as possible. Ideally, you shouldn't be able to see your own hand in front of your face.

→ Keep the temperature a little cooler at night. Around 65°F works well for most.

→ Limit or eliminate caffeine intake within 6 hours or less before bedtime. Even if you have no problems falling asleep when consuming caffeine at night, the *quality* of your sleep will still be affected. [12]

→ Limit or eliminate alcohol before bed. Alcohol is a sedative, so it will help you fall asleep faster, but it reduces the *quality* of your sleep, by reducing total night REM sleep. [13]

→ Avoid eating a large meal right before sleeping.

→ Get early sunlight exposure in the morning when possible. If not, consider using a 10,000+ lux light therapy lamp to get full spectrum light early in the day. This will help set your circadian rhythm.

Other things to try:

→ Read or listen to fiction for 15–30 minutes before sleep. This tip will help a lot if you tend to ruminate at night. Escape to another world and get your mind off things. Bedtime stories aren't just for kids!

→ Taking a warm bath before bed may help you sleep better as your core temperature will actually *drop* afterwards to compensate, resulting in increases in sleepiness, slow wave sleep, and stage 4 sleep. [14] The optimal timing for this seems to be around 1–2 hours before bed. [15]

→ Limit the activities you do from bed—sleep and sex, or maybe some reading before falling asleep. Don't get in the habit of staying in bed all day.

→ Reduce exposure to electronics before bed—too much blue light may inhibit your body's natural release of melatonin. Use the computer program f.lux and the "nightshift" mode on your phone to warm the colors of your screens.

→ If possible, build an extra day into your schedule for sleep when traveling—amazingly, in a phenomenon known as the *first-night effect*, your brain stays half-awake during the first night of sleep in an unfamiliar location. [16] So, if you travel to a tournament, sleep one night in a cheap motel, and then play your matches the next morning, you're not likely to be at your best!

→ Consider supplementing with magnesium. If you happen to be deficient in this mineral (an occurrence that is more common in athletes because it is lost through sweat), then your sleep quality may be impaired. A standard dose for magnesium falls in the range of 200–400 mg taken daily. Magnesium does not have a sedative effect, so it may be taken any time of the day.

→ If you have done all the above and still take a long time to fall asleep, taking some melatonin before bed may be helpful to reduce sleep latency. [17] Take 1–5 g of melatonin (start with the lower end of the range to determine the lowest effective dose) 30 minutes before bed.

I know sleep is important, but I usually only get 6–7 hours per night and I feel fine. My body has adjusted!

One of the most nefarious consequences of sleep deprivation is that you begin to lose your ability to accurately gauge your own performance. You become out of touch with what "normal" really feels like. This is especially tricky because you typically feel worse when first becoming sleep deprived, but then if sleep deprivation continues, you start to feel *better*. This leads one to think they have adjusted. What has actually happened, however, is you only *feel* like you're back to normal. When measured objectively, your performance and cognitive functioning are still suppressed, despite your positive self-evaluation. [18–19]

Can't I just "catch up" on the weekends?

It seems not. One study found three consecutive nights of 8-hour "recovery sleep" was not enough to restore performance after a week of only getting 7 hours of sleep. [20] So running a sleep deficit during the week and attempting to "catch up" on the weekend is not a winning strategy.

You can, however, use sleep extension to create a "sleep bank" that you can draw from in times of need. This will protect against some of the effects of temporary sleep deprivation. [21–22] Aiming for the standard 8 hours during the week, and more like 9–10 hours over the weekend could be an effective strategy to both boost performance *and* reduce the impact of any random off nights you may happen to have.

Instead of treating sleep like a credit card by running up a deficit and attempting to pay it off over the weekend, treat it like retirement savings—pay your bills, and if you can save a little extra here and there, do it!

BIORHYTHMIC OPTIMIZATION

Practicing good sleep hygiene and getting sufficient duration of sleep should be your priority, but if you want to optimize things further, you may want to consider shifting your "night owl" sleep pattern back a bit. Our bodies have an internal clock, a *biorhythm*, if you will, that prefers us to be most active during the daylight hours. I know quite a few night owls who swear they feel better staying up all night and sleeping during the day, but upon closer inspection, this is rarely the case.

A notable study by Facer-Childs and colleagues, found that shifting the sleep-wake cycle of night owls back by around two hours decreased self-reported ratings of depression and stress, reduced sleepiness in the morning, and *improved* cognitive and mental performance (reaction time and grip strength specifically). [23]

Keep in mind, the subjects did not improve their sleep quality or quantity, they simply changed the timing. The strategies used to achieve this phase shift will seem familiar as they are similar to the recommendations I suggested earlier (early light exposure, strategic timing of caffeine, limiting blue light exposure in the evening), but one additional tip is they advised the subjects to eat breakfast soon as soon as possible after waking, keep lunch at the same time each day, and not to eat dinner past 7 p.m.

So, if you're the type who can't seem to fall asleep before 2:00 a.m., consider using some of these strategies to get to bed earlier. You'll likely feel and perform better as a result!

WHAT ABOUT NAPS?

In a comprehensive review paper, [24] Catherine Milner and Kimberly Cote poured over the research regarding naps and found the following:

→ Naps have beneficial effects even for *well-rested* individuals in areas such as logical reasoning, reaction time, mood, and subjective levels of sleepiness.

→ Napping is generally easiest during the afternoon due to a natural circadian dip in alertness.

→ The ideal length of time for a "power nap" is between 10–20 minutes. This will minimize sleep inertia (feeling groggy upon waking) while still imparting performance benefits.

→ Longer naps in the 60–90-minute range often result in a temporary period of *reduced* performance due to sleep inertia upon waking. Once this grogginess goes away, performance improvements and feelings of wakefulness increase.

→ Longer naps that result in REM sleep may have a uniquely beneficial effect on memory consolidation and skill acquisition for habitual nappers.

→ Combining caffeine + a power nap results in a synergistic, 1+1 = 3 scenario where the combined treatment was superior to either intervention alone.

Clearly napping can be an effective strategy to boost performance, but it should be viewed as a supplemental strategy to a good night's sleep, not a "workaround." If daytime napping consistently causes disruptions to your nightly sleep, then it is likely to have a net negative impact. Don't put the cart before the horse.

Personally, I find a short siesta after lunch to be the ideal time for a power nap. Taking the nap earlier in the afternoon helps to ensure it doesn't interfere with your sleep, and there is often a postprandial dip in energy after eating that makes the post-lunch period perfect for a snooze.

To really take things to the next level, taking some caffeine immediately before the nap is an extremely effective strategy. Since caffeine typically takes around 30–60 minutes to reach peak levels in the blood, you can use that window to nap. Then, just as you're waking up, the caffeine begins to kick in. This is a powerful way to maximize the benefits of a nap while eliminating the post-nap grogginess and confusion.

One final note on naps: Do not attempt to force the nap and stress about whether you're falling asleep in time or not. Simply lying down in a quiet, dark room and closing your eyes for 10–20 minutes as a "sensory reset" is beneficial on its own. If you spend that time in a stressed state because you can't fall asleep, you've defeated the purpose entirely!

FIGHTING JET LAG

If you are traveling across multiple time zones for a tournament, you may experience some degree of jet lag upon arriving at your destination. If possible, give yourself a 1–2 day buffer before playing any important matches so that you have time to adjust. Remember, the first night's sleep in an unfamiliar location is not likely to be very restful, regardless of whether you are jet-lagged or not, so having this buffer should be a no-brainer.

To speed your adjustment to the new time zone, you can combine melatonin supplementation with light therapy. One systematic review [25] found that melatonin, taken close to the target bedtime at the destination, decreased jet lag from flights crossing five or more time zones. The benefit appears to be greater the more time zones crossed, but less effective for flights westward.

Since early full-spectrum light exposure is a powerful way to help set your circadian rhythm, and you can't be guaranteed your destination will be sunny in the mornings, packing a light therapy lamp (there are quite a few in the $20–$40 range that are quite small and easy to pack) is a good way to cover your bases. Your first choice should be getting outside early in the morning and getting plenty of actual sunlight, but having a light therapy lamp as a fallback is wise. This, plus melatonin is a great one-two punch for dealing with jet lag!

CONCLUDING THOUGHTS AND A FINAL CONCESSION

My intention with this chapter was to show you just how impactful sleep can be on your health, performance, and recovery. That said, I don't want you getting scared and developing sleep-related anxiety if you can't manage to consistently hit 8 or more hours per night. There *is* a small subset of people who may function just fine on less sleep. All I ask is before deciding that *you* fit into this category, give the sleep strategies outlined in this chapter a real go for at least 2 or 3 months. If you don't find any benefit to the extra sleep, then return to your habitual levels. Fair enough?

CHAPTER SUMMARY:

→ Getting the proper amount of sleep is not just vital for your health; it can acutely improve your athletic performance.

→ Truly serious athletes should aim for 8–10 hours of sleep per night.

→ Many people think they function just fine with 6–7 hours of sleep per night, but when measured objectively, their performance and cognitive functioning are suppressed.

→ Playing "catch up" on the weekends cannot erase poor sleep habits during the week.

→ Napping can be an effective strategy to boost energy levels and performance, but if it consistently causes disruptions to your nightly sleep, it is likely to have a net negative impact.

→ Melatonin supplementation and light therapy may help combat jet lag.

BECOMING BULLETPROOF: INJURY PREVENTION, ADVANCED RECOVERY TACTICS, AND DEALING WITH SICKNESS

All serious athletes risk injury to some degree. This is an inevitable part of trying to push performance to elite levels. You can try to minimize this risk to the extent possible, but the key to becoming a strong and resilient individual lies in a somewhat counterintuitive truth about the human body and mind: you are *antifragile*.

Something that is fragile becomes weaker and weaker the more it is stressed and jostled about. If you need an example, just think of the early prototypes of those darn plastic balls! Being antifragile is precisely the opposite. In his book *Antifragile*, Nassim Taleb describes it in this way: "Antifragility is beyond resilience or robustness. The resilient resists shocks and stays the same; the antifragile gets better." Too often we acknowledge the risk of action, but overlook the risk of *inaction*. Yes, you might get injured if you go outside and exercise, but just sitting around on the couch all day is equally damaging. The best way to protect oneself from injuries is not to play it safe and avoid anything that might risk harm; instead, you should proactively seek out training designed to push you *just* past your current capabilities.

With the strategic application of stress, you can incrementally make yourself stronger and more resistant to injury, but clearly, it's possible to both acutely or chronically overwhelm your body's ability to adapt and recover from stress—bend a bone just a bit and it stimulates osteoblasts to lay down more collagen fibers which then mineralize and strengthen the bone. Bend it too much, and it snaps. Thus, it is the purposeful application of the right amount of stress applied at the right time that will lead you safely down the path to becoming stronger and more resistant to injuries.

The first step to achieving this balance is maintaining an awareness of the global levels of stress placed on your body and ensuring you are adjusting your training accordingly. There is a lot more interplay between stressors in different domains of your life than you might think. Remember, your body does not necessarily know the difference between shoveling snow, working out, and playing table tennis. All these things will take their toll on you in their own way.

Even seemingly unrelated stressors from everyday life will have physiological ramifications on your ability to perform and recover. Division I football players, for example, have been shown to get injured nearly twice as often during periods of high academic stress. [1] The additional academic stress of exams, coupled with a (likely) reduction in sleep, creates a situation in which the athlete is not able to perform at full capacity on the field, resulting in an increase in injuries.

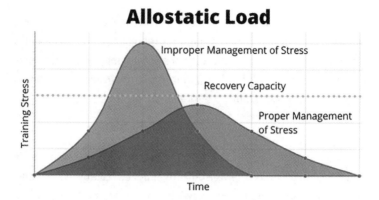

Allostatic Load

Taken together, the sum total of the stresses experienced in your life can be referred to as the *allostatic load*. One of the best ways to help prevent injuries is to "flatten out" the spikes of this load as much as possible. This is quite similar to the "flatten the curve" policy enacted during the COVID-19 pandemic. Notably, the total "area under the curve" can be the same. You just want to spread out the volume so that it never spikes to the point where it exceeds your recovery capacity.

You should always aim to build up to a given level of training volume *incrementally*—and just as importantly—don't allow yourself to decondition and then try to jump right back into your previous peak levels of training. Research shows up to a 10% increase in training volume per week is a good rate to minimize risk of injury. [2] If you are deconditioned due to a break from training, a good rule of thumb is to spend as much time ramping back up to full volume as you spent off from training. If you were out for a month, take a month to ramp back up. Finally, you should periodize your training so that purposeful periods of rest and recovery are interspersed throughout the year. Doing these things will result in a tremendous reduction in your risk for injury.

At any given time, there will be certain components of your allostatic load that will be out of your control: illness, work- and relationship-related stress, disrupted sleep from travel, etc. When this is the case, you must do what you can to "shore up" your recovery in the areas that you *can* control, while adjusting your training if necessary. Taking those previously mentioned football players, rather than continuing their normal training and practice schedule right through exams, a better approach would be to take a week to deload and pursue some lighter, "active recovery" protocols. This would preserve performance, minimize the risk of injury, and likely allow for better performance on the exams to boot!

In a nutshell: You become stronger and more injury resistant by incrementally exposing your body to increasingly demanding tasks, forcing it to adapt. Using a graded prescription of volume at an appropriate rate will minimize injury risk. Regularly scheduled periods of rest and recovery are necessary to allow for more complete healing and tissue repair. Stress from all parts of your life affects your performance, recovery, and injury risk. The total combined stressors from all areas are the *allostatic load*.

APPLICATIONS TO TABLE TENNIS

Compared with other sports, table tennis carries a low risk of injury. But while the uninitiated might scoff at the idea of getting injured while playing "ping pong," serious players know the toll high-level play can take on your body. And as you improve, your risk of injury will only *increase*. Table tennis athletes at the national/international level present higher indexes of injury than those at lower levels. [3]

This is because in order to get to the highest levels, the training you must pursue becomes increasingly rigorous and thus riskier as well.

Although acute injuries do occur, I've found table tennis players tend to experience injuries related to *overuse* far more frequently. Overuse injuries nearly always occur from simply doing too much too quickly and not allowing for sufficient recovery between bouts. Because of this, utilizing the strategies outlined above is particularly relevant to table tennis players. As they say, an ounce of prevention is worth a pound of cure!

Take a stroke like the chiquita (banana flick), for example. Because it's not particularly fatiguing and is a quick stroke, it can be repeated with a very high frequency when training with a robot or multi-ball feeding by a training partner. This is great from a learning perspective since you can easily perform a high number of repetitions, but it can also set you up for overuse injuries. So, if you become determined to learn the banana flick after watching a few Dimitrij Ovtcharov matches on YouTube, perhaps don't go straight into a solid hour of repetitions with your robot. It's easy to let your eagerness and enthusiasm get the better of you when first learning a new stroke, but once you've crossed that threshold and your elbow or wrist starts bothering you because you did 10,000 repetitions on day one, there's no going back. The only solution will be to rest it until it heals and now you've taken one step forward and two steps back!

HOW MUCH IS TOO MUCH? OVERREACHING VERSUS OVERTRAINING

An accomplished athlete will train both smart *and* hard. This means giving 100% during training but also being mindful of one's limits and giving just as much focus to less glamorous things such as sleep and recovery. When the latter is ignored, the consequences can be severe. This section will outline a few of those consequences and discuss the differences between overreaching and overtraining.

Overtraining is a word that gets tossed about fairly frequently, but it's rarely discussed in an accurate way. On the one hand, you have people who use it as a bogeyman—they *overstate* the likelihood of it occurring and use it as an excuse to do less than they should. These are the types who make absolute claims like "you can't exercise longer than an hour," or "a muscle should never be trained for two days in a row." On the other hand, some claim that overtraining doesn't exist—that one is simply "underrecovering" and/or not "hardcore" enough. This is equally untrue.

For each athlete, there exists a certain amount of training that is simply too much, even if recovery and sleep are maxed out. If an athlete consistently fails to recover from training over a prolonged period, they may eventually develop a condition called "overtraining syndrome" (OTS). To truly understand the progression toward OTS, it is helpful to first understand the interplay between three concepts: the fitness-fatigue model, overreaching, and overtraining.

The fitness-fatigue model is a crucial concept in sport science and is a key part of periodization. The theory behind this model is relatively straightforward: your performance will temporarily *decrease* after training because of the concomitant buildup of fatigue. Your body is not able to "cash in" on the physiological adaptations from training until this fatigue dissipates. Most understand this intuitively within the context of a single workout—if you give maximum effort during a single set and manage to lift 100 lb for ten repetitions, it's only common sense that you won't be able to repeat that same performance 30 seconds later. What many fail to realize, however,

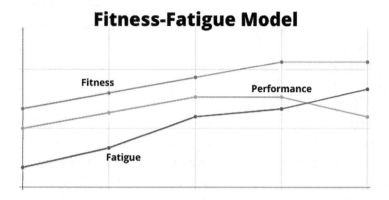

is there is a certain amount of low-level fatigue that persists week-to-week that will *also* mask your fitness. So, even if one is allowing sufficient recovery between sessions, there is a broader scale "systemic fatigue" that builds up over time as a natural consequence of hard training.

As you can see from this graph, at the beginning of a training block, you will often see a concurrent increase in both your performance and your fitness levels. As fatigue increases, however, your performance will begin to level off and may even start to decline a bit—even if your actual *fitness* level is still increasing or at least maintaining.

Once this begins to occur, you are in what's referred to as an *overreached* state. You are *not* overtrained just yet. You've simply temporarily pushed beyond your recovery abilities and are starting to plateau or regress in performance as a consequence. Some programs will intentionally include an overreaching week at the end of a mesocycle to explore the boundaries of an athlete's recovery and attempt to present a superlative stimulus. Necessarily, this week is followed by a deload week where volume and intensity are reduced so recovery can occur. This is what's referred to as *functional overreaching*. If pushed too far, or done in a haphazard or unintentional manner, the athlete risks *non-functional overreaching*. Non-functional overreaching should be avoided because it reduces training quality to an undesirable degree and increases the risk of injury. It also typically requires longer timescales to fully recover from, and performance may still be plateaued or reduced even after the fatigue is gone.

If nonfunctional overreaching occurs for weeks and months on end, it could eventually develop into OTS. Some of the symptoms to look for include:

→ Lack of energy
→ Sudden drop in performance
→ Insomnia
→ Headaches
→ Depression/moodiness
→ Loss of passion for training/sport
→ Decreased appetite
→ Increased incidence of injuries
→ Decreased immune system
→ Menstrual cycle dysfunction

True overtraining can take several months or longer to recover from. And, unlike functional overreaching, there is no rebound effect where performance increases above previous levels after recovery. If you feel like you've overtrained and you take a week off and feel great afterwards, then you did not have OTS. You were likely just a bit overreached. Pay attention to your recovery and include periodic deloads in your training and your chances of developing OTS are generally very small.

ON HEART RATE VARIABILITY (HRV)

Tracking HRV via is a popular method of assessing readiness to train in some circles, but it's not one I recommend to most athletes. In nearly all cases, subjective measures will be more than sufficient to measure recovery. HRV tends to be a lagging indicator. By the time it tells you something useful, you're already too deep in the hole!

THE FEMALE ATHLETE TRIAD

The female athlete triad is an unfortunately common condition affecting physically active girls and women. It involves three components: low energy availability, decreased bone mineral density, and menstrual cycle dysfunction. If left untreated, the consequences of this condition can be quite severe, including osteoporosis, amenorrhea, and clinical eating disorders. [4] Thus, it is particularly important for female athletes to pay close attention to their recovery and ensure they are maintaining a healthy body weight and consuming sufficient energy to fuel performance. The female athlete triad occurs more commonly in females involved in sports that emphasize aesthetics or leanness, but it is not limited to those arenas. As this is a complex condition that can be difficult to diagnose early on, female athletes should make sure they receive regular health checkups and ask for screenings for all three of the related conditions.

WARMING UP, MOBILITY, AND FLEXIBILITY: HOW TO PREPARE FOR PHYSICAL ACTIVITY

"You must unlearn what you have learned."
—*Yoda*

Now that we've talked about how to prevent injury from managing your training on a more global level, it's time to dive into some specific things can do to reduce your chances of injury. We'll start with the warm-up. There are a lot of conflicting recommendations when it comes to the proper way to prepare your body for physical activity. Unfortunately, most of what we learned in gym class as kids was wrong: static stretching (holding a stationary stretch for time) does not seem to help prevent injury. [5–6] In part, this is because most injuries occur within a normal range of motion. This isn't to say static stretching serves no purpose. You just want to avoid the mindset that stretching alone is sufficient as a warm-up and will safeguard you from injury. Static stretching can still be an important part of your warm-up, it just shouldn't be the *only* part.

So, what does help prevent injury? As it turns out, the most important thing a warm-up does is literally *warm you up*. Its purpose is to both raise your core temperature and to safely take your joints through a range of motion similar to the activity you will be performing. This is accomplished most efficiently by performing a combination of light, aerobic activity (jumping jacks, lunges, light jogging, etc.), dynamic stretching, and strategic mobility work. Your initial warm-up should leave you feeling loose, springy, and ready for action. In fact, a good warm-up does more than simply reduce your chance of injury, it will also acutely *improve* performance. [7]

There are two main components to a full warm-up: A general warm-up and a *specific* warm-up. In table tennis, the average club player typically jumps right into a specific warm-up and foregoes the general warm-up phase. To be honest, I'm guilty of this myself. I'll often just spend a few minutes warming up the forehand and backhand, maybe perform a few drills if there's time, and then begin a match. Because table tennis is not as physically demanding as other sports, this is something that can be "gotten away with" to some extent.

If, however, you are serious about performing your best while reducing your chances of injury, you need to perform a *general* warm-up too. The problem with not warming up off the table is by the time you realize you should have spent some time getting warm and loose, it's too late. We've all warmed up with an overzealous partner who seems intent on "winning" the warm-up. Suddenly, you're lunging for balls you didn't expect to have to hit and something pulls. Injuries can be very hard to recover from and often force you to reduce or eliminate your table tennis training until you heal. Spending a few minutes performing a general warm-up can help prevent this from happening.

And, to my previous point, you'll also play better after warming up properly. A 2020 study on elite table tennis players found that a warm-up that included a combination of dynamic stretching, foam rolling, and static stretching significantly improved flexibility, power, *ball speed*, and agility. [8]

In one study, researchers interviewed over 100 table tennis players regarding their experiences with injuries. Over *half* of the participants admitted that the most likely reason they received an injury was an *inadequate warm-up*. [9]

THE DANGERS OF A POOR WARM-UP

We've established the benefits of a good warm-up, but are there potential drawbacks? Unfortunately, yes. If performed improperly, your warm-up could just as easily *decrease* performance. Holding static stretches for longer durations (around a minute or longer) has been shown to temporarily inhibit muscular performance. [10–11] So, if your idea of warming up is to do some long bouts of stretching and hop right into your training, you've not only failed in lowering your risk of injury, you've also *decreased* your performance! Fortunately, the negative effects of static stretching can be circumvented if followed by a sport specific warm-up; [12] thus, if you personally find static stretching to help, it can still have a place if positioned correctly.

In this next section, I will outline a potential general warm-up that can be used to prepare you for action. Think of these stretches and drills as tools for you to use as needed. You may not have to perform everything on the list each time you warm-up, but it is important that you learn the areas in which your mobility is lacking and then address those deficits accordingly.

THE WARM-UP

Because each person is different, it is impossible to provide a single warm-up that will perfectly meet the needs of every trainee; thus, I will first outline the basic components of a good warm-up in general terms.

A good warm-up will have some combination of the following basic components:

→ Raise the temperature of your body.
→ Soft-tissue work as needed—often accomplished by self-myofascial release via the use of a foam roller or lacrosse ball.
→ Dynamic stretches.

→ Static stretches.
→ Activation of muscles (often accomplished with bands).
→ Movement prep (shadow strokes, agility drills, etc.).

How long it takes you to warm-up will vary day to day: some days you may be particularly tight and will need to take extra time, while other days you may be pretty loose and ready to go. Here is a sample warm-up that contains all the key components of a good warm-up, and specifically addresses some common problem areas for table tennis players:

The Table Tennis Ten[11]

1. Light cardio of choice: Jumping jacks, jump rope, easy jog, etc.) 3–5 minutes (or as long as needed to feel warm).
2. Foam roll trouble spots as needed: (hip flexors/quads, piriformis, thoracic spine, etc.) 30–60 seconds.
3. Fire hydrants: 5–10 rotations each direction, each leg.
4. Groiners with overhead reach: 8–10 reps.
5. Hip flexor stretch: 30 seconds each side.
6. Side lunge: 5–10 reps.
7. Rocking ankle mobilization: 5–10 reps each side.
8. Wall slides: 5–10 reps.
9. Band pull-aparts/dislocates: 8–10 reps.
10. Wrist rotations: 30 seconds.

Doing all the above will result in a thorough full body warm-up that can be performed before both table tennis and resistance training. Remember, to personalize this and adapt this as needed.

---

11   For a video demonstration of this warm-up, head to peakperformancetabletennis. com/resources.

Here is an example of what a scaled-down warm-up might look like:

→ Jumping cross body slaps: 8–10 reps.
→ Butt kicks: 15–20 reps.
→ Knee ups: 10–15 reps.
→ Cossack squat w/ overhead reach: 5–10 reps.
→ Spidermans: 5–10 reps each leg.
→ Arm circles: 8–10 reps each direction.
→ Lateral + in/out footwork drill with shadow strokes.

This warm-up will still loosen up your ankles, knees, hips, and shoulders, but is a lot simpler and faster to perform.

Kalinikos Kreanga likes to warm-up with light resistance bands before training: *"It's really helping me a lot. Since I started to use it, it's a much better feeling."* [13]

BUILDING YOUR ARMOR THROUGH RESISTANCE TRAINING

One of the most underrated aspects of becoming stronger through resistance training is the benefit of injury prevention. In addition to strengthening your muscles, resistance training also strengthens your bones, tendons, ligaments, and other connective tissues. With an intelligent, targeted resistance training program, you are literally armoring yourself against injury. Research consistently shows a strong reduction in injury risk for athletes who engage in strength training. [14–15] One review article concludes the following:

> Based on the extant literature, it appears that there may be no substitute for greater muscular strength when it comes to improving an individual's performance across a wide range of both general and sport specific skills while simultaneously reducing their risk of injury when performing these skills. [16]

I will build an even stronger case for resistance training in the physical training section, but its injury-reducing benefits alone make it a worthwhile investment for the serious table tennis athlete.

SPIDERSILK TENDONS

If you're the type who has had issues with frequent strains, you might want to consider paying a little extra attention to strengthening and caring for your tendons and ligaments. Fortunately, many of the same things that help your muscles grow stronger and more robust also serve to strengthen your tendons and ligaments. Research shows that higher protein diets along with resistance training are beneficial for improving your tendon and ligament health. [17] So, just by eating a protein-rich diet (particularly one that's high in the amino acid, leucine) and getting in some solid resistance training, you're already well on your way toward making your tendons and ligaments stronger and thus more resistant to injury.

One thing to note is that muscles can adapt and heal much faster than your tendons and ligaments can. This is partly because muscles have a much better blood supply as they are nourished by vascular perfusion, while tendons are nourished primarily by synovial fluid diffusion. [18] In other words, while your muscles receive a strong supply of blood even at rest, your tendons rely on a more passive supply of nutrients via physical movements. These differing rates of recovery should be taken into account when assessing readiness to train.

The ethos of *"No pain, no gain,"* is a common one in athletics, but one must know the difference between the kind of pain you can push through and the kind you shouldn't. If you're doing a high rep set of squats and your legs are burning from the accumulation of metabolites in the muscle, by all means, push through the pain. If you are experiencing pain in a joint or tendon, however, you should *not* push through that pain. You must adapt your training so that you can train in a way that doesn't bother your joints and connective tissues. Fortunately, there are several useful strategies at your disposal which we will now look at in turn.

FLEXIBLE EXERCISE SELECTION

Unlike powerlifters and weightlifters who must perform specific lifts in order to compete, for the table tennis athlete, exercises are merely a means to an end. If you experience pain or discomfort with a given movement, despite sound form and an appropriate intensity of effort, then simply find an alternative movement that is more comfortable.

Movements such as the squat, bench press, and deadlift are excellent exercises, but there's nothing magical about them. There are many ways to strengthen the same movement patterns with different exercises, so don't feel pressured to perform an exercise that doesn't agree with you.

UTILIZING HIGHER REP RANGES

Although training with heavier loads will result in better strength gains, you can still increase your strength and athleticism using higher reps in the 15–30 range. In fact, in terms of muscle growth, high reps have been shown to be equally as effective as low reps. [19–20] If you find heavier weights bother your joints, you can still tap into the benefits of resistance training with smart exercise selection and the utilization of higher rep protocols.

BLOOD FLOW RESTRICTION TRAINING

Blood flow restriction (BFR) training is a training technique that may sound extreme at first blush, but is actually very well researched and quite safe. [21–22] In BFR training, one uses a wrapping implement of some kind to temporarily restrict venous blood flow return (not arterial) from the arms or legs.

This exposes the muscles to high levels of metabolic stress as metabolic by-products accumulate and become trapped around the muscles. This enhances muscle fiber recruitment and activation. The main benefit of BFR training is that it allows muscle growth and strength gains to be made with weights as low as 20%–30% of your one rep max. It also results in a massive influx of blood in the area being trained, which can be taken advantage of to help recovery. [26] Since tendons rely on movement and exercise to receive nutrients from the blood, BFR training kills two birds with one stone by both giving them a break through the use of lighter weights *and* by bathing the area with a large supply of blood.

SUPPLEMENTATION PROTOCOL

There is some evidence that supplementing with gelatin alongside a small dose of vitamin C might help with injury prevention and tissue repair. In one study, [23] they gave participants a dose of 0g, 5g, or 15g of gelatin, along with some vitamin C one hour before training. The group that received 15 g of gelatin showed *double* the collagen synthesis rate of the placebo group. Another study [24] showed that a 10 g collagen supplementation led to improvements in joint pain in athletes over 24 weeks.

If you are looking to specifically strengthen and repair your tendons, you can try supplementing with 15 g of gelatin with 50–100 mg of vitamin C an hour or so before exercise. Theoretically, the movement and increased blood flow from your training should assist with nutrient uptake into the tendon. Because high dose (1,000+ mg) vitamin C supplementation may reduce adaptations from exercise, [25] a smaller dose of 50–100 mg of vitamin C should be used.

This protocol is theoretical and based on somewhat thin evidence, but I would consider it a low-risk and relatively cheap endeavor to try. The modern diet rarely includes things like bones, tendons, and other connective tissues, as we typically just throw these things away and only eat the muscle meat. Because of this, there's a chance you may be slightly deficient in amino acids such as glycine. By supplementing with gelatin and/or including some food sources such as bone broth and more gelatinous cuts of meat, you can round out the amino acid profile of your diet, potentially improving your health overall.

NOVEL METHODS TO BOOST RECOVERY

Train hard, recover harder.

The number one thing you can do to maximize recovery is to simply make sure you've got the "big rocks" in place:

→ An appropriate total amount of training volume (i.e., the *allostatic load)*, should not consistently exceed your ability to recover from it. This seems like common sense but it's one of the most common mistakes I see. More is not always better!
→ Get enough sleep (8+ hours).
→ Provide high quality fuel for recovery—eat sufficient calories from a variety of nutrient-dense sources. Carbs, in particular, are key here.
→ Manage stress.

These things will account for 90% or more of your recovery. With that said, there are a few other things you can do to help things along a bit. If the above is the cake, here's the icing:

→ A 2018 meta-analysis looked at different methods for increasing recovery and found that a post-workout massage was the best option for reducing muscle soreness and perceived levels of fatigue. [26]
→ Wearing compression garments for around 24 hours after an intense session that causes soreness was also found to be an effective recovery tool. In fact, another study showed that it can improve your strength performance in the subsequent session. [27]
→ Just ten minutes of low-intensity cycling after training your legs can help improve markers of recovery. This was found to be just as effective as cold-water immersion. [28]

→ There is an emerging body of evidence supporting the efficacy of tart cherry juice in aiding recovery after intermittent exercise. [29–30]. Taking around 8 to 12 oz (1 oz if in concentrate form) twice a day, 4–5 days before an event, as well as 2–3 days after, can help accelerate recovery.

It's easy to get overzealous when training and overdo it from time to time, so it doesn't hurt to have a few extra tricks up your sleeve for those occasions. Just to reiterate, don't expect these things to make a night and day difference. One of the most important things you can do to acutely recover from a training bout is to simply get yourself into a relaxed state, eat some food, and get a good night's sleep. One of the main benefits of protocols like the above is the *psychological* relief you get from feeling like you're actively "doing something" to help your recovery. Personally, wearing compression garments and drinking an "elixir" of tart cherry juice helps me *feel* like a serious athlete. I'm then able to relax a bit more and recover even *better* as a result—a bit of science, a bit of placebo. Since consistently training while your muscles are still sore may impair motor learning, [31] it pays to take your recovery seriously!

Did you know the placebo effect can work even when you *know* it's a placebo? [32] The placebo effect isn't just "in your head" either— the altered expectations that occur as a result of the placebo can result in measurable, physiological changes to your body. In one study, [33] lifters were given *fake* steroids and the participants gained strength at a dramatically faster rate as a result. If you feel something works well for you and there isn't a significant cost associated with it (whether in time, money, or performance), it's okay to continue implementing it even in the absence of much empirical support.

This is something especially important to keep in mind if you are a coach. You may be able to identify a dozen things your athlete does that are useless on paper, but coming in like a wrecking ball and taking everything away may do more harm than good. Pick your battles!

AN "EMERGENCY PROTOCOL"

You might have noticed that two pretty popular options for reducing muscle soreness and/or joint pain are conspicuously absent from this section, namely NSAIDs (such as ibuprofen) and ice baths.

There's a reason for this. Your body has a "sweet spot" for inflammation; reduce it too much, and you reduce the very adaptations you hope to gain by training in the first place! Research shows that getting too heavy-handed with NSAID usage over an extended period can inhibit muscle hypertrophy and strength. [34] This is because there is a bit of overlap between the mechanisms by which NSAIDs suppress pain and inflammation and the pathways through which your body repair and grow tissue. Similarly, cold water immersion techniques, such as ice baths, have also been found to reduce muscle growth and strength gains when taken after training for the same reasons. [35]

It's not that these two methods can't help with recovery—they can. The problem is the *cost* of that recovery! If you're pushing yourself to the extent that you require heavy use of NSAIDs and frequent ice baths just to recover from your training, you're just shooting yourself in the foot. Any extra adaptations you may receive from the additional training are *washed out* by the interference from the recovery protocol. Don't spend 10 dollars to earn eight!

There are still situations in which you might want to use these types of protocols, however. If you need to quickly drop fatigue and/ or soreness before an important scheduled event, you can utilize NSAIDs and/or ice baths. In this situation, the short-term cost is outweighed by the importance of you being in peak shape for your match. It should not, however, be something you habitually use to recover from normal training sessions.

NUTRITION PROTOCOL FOR RECOVERY WHEN INJURED

So, you didn't listen to me and you went ahead and got yourself injured. Typical! Well, what do you do now? Should you change what you eat? Should you eat less since you won't be able to stay as active? How can you support your body nutritionally in order to maximize your rate of healing?

First things first, always get checked out by a medical professional and then follow their instructions to a T. There's no way for me to outline a protocol that will be suitable for all types of injuries—there's simply too much variability. Instead, this section will outline some broad strokes principles you can apply and adapt to your particular situation as needed.

ENERGY INTAKE

The process through which your body repairs and remodels tissue has an energetic "price tag," so make sure you're eating enough to pay the bills. Being in an energy deficit also affects your body's hormonal production, shifting it to a more catabolic state where healing may not be optimized. While recovering from an injury, you should aim to maintain your weight, and it may even be beneficial to allow for a little weight gain. Although concerns about fat gain are warranted, particularly because you'll likely be less active overall as you rest, remember that fat can be stripped off very quickly once the healing process is complete. Priority number one should be healing as quickly as possible and avoiding significant lean body mass losses.

Regarding the "energy out" portion of the equation, it's important to maintain *some* level of activity—assuming your doctor has cleared you. Don't fall into the "all or nothing" mindset; complete bed rest is rarely the best option. Did you injure your foot? Fine. Nothing's stopping you from exercising your *upper* body. There's even research that shows if you continue to train the other, uninjured limb you'll get a crossover effect and still get a benefit in the injured limb! [36] So, if you strain a tendon in your right arm, if you still continue to train your *left* arm, you'll better maintain your strength in your right, even though you're not training it. How cool is that?

Learn to train safely around an injury and you'll be surprised at how quickly you can get back up to speed once healed. This does *not* give you license to be an idiot; if you broke your foot, don't attempt to perform an exercise that puts you in a precarious position because you're balancing on one leg. Use common sense, and make sure you are only exercising under the guidance of your doctor or physical therapist.

MACRONUTRIENTS, MICRONUTRIENTS, AND MEAL TIMING

If you're already consuming a high protein diet as outlined in the nutrition section (0.72–1.2 g of protein per pound of body weight per day), there's no need to change your macronutrient breakdown while healing from an injury. If your habitual intake falls *below* the levels I recommended, then you should consider upping your protein intake to help facilitate the healing process. In addition to helping with the healing of the injured tissue, a higher protein intake may help to mitigate the muscle loss that can occur while injured.

Similarly, you should continue to focus on including plenty of nutrient-dense fruits and vegetables in your diet. At the very least, you may want to consider taking a daily multivitamin as a little extra insurance policy, or selectively supplementing if you happen to know your diet is lacking in certain vitamins or minerals (calcium comes to mind).

Meal timing is not a major factor other than ensuring you are timing your food intake with any medications you may be taking in accordance with what is recommended on the label (take on an empty stomach, take with food, etc.).

SUPPLEMENTS

There are a few supplements that may become conditionally useful while injured. Specifically, you may find it slightly beneficial to utilize some compounds that will help modulate inflammation without eliminating it.

Remember, inflammation is not necessarily a bad thing. It's a necessary part of the healing process. And while you may benefit from the use of stronger anti-inflammatory measures at the first onset of an injury (NSAIDs, ice, etc.), continuing with those measures beyond the doctor's recommendation is not a good long-term solution. I like to use the following compounds to help keep inflammation in the "sweet spot"—bridging the gap between the first stage of injury and recovery:

→ Fish oil: 2–3 g combined EPA/DHA per day. This is a higher dose than the 1–2 g I would normally recommend (remember this can be achieved by eating fatty fish several times per week as well).
→ 500 mg curcumin + 20 mg piperine (to enhance absorption) taken three times per day with food.

I've found these supplements can help control inflammation without eliminating it. I'll typically use this stack after I've discontinued the use of NSAIDs but don't feel ready to go cold turkey. Again, these are *not* a substitute for medicine, and if you decide to experiment with them, make sure you keep your doctor in the loop.

REDUCING ILLNESS: STEPS FOR PREVENTION AND "THE CURE"

Getting sick is an unfortunate reality of existence. You can do everything in your power to prepare optimally for an important tournament, but if you come down with the flu, you'll be lucky to play at 70% capacity, if at all. Frequent bouts of illness also result in a greater number of poor quality and/or missed training sessions. Cumulatively, this could have a significant impact on your rate of development as an athlete. In this section, I will outline some strategies for both preventing illness from occurring in the first place and reducing the duration of illness.

ILLNESS PREVENTION

There is a paradoxical relationship between exercise and the immune system: regular exercise tends to improve immune system function, [37] but intense exercise—particularly among elite athletes—can also have temporary immunosuppressive effects. [38] If an athlete is traveling frequently for competition and experiencing disruptions to sleep while being exposed to a large number of people, the risk of illness is increased even further. So even though your baseline immune function may be excellent as an athlete, it's wise to take some extra measures to bolster your immune system so you stay healthy during intense periods of training.

The first order of business is to get the "big rocks" in place. Getting regular exercise, sleeping well, managing stress, and eating a nutrient-dense diet (with plenty of fluids) is the foundation upon which a strong immune system is built. Beyond that, practicing proper hygiene and getting an annual flu vaccine is also important. Everyone heads to the supplement aisle when it's time to "boost" the immune system, but supplementation isn't going to do a thing unless you have those big rocks sorted out first. With that in mind, there *are* some supplements which may help decrease the occurrence of illness.

Regular consumption of garlic has been shown to significantly reduce your chances of infection. [39–40]. Eating a clove of garlic 2–3 times per day with your meals or supplementing with aged garlic extract (1,000 mg 2–3 times per day with food) is a good minimum effective dose. When preparing the garlic, make sure you slice or crush it, and then grill or roast it rather than microwaving it as this will better preserve the beneficial bioactive compounds.

Athletes who supplement with vitamin C have been shown to be *half* as likely to catch the common cold as those who don't, but this effect is seen only in those who regularly participate in intense physical exercise. [41] Recall, however, that other research shows high-dose vitamin C supplementation may interfere with adaptations from exercise, [25] so you will have to determine for yourself if this is a trade-off you want to make. If you tend to get sick on a frequent basis and you are extremely active, it may be worth taking vitamin C as it could increase the total number of quality training sessions you perform. This would likely outweigh any slight negative effects the supplementation may have on your training results. Personally, I supplement with vitamin C proactively during the flu season and forgo it the rest of the year. For the preventative effects, a dose of 500 mg, three times per day should be consumed.

Vitamin D and zinc have also been shown to reduce your chances of getting sick, with vitamin D being shown to help prevent upper respiratory tract infections, [42] and zinc shown to reduce the risk of infection overall. [43] Since zinc is lost through sweat, and optimal levels of vitamin D are difficult to obtain from sunshine alone (particularly in the winter when the risk of sickness tends to be highest), these two supplements are particularly relevant to hard-training, indoor athletes such as table tennis players. Alcohol has been shown to *suppress* immune system function, [42] so consider reducing or eliminating alcohol consumption during periods of increased risk of sickness.

Finally, there is *some* emerging evidence from a systematic review on probiotic supplementation that probiotics may help reduce the risk of respiratory tract infection while bolstering immune system function in athletes. [45] There is also some meta-analytic data that suggests supplementing with probiotics in the weeks before and after getting your flu shot may have a synergistic effect, boosting its effectiveness by up to 20%. [46] Importantly, the authors of the first study point out that because many of the studies vary quite a bit in design and purpose, with some having small samples sizes and failing to show a benefit, we are left with "inconclusive results for standardized supplementation protocols." Thus, it is difficult to provide specific recommendations just yet regarding probiotic supplementation.

So, to distill all the above, here is my standard prevention protocol:

→ Manage the "big rocks" first and foremost (sleep, nutrition, hydration, stress, activity levels).
→ Practice good hygiene.
→ Get your annual flu vaccine.
→ Ensure zinc vitamin D levels remain in an optimal range year-round.
→ Regularly include garlic in your diet and/or supplement.
→ Minimize or avoid alcohol intake.
→ Consider supplementing with vitamin C regularly during flu season if you are highly active.
→ Consult with doctor and explore probiotic supplementation, possibly "sandwiching" your flu shot with 3–4 weeks of supplementation before and after.

There is, of course, an element of luck involved in whether you happen to get sick, but implementing the above is a good way to help "make your own luck," as they say.

THE CURE

Note: *The Cure* is tongue-in-cheek. The suggestions in this section have been effective for me and for the clients whom I've trained, but they are *not* a substitute for medical advice. If you're sick, go to a doctor. Get a proper diagnosis, and follow your doc's instructions to a T, even if that means ignoring everything I suggest here! Once you've done that and been cleared by your doctor, you can implement what I suggest below.

With all that said, if you have a basic cold or the flu, there are several steps you can take that may help you get back on your feet a bit faster. I like to focus on interventions that actually speed healing rather than just masking symptoms.

At first sign of symptoms, here's my protocol:

1. Buy a gallon of purified water—I try to polish this off between meals by the end of each day.

2. Pick up some zinc lozenges and take as directed on the box. This should help reduce the duration of the cold. [47] Note: you must use the lozenge form so the zinc has prolonged exposure to the throat. If you supplement with zinc via a vitamin, cease supplementation while taking the lozenges as too much zinc can have detrimental effects.

3. Supplement with African geranium (*Pelargonium sidoides*). There is some evidence it will help reduce the duration and severity of the common cold, [48] and good evidence that it will greatly reduce all symptoms of acute bronchitis. [49] I'll defer to *Examine* for the dosing protocol:

    To supplement Pelargonium sidoides, take the patented extract EPS7630, which is an 11% ethanolic root extract.

    The extract is concentrated to 1:8–10, so there is some variability with the recommended dosages. To supplement the extract, take 4.5 mL of the tincture (30 drops) or 30 mg of the capsules. Dosages vary by age:

→ *10 drops (1.5 mL) or 10 mg of EPs7630 is taken thrice daily before meals for those under six years of age*
→ *20 drops (3.0 mL) or 20 mg of EPs7630 is taken thrice daily before meals for those between six and twelve*
→ *30 drops (4.5 mL) or 30 mg of EPs7630 is taken thrice daily before meals for those above twelve years of age*

While the vast majority of studies have used EPs7630 specifically, any hydroalcoholic (water and ethanol) extraction equal to 800mg of the plant can be used as an alternative. [50]

4. Aim for an extra 1-2 hours sleep each day (as much as can be managed).

5. Cook up some **Witch's Brew**:

Eye of newt, and toe of frog,

Wool of bat, and tongue of dog,

Adder's fork, and blind-worm's sting,

Lizard's leg, and howlet's wing,

For a charm of powerful trouble,

Like a hell-broth boil and bubble.

—Macbeth (IV, i, 14–15)

Or, alternatively, head down to your local butcher and pick up some marrow bones and chicken feet, and get a nice bone broth brewing on the stove. I like to add lemon, garlic, onions, carrots, and whatever other herbs and spices that happen to sound tasty. If you're not much of a chef, you can simply pick up some pre-made bone broth from the store.

Sipping on broth is a home remedy that actually has some science behind it. Besides being comforting and savory, it also helps to open up the respiratory tract [51] and exert some anti-inflammatory effects on the body. [52]

Since I began doing these five things, I've been able to cut the duration of illness by 30–40% on average. Your mileage may vary, but anecdotal reports from clients who have implemented this have been favorable as well.

CHAPTER SUMMARY:

→ You become stronger and more injury resistant by incrementally exposing your body to increasingly demanding tasks, forcing it to adapt.

→ Using a graded prescription of volume at an appropriate rate will minimize injury risk.

→ True overtraining is rare, but you should be aware of signs of nonfunctional overreaching.

→ Females, in particular, should pay close attention to their recovery and nutrition to ensure they do not put themselves at risk of the female athlete triad.

→ Regularly scheduled periods of rest and recovery are necessary to allow for more complete healing and tissue repair.

→ A proper warm-up is essential for reducing injury risk.

→ Increased flexibility will not necessarily reduce risk of injury.

→ Including resistance training as a regular part of your training is a powerful way to "armor" your body and protect it from injury.

→ Things like a post-workout massage, compression garments, low intensity cycling, and tart cherry juice may have a small beneficial effect on recovery.

→ Heavy use of NSAIDs and/or ice baths should be avoided unless you quickly need to regain performance for an important event.

→ Do not diet through injuries. Switch to maintenance calories and keep protein high.

→ Be proactive in avoiding sickness: practice good hygiene, get your flu shot, get enough sleep, etc.

→ Supplements such as vitamin D, zinc, garlic, and vitamin C may give athletes a small boost to their immune system.

→ If you come down with a cold, taking zinc lozenges, African geranium, and sipping warm broth may help shorten its duration by a few days.

SECTION IV
SPORTS NUTRITION

SECTION OVERVIEW

One of the fastest ways to start feeling and performing better as an athlete is to improve your diet. Unfortunately, it's hard to think of an area more rife with misinformation! The average person's knowledge of nutrition typically consists of tidbits of information picked up from friends, magazines, social media posts, and news stories. As a result, their beliefs about what constitutes a healthy diet are a patchwork of one-liners and soundbites that lack the depth and nuance necessary to make informed decisions.

Here's just a short list of common myths that get tossed around:

→ If you eat a high-fat, ketogenic diet you will become "fat adapted" and burn off more body fat.
→ You need to cleanse or "detox" the body periodically to get rid of accumulated toxins.
→ Organic foods are significantly more nutritious than conventionally grown food and don't use pesticides.
→ You must eat smaller, more frequent meals to keep your metabolism burning.
→ Sugar is addictive and toxic.
→ Artificial sweeteners cause cancer.
→ GMOs are dangerous.
→ Carbs spike insulin and make you store fat.
→ Gluten is bad for you.
→ If you skip meals, (or drop your calories too low) your body goes into "starvation mode" and will start *storing* fat.
→ Food eaten late at night will automatically be stored as fat.

The problem with these myths is not so much their individual impact; rather, it's the cumulative weight of these misconceptions that tends to cause problems. With so much conflicting information out there, it's almost easier to just do nothing. And that's precisely what so many of us do. We're crushed by the weight of an endless stream of (mis)information and are paralyzed into inaction.

But that's not going to fly if you're truly serious about becoming the best athlete you can be.

In the chapters that follow, I will provide a framework upon which you can build a healthy, sustainable, and *performance-enhancing* diet that is based on science and facts rather than sensationalism. To help with this, I will be framing this discussion using the nutritional pyramid model created by Dr. Eric Helms:

This model is useful because it provides a nutritional hierarchy, allowing you to prioritize the most impactful parts of your diet while ignoring the trivial. No longer will you be left floundering in a sea

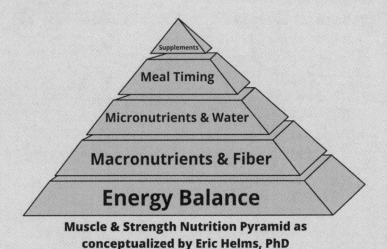

Muscle & Strength Nutrition Pyramid as conceptualized by Eric Helms, PhD

of uncertainty, weighed down by minutiae. With the knowledge I'm about to share, you will be armed with a dietary Archimedes' lever. You will know precisely where to push in order to make *incredible* changes to your health and performance.

The chapters within this section will discuss nutrition in a meticulous and thorough way. Feel free to skip around as needed. For many of you, this level of micromanagement will not be necessary. Some, however, may find this to be the one key area holding them back.

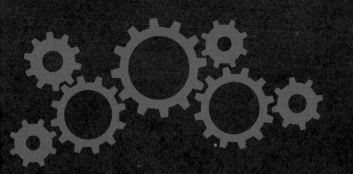

LEVEL ONE: ENERGY BALANCE, CALORIC INTAKE, AND RATE OF WEIGHT CHANGE

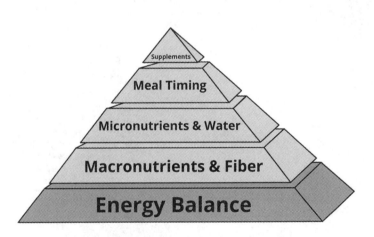

As you can see, at the bottom of the pyramid we have *energy balance*. In this hierarchical model, the categories at the bottom have the most significant impact on your results whereas the items at the top are of decreasing importance. As the foundational level of the pyramid, energy balance is the most important variable that will impact your ability to attain peak performance levels, recover from training, build muscle, and lose fat. In line with the Pareto principle, it is the 20% that will produce 80% of your results.

Ironically, despite its importance, energy balance typically receives the *least* amount of attention in the world of nutrition. Too often, this model is flipped upside down and we get caught up in details that don't have a significant impact on results: *What supplements should I take? What's the glycemic index of this carb? How often should I eat?*

These types of questions have some significance in specific situations, but their relevance is *contingent upon* maintaining an appropriate energy balance. With that in mind, here are a few of the things we will cover in this chapter:

→ Why you may benefit from losing some weight even if you're not technically overweight.
→ How to find your ideal body weight.
→ What *really* causes changes in weight?
→ How quickly should you gain/lose weight?

In a nutshell, this chapter is about your weight and how to control it.

Why should this matter to a table tennis player? So glad you asked. . .

SWEDEN'S SECRET WEAPON

The year was 1987. The World Table Tennis Championship was underway in New Delhi and Jan-Ove Waldner had just beaten Chen Longcan and advanced to the semifinals to face off against Teng Yi. But something was different about Waldner that day. He was completely in the zone—focused and lightning quick. His footwork and speed were incredible and he was able to utilize his forehand like never before.

His secret? He had gotten a stomach bug the week prior and lost 15 lb. (7 kg)!

After analyzing his match, his coaches decided to start implementing weight training for 6 hours per week in addition to his table tennis training. Their rationale was simple: Since his body weight was artificially low due to the illness and he was heavier now, they needed to strengthen his legs so he could regain that speed and quickness he displayed in New Delhi!

If you look at footage of Waldner during that time, you would see that he could easily *gain* 15 lb. and still be far from what most would consider to be overweight. But there's a difference between health and performance. What Waldner's coaches were learning to manipulate was Waldner's *relative strength*.

Relative strength—the ratio between your body weight and your strength levels—is strongly correlated with athletic performance. [1] Getting rid of excess fat on your body while maintaining your current strength levels will automatically improve your relative strength, but if you can attack the problem from both ends and get *stronger* in the process, even better. So, the question is. . .

How do I know how much fat (if any) I need to lose?

This is a good question because just as there are health consequences of maintaining too high a body fat percentage, there can also be downsides to keeping your body fat percentage too low. In the following section, I will outline how to find the range in weight at which you are likely to perform best.

FINDING YOUR "FIGHTING WEIGHT": BMI AND BODY FAT PERCENTAGES

If you are relatively inactive outside of table tennis and you do not have a background in athletics, aiming for a "normal" score in your body mass index (BMI) is a good place to start in terms of your weight. If you are a serious athlete and/or have been weight training for several years, however, getting an estimate of your body fat percentage will be a more useful way to determine your ideal weight because it will distinguish between the amount of fat and lean body mass you have.

For reference, the American Council on Exercise provides the following chart to illustrate the range of body fat percentages:

Classification	Women (% fat)	Men (% fat)
Essential Fat:	10%–12%	2%–4%
Athletes:	14%–20%	6%–13%
Fitness:	21%–24%	14%–17%
Acceptable:	25%–31%	18%–25%
Obese:	32% plus	25% plus

For the table tennis player looking to achieve *peak* performance, my recommendation for men is to stay within a range of 8%–13% body fat and for women to stay within 16%–22%.

This range strikes a balance between having a healthy and sustainable level of body fat while still ensuring that you're not carrying more weight than you need to be. This does *not* mean if you are one or two percentage points above this range, you are automatically "unhealthy" or will experience huge decreases in performance. It's just a general range for you to shoot for.

A NOTE ON LOW ENERGY AVAILABILITY

Serious athletes tend to burn far more calories than the average person due to their higher-than-normal activity levels. Because of this, they are at an increased risk for *low energy availability* (LEA). [2] LEA occurs when the amount of dietary energy left after training is insufficient for the remaining metabolic processes the body requires for daily living, growth, and repair. Chronic LEA will result in not only acute performance decreases but also decrements to your health. This is a particular concern for female athletes, where LEA-related disruptions to the menstrual cycle can result in decreases in bone mineral density. [3]

I mention this to point out that just as eating too much can cause issues (weight gain, health complications, etc.), eating too little can be equally problematic. Well-intentioned athletes who are intent upon "cleaning up" their diet need to understand that first and foremost, energy needs must be met. And that may mean eating *more.*

A 2019 study [4] on the body composition and diets of female athletes found that the women tended to under consume both calories and carbohydrates. I examined the raw data for the table tennis player subgroup and found they were also well below the optimal intakes of protein and water.

CALCULATING BODY FAT PERCENTAGE

Unfortunately, body fat percentages are not as easy to calculate as a BMI. Common methods include assessments via fat calipers, a Bod Pod, a DEXA scan, or a visual estimate (ideally from an experienced coach). Let's say you go with a visual estimate and determine you're around 20% body fat at a weight of 180 lb. (82 kg). This means you have about 36 lb. (16.4 kg) of fat on your body (180 lb. or 82 kg x .20), and you have approximately 144 lb. (65 kg) of lean body mass or fat free mass (muscle, bones, organs, tissue, etc.).

To find out how much weight you'd need to lose to get within the recommended range, you can use the following formula:

Lean Body Mass divided by (one minus desired body fat percentage)

If your initial goal was to get down to 13% body fat, you'd do the following calculation:

144 lb. (65 kg) divided by [1 − 0.13] = 165.5 lb (75.2 kg)

If you were to drop down to 8% (which I would not recommend in a single dieting phase), the numbers would look like this:

144 pounds (65 kg) divided by [1 − 0.08] = 156.5 lb (71.1 kg)

This means your ideal "fighting weight" will likely be somewhere in the range of 155–165 lb. So, you would need to lose anywhere from 15–25 lb. in order to get to your goal of 8–13% body fat—assuming you maintain your lean body mass in the process. If you end up gaining lean body mass through resistance training (more on that later), then your body weight can scale upward a bit. Remember, the goal should not be to get your body fat percentage as low as possible. The range shown above is quite large for a reason. Some people are quite comfortable hovering around 8% body fat (16% for women). For others, this will be excessively low and may actually *harm* performance. Experiment and find the spot that feels best for you.

Now that you know how much weight you need to lose, we will now discuss what causes changes in weight, and more importantly, how to precisely control those changes.

ENERGY BALANCE: THE KEY TO CONTROLLING YOUR WEIGHT

There are no bad foods, only bad diets.

In 2010, a nutrition professor at Kansas State University named Mark Haub made waves in the world of nutrition by successfully losing weight on a diet primarily consisting of Twinkies and other convenience store junk foods. While on this "Twinkie diet," he managed to lose 27 lb in 10 weeks *and* improve his cholesterol and triglycerides levels. How is this possible?

Professor Haub simply consumed fewer calories than he burned. He stuck to a strict intake of 1,800 calories per day and was able to lose weight just fine, despite eating a diet mostly composed of highly processed, sugary foods. If you think this little informal experiment was a fluke, think again. The science is overwhelmingly clear on this issue:

When merely seeking to regulate your weight, the composition of the diet itself does not matter provided your caloric intake is equalized. [5–10]

Does this mean that Haub's diet was ideal for health and performance? Of course not. But it does demonstrate the overwhelming importance of *energy balance*. That's why it's the foundational level of the pyramid. Get this one right, and you can get away with a lot; get it wrong, and you're going nowhere fast.

In the following sections, I will explain the components of energy balance and how you can precisely manipulate them to reach your goals.

ENERGY BALANCE 101: "CALORIES IN"

All the foods we eat, regardless of their composition and nutrient profile, contain a certain number of calories. A *calorie* is the term we use to indicate the amount of energy that a given food will produce in the body. That's all calories are—units of heat energy.

Your body breaks down the foods you eat and uses the energy to keep you alive and fuel performance. If you consume too much food, the excess energy is stored as fat to be used for later. If you consume too little, your body taps into your fat stores to make up the difference.

So, all else being equal. . .

→ Weight loss occurs when calories in < calories out.
→ Weight gain occurs when calories in > calories out.
→ Weight maintenance occurs when calories in = calories out.

This is what's known as *energy balance*, or the "calories in, calories out" (CICO) model. And while this model may be viewed as controversial among internet gurus and pop diet book authors, in the scientific community, it is not.

The common denominator for *all* successful diets is the ability to create and sustain an appropriate energy intake.

I could pull up *many* studies demonstrating the integrity of the CICO model, but one that is particularly enlightening is the landmark DIETFITS study. [11] This was a year-long randomized controlled trial with over 600 participants. In this study, they tested a healthy low-carb diet versus a healthy low-fat diet. Calories were *matched* between groups. The only difference was the number of fats and carbs each group consumed. Participants were carefully monitored and were instructed to attend 22 dietary counseling sessions with a dietician to ensure maximal compliance.

In the end, they found no significant difference in weight change between the groups. They even tested the participants' genotypes and insulin production and found they had no impact on predicting weight loss success or failure, regardless of the group. This is instructive because most popular fad diets either demonize carbs or fats. Turns out, they're both wrong! Once you sort out your calories and protein (more on that later), you have a ton of flexibility regarding how you decide to split your remaining calories, be they carbs or fats.

ENERGY BALANCE 101: "CALORIES OUT"

Now that we've covered the "calories in" portion of the equation, let's take a moment to examine the "calories out" side of things. This part of the equation is far more complicated and is typically the part critics use to "disprove" the integrity of the model. They will, for example, point out that if you calculate a deficit and consume that number of calories consistently, you will lose weight at first but then weight loss will slow and eventually stall.

This isn't evidence that the energy balance theory is wrong, however, it's just a failure to understand that the "energy out" portion of the equation *changes* as your body changes.

Let's break it down by looking at the individual components of your metabolism:

→ **BMR** = Basal metabolic rate. This is the energy your body burns just "keeping the lights on."
→ **TEA** = Thermic effect of activity (calories burned from intentional exercise/activity).
→ **NEAT** = Non-exercise activity thermogenesis (calories burned from subconscious movements such as fidgeting, muscle spasms, daily living, etc.).
→ **TEF** = Thermic effect of food (calories burned from processing and digesting the food you eat).
→ **TDEE** = Total daily energy expenditure (the sum of all the above).

As you can see, there are several factors that go into how many calories your body will burn each day, and each of these factors can be affected by changes in your diet. For example, here is a breakdown of what happens to each component of your metabolism when you enter an energy deficit and begin to lose weight:

→ **BMR:** As you lose weight and become smaller, and your energy needs are *reduced* (a smaller house requires less electricity). Calorie needs go down.
→ **TEA:** A smaller body burns fewer calories when exercising. As you lose weight, your body becomes more efficient and calorie burn through exercise is reduced.
→ **NEAT:** When your body is exposed to a prolonged energy deficit, spontaneous movements are decreased to preserve energy. This further reduces calorie needs.
→ **TEF:** Less food eaten = less energy burned through the digestion of food. Once again, calorie needs go down.

To further complicate things, fullness and hunger-regulating hormones such as leptin and ghrelin will begin to shift as you attempt to change your weight. This will affect your ability to adhere to your diet and can result in undesired changes in the "energy in" portion of the equation!

Taken together, the above factors clearly show your body does *not* want to change. Its default mode is to fight for homeostasis, and fight it will! The fact that calories must be adjusted in order to maintain weight loss is not a sign the CICO model is wrong, it just shows that it is a *dynamic system*. You must continually adjust both your diet and activity levels to account for these changes. This is unfortunately easier said than done, but with foreknowledge of how this all works, it *can* be achieved!

There are three main reasons people struggle to change their weight using a "by the numbers" approach:

1. OVER-/UNDERESTIMATING CALORIC INTAKE

As it turns out, we are *really* bad at estimating our own caloric intake. In one notable study, subjects were found to be underestimating the number of calories they had eaten by about 50%! [12] The simple truth of the matter is this: if you struggle to lose weight, odds are you are eating more than you realize. And the same thing goes for if you struggle to *gain* weight—you just need to eat more. Even registered dieticians fail to accurately report their own calorie intakes. [13] This doesn't mean tracking has no utility; it's just important to recognize and account for the inherent margin of error.

2. OVER-/UNDERESTIMATING CALORIES BURNED THROUGH EXERCISE

As if the above wasn't enough, we also happen to be pretty bad at estimating how many calories we've burned through exercise. In that same study mentioned above, participants over-estimated calories burned through exercise by a whopping 50%. Generally speaking, relying on exercise to make up for a poor diet is a fool's errand. There is quite a bit of truth to the saying *"You can't outrun a bad diet."*

3. UNACCOUNTED FOR CHANGES IN NEAT

The most pernicious of the four components of your metabolism is NEAT. While individual resting metabolic rates typically only differ by about 200–300 calories, [14] changes in NEAT (particularly in the context of overfeeding) do vary quite a bit. So, when people say there is no such thing as a "fast" or a "slow" metabolism, they may be right from a technical standpoint, but they are *wrong* if they don't recognize that some people's energy needs may be drastically different from what a generic TDEE calculator might suggest.

As a case in point, in one study, [15] subjects were overfed by 1,000 calories. At the end of the study, some subjects had gained less than 1 lb. of fat, while others gained nearly 10 lb. of fat. Why the large disparity? It all came down to differences in NEAT: The highest NEAT responder in the study burned almost *700* calories extra due to increases in NEAT, whereas the lowest NEAT responder in this study actually saw a decrease in NEAT of about 100 calories. The reason I call NEAT pernicious is because we mostly don't have any control over it,[12] and it can work in sneaky ways to counteract efforts to modify your weight.

A well-intentioned dieter may go for a jog and burn an extra 200 calories, but then is so tired for the rest of the day, he/she ends up on the couch watching Netflix. In the end, the additional calories burned through exercise are washed out by the *decrease* in activity levels later in the day.

If all the above seems to paint too grim a picture, fear not. There are ways to circumvent these problems, and simply understanding the *why* behind them is the first step. Changing your weight is simple, but it's certainly not easy. In the next section, you will learn how to take that first step.

---

12   Tracking your daily step count using a pedometer can be one way of attempting to account for changes in NEAT as you diet. This is effective because it serves as a decent proxy for "global" activity levels instead of only focusing on calories burned through intentional exercise.

GETTING THE SCALE MOVING IN THE RIGHT DIRECTION: PRACTICAL STEPS

In this section I will primarily be outlining a "by the numbers" approach where various metrics are tracked in order to ensure consistent progress, but I will also be providing more general guidelines for a more intuitive approach where tracking at that level of detail is not required (see the "Dietary Heuristics" section for more). If you have no problems regulating your weight and are happy with your current appearance and body fat percentage, then feel free to just skim over this section for now.

If, however, you consistently struggle to either gain or lose weight, or you have more advanced physique goals (you want a six-pack), then I highly recommend you take the time to implement the strategies discussed here. Learning how to control your energy balance is a critical first step in improving your ability to perform as an athlete.

FINDING MAINTENANCE CALORIES

You need to know where you are before you can get to where you want to go.

The first step to controlling your weight is determining your *maintenance calories*. This is the amount of food you need to eat to roughly maintain your weight. Once you have established a maintenance level intake, you will have a reference point from which you can adjust.

There are several free online calculators that you can use to estimate your maintenance level calories, but to get in the ballpark, you can just multiply your current body weight by 15. The *best* way to determine your maintenance calories, however, is to take a two-week period to record some data on yourself. Even the most detailed of calculators can only provide a "best guess" based on averages. By taking the time to record some data on yourself, you will be much more likely to obtain valid results.

Here's how to do it:

→ Record your body weight daily for two weeks:
  • Wake up, use the bathroom, and weigh yourself in the nude. Maintain these conditions each day so variables are minimized.
  • At the end of each week, average the seven weigh-ins so you have a weighted, weekly average.
→ Keep a daily food journal:
  • Without changing your diet, track your calories as accurately as possible (weigh foods to the gram using a digital food scale) and keep track of total calories consumed each day.
  • Keep a rolling average of each day's caloric intake so at the end of the two weeks you know your average caloric intake.
→ Find the difference in weight between your week one average and your week two average.
→ Multiply the difference in weight between week one and two by 3,500 (which is the number of calories contained in 1 lb. of fat) and divide by seven to find out how far above or below maintenance you are.
→ Subtract/add that number to your average caloric intake for those two weeks to find your maintenance.

Here's a hypothetical example using a made-up person. Let's call him "Timo."

Week One	Week Two
Average weight: 161.2 lb. (73.3 kg)	Average weight: 161.8 lb. (73.5 kg)
Average caloric intake across both weeks: 2,950 calories	

The difference in Timo's weight over this two-week period is 0.6 lb. (0.2 kg).

→ 3,500 x 0.6 = 2,100
→ 2,100 / 7 = 300

Since Timo's weight went *up,* we know he is above his maintenance, so we need to subtract the 300 calories from his average caloric intake to find his maintenance:

→ 2,950 – 300 = 2,650 calories

This number represents Timo's current TDEE. From here, we can add or subtract calories to achieve the desired body composition changes:

To lose weight, subtract 10%–25% from your maintenance level intake.

Your goal should be to lose no more than 0.5%–1% of your total body weight per week—for most people this falls in the 1–2 lb (0.5 –1 kg) range. This rate of weight loss will help ensure you are able to minimize muscle and strength loss and mitigate decreases in athletic performance. [16]

If you want to gain weight, then add 10% to your maintenance level intake.

Your rate of acceptable weight gain (meaning maximizing lean body mass gains while minimizing fat gains) will vary based on the amount of lean body mass you've already added to your frame.

Suggested Rates of Weight Gain by Experience Level	
Rank Beginners (no history of resistance training)	1.5%–2% of body weight gained **per month**
Beginner/Intermediate: (1–2 years proper resistance training)	1%–1.5% body weight gained **per month**
Intermediate/Advanced (3–5 + years proper resistance training)	0.5%–1% body weight gained **per month**

Remember your TDEE is a moving target—as your body weight changes over time, your TDEE will change as well! If you are consistent with your diet and exercise and don't see any changes in weight for two weeks in a row (females may need to wait four weeks), then you must adjust your calories up or down accordingly.

For example, a male beginner who is trying to gain 3 lb. (1.4 kg) per month should do the following:

→ Find his TDEE and add 10% to his caloric intake.
→ Weigh himself multiple times throughout the week (daily would be even better) under the same conditions. At the end of the week, average the weights. Going forward, use a weekly average to compare progress.

→ Gaining 3 lb. (1.4 kg) per month requires an average weight gain of 0.75 lb. (0.34 kg) per week.

→ Every 2 weeks he should be approximately 1.5 lb. (0.68 kg) heavier.

→ If this rate of weight gain is achieved, change nothing.

→ If the rate of weight gain is *less*, add 100–200 calories to daily intake.

→ If the rate of weight gain is *more*, subtract 100–200 calories from daily intake.

Here's an example of how you might adjust if you are looking to *lose* 1–2 lb. (0.5–1 kg) per week:

→ Subtract 20% from your TDEE.

→ Track your body weight daily and take a weighted weekly average at the end of each week.

→ After 2–4 solid weeks of data with good adherence, compare your weighted weekly averages.

→ If you have lost weight in the desired range, change nothing.

→ If your rate of weight loss is below the desired rate, subtract 100–200 calories from your intake.

→ If the rate of weight loss is too high, i.e., you're losing weight too quickly, add 100–200 calories to your daily intake.

Adjustments to calories should be made gradually and in small increments rather than big jumps. Changes in body composition are often masked by water retention, so it's important not to become caught up in the day-to-day fluctuations of the scale. Go by the weekly averages and each time you make an adjustment to your calories, allow 2–4 weeks to pass before deciding to adjust again.

This all may seem a little overwhelming if you aren't accustomed to tracking your diet and weight in such a detailed manner, but you might be surprised at how quickly you can adjust. We live in a time where it's easier than ever to track calories. Restaurants are becoming more and more transparent with their nutritional information, and the rise of smartphones, apps, and online databases have made the nutritional information of nearly any food a mere click or two away. In fact, with a little practice, tracking your calories should only take an extra 5–10 minutes per day.

If calorie counting is too tedious, tracking your body weight and keeping a simple food journal can also be an effective means of identifying trends and providing yourself with the data necessary to make adjustments. The most important thing is to ensure you're able to get your body weight into the optimal range, at an appropriate rate, and that you're providing your body with enough calories to fuel performance and support recovery.

CHAPTER SUMMARY:

→ Increasing relative strength is a fast way to improve athleticism.
→ Even if you are not overweight, you may still see performance improvements by leaning out a bit.
→ A theoretical "optimal" body fat percentage for table tennis players is in the 8%–13% range for men and the 16%–22% range for women.
→ Your energy balance—the number of calories you consume versus the number burned— will dictate whether you maintain, gain, or lose weight.
→ The *rate* at which you gain or lose weight is important.

→ To lose weight, subtract 10%–25% from maintenance caloric intake.

→ Aim to lose 0.5%–1% of total body weight (or 1–2 lb / 0.5–1 kg) per week.

→ To gain weight, add 10% to maintenance caloric intake.

→ Rate of weight gain depends on amount of lean body mass already added to frame.

→ Calorie counting or food journals, along with tracking body weight, can be used as a tool to ensure correct energy intake and rate of weight change.

LEVEL TWO: MACRONUTRIENT AND FIBER INTAKE

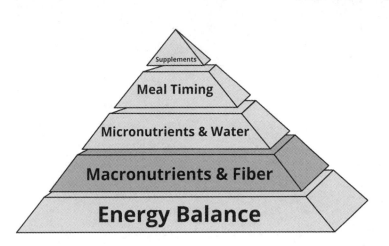

We've established that, yes, calories do count, but are they *all* that count? Once we know roughly how many calories to eat each day, how do we go about deciding where those calories should come from? Does it matter?

Too often, people create a false dichotomy between the importance of calories and the importance of eating the right types of foods. The reality is *both* are important. You can't just hit your energy needs for the day with a bunch of empty calories and expect to look, feel, and perform your best. And likewise, you can't just eat "healthy foods" and be certain your energy and nutrient needs are being met. Both energy needs *and* nutrient needs are important pieces of the puzzle, which is why they are the first and second levels of the pyramid respectively.

In this chapter, you will learn precisely how these two puzzle pieces fit together. You will learn the three main sources of calories, their impact on your health, and how to balance them in the correct proportions to achieve peak performance.

Before diving into the specifics of these roles, however, it's useful to first examine how your body's energy and nutrient needs interact on a broader scale. As an athlete, this concept will be especially important to understand because there are ramifications on your ability to perform if you don't get this right. Consider, for example, a trap I fell into several years ago.

THE ATHLETE'S "CLEAN EATING" FALLACY

Many moons ago, before I knew what I know today about nutrition, I got sick of my junky diet full of processed foods, takeout, and sweets, and decided I needed to clean things up. I read a blog post about how I was supposed to eat like a caveman, so I went to the food store and stocked up on fruits, veggies, meat, and basically anything else that seemed to fit into the category of healthy and "primal." I heard carbs were bad, so I cut out bread, rice, and potatoes. I stopped salting my food. I completely overhauled my diet, and I couldn't wait to see how it would pay off on the court and in the gym.

But then something strange happened. . .

After the first couple of weeks or so, my performance began to plummet. I couldn't make it through my training sessions like I used to, and I would consistently gas out when playing consecutive tough matches. I felt like my energy levels were suffering, so I started to eat more to compensate, but then I started having issues with bloating and gassiness.

Wanting to troubleshoot things, I started tracking my calories and paying attention to my body weight. Low and behold, I was barely cracking 2,200 calories per day and my body weight was down over 5 lb. To give some perspective, as an adult male who happens to be a high NEAT responder (think your classic hardgainer), I usually require over 3,000 calories to even *maintain* my weight when I'm training hard. So, what happened? How had I unknowingly slashed so many calories from my diet?

It's simple. Many healthy foods happen to be high in nutrients but also *low* in calories. Additionally, the high fiber and water content of fruits and vegetables make them incredibly filling. This is why they are such good choices when trying to lose weight. Unfortunately for me, I did *not* need to lose weight! I was training harder than ever and my body was in desperate need of fuel. And by cutting out salt to the extent that I did, I was also failing to fully replace the sodium I was losing through sweat. By deciding to solely focus on "eating clean," I had increased the quality of the food I was eating, but inadvertently *decreased* my total energy intake. This is despite the fact that the sheer volume of food I was eating was higher than it was previously.

To fix this, I kept most of the fruits, veggies, and protein in my diet, but I *added* easy-to-digest carb sources like white rice, potatoes, and pasta to help fill in those missing calories. I started putting some salt on my food again. I even started including some sweets and sugary cereals in moderation. Within a week I was back to normal and feeling better than ever. It may seem counterintuitive that a diet that includes some foods typically viewed as unhealthy may actually be *superior* to a diet composed solely of "clean foods," but the key to understanding this is recognizing the utility of what the United States Department of Agriculture (USDA) refers to as *discretionary calories*.

Discretionary calories are the "leftover" calories in your diet that remain after you have already met your nutrient needs. It's the difference between *total* energy requirements and the energy consumed to meet your *nutritional needs*. Here is a graph illustrating this concept:

Once you have fulfilled your nutrient needs for the day, you don't get bonus points for continuing to consume only healthy, nutrient-dense foods. Eating so-called "junk food" is primarily an issue when you do so at the *expense* of other nutrients. As long as you're eating your fruits/veggies, getting enough fiber and protein, and staying within your calories for the day, there is nothing wrong with enjoying some treats in moderation—especially if it helps you meet energy needs that wouldn't have been met otherwise.

Energy Needs vs. Nutrient Needs

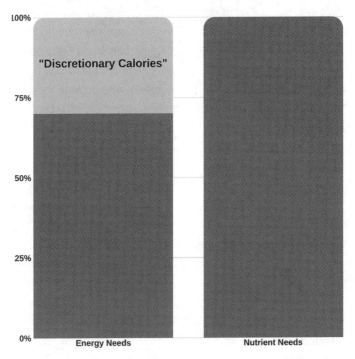

A good rule of thumb is to limit these types of indulgences to no more than 10%–20% of your total calories for the day.

Still not convinced? Here's some research to back it up:

Overly rigid dieting practices where foods are viewed as "clean" or "unclean" are associated with higher BMIs and more instances of disordered eating, whereas utilizing flexible dieting strategies are associated with more successful weight loss outcomes and better maintenance of a healthy body weight. [1–2] One study even directly compared the typical "clean eating" bodybuilding diet with a more flexible approach that was based on macronutrients and calories.

Overall, they found no significant differences between the groups, but there was a slight trend for *less* micronutrient deficiency in the females who followed the flexible dieting approach. [3]

So now that we've established the importance of balancing energy needs and nutrient needs while utilizing a flexible and inclusive dietary approach, we can finally start getting into the nitty gritty of this second level of the pyramid. The following section will briefly describe each macronutrient's purpose in your diet and will provide some specific recommendations for your daily intake.

BALANCING THE THREE MACRONUTRIENTS

Calories come from three different macronutrient sources: protein, fat, and carbohydrate.[13] So, while we have a total number of calories to shoot for each day, those calories will be composed of some combination of protein, fat, and carbs. If you've been around long enough, you've likely seen each one of these macronutrients get their time in the limelight.

In the 1980s, fat was the enemy. After that, carbs became the bad guy—something that is still quite common to hear today. Even protein has had its fair share of vilification with accusations that it causes kidney damage, cancer, and smelly farts (okay, so maybe that last one has some truth to it!).

The truth is, all three macronutrients have an important role to play in a well-balanced diet.

We will now take a look at each of these roles in turn.

---

13   Technically, alcohol is also a unique source of calories with 7 calories per gram.

PROTEIN

Protein gets its name from the Greek word *protos*, which means "first," but that's not the only reason to start this discussion with protein. Dietary protein is vitally important for maintaining a good body composition as it provides the raw materials for building, repairing, and maintaining skeletal muscle. As an athlete, this is important because your base athleticism is affected tremendously by the ratio of fat to muscle in the body. Although you may have heard people tend to eat *more* protein than they need, there is a difference between how much protein your body needs for daily living and how much is needed to optimize your performance as an athlete. I call this phenomenon *the protein gap*.

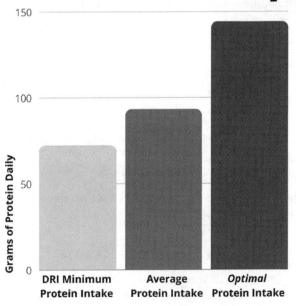

Polling data from the Centers for Disease Control and Prevention (CDC) indicate the average American adult male weighs around 198 lb. (90 kg) [4] and consumes 93 g of protein per day. [5] To meet the dietary reference intake (DRI) of 0.8 g of protein per kg of body weight, the average male would only need to consume around 72 g of protein per day.

As you can see in the graph above, the average male in the United States already exceeds the DRI recommended protein intake. This is where those headlines about Americans getting "too much protein" come from. But remember, the DRI is just a bare minimum to maintain a positive nitrogen balance in the body and promote general health. When *athletes* are studied, research consistently shows performance benefits all the way up to 1.6 g/kg or 0.72 g/lb. [6] As activity levels go up, so do your protein requirements. [7] So that same 198 lb. (90 kg) male would actually need to consume a minimum of 144 g of protein per day in order to optimize performance and recovery.

OPTIMAL PROTEIN INTAKE

In order to optimize body composition and performance, I recommend table tennis players consume **0.72–1.2 g of protein per lb. of body weight daily (or 1.6–2.6 g per kg)**. This daily dose should be split evenly between three or more meals per day. You may have noticed the upper end of this range goes beyond the 0.72 g/lb. minimum threshold recommended by the research. This is because there can be additional advantages to higher protein intakes in certain contexts.

For starters, high protein diets have been shown to promote satiety [8] and increase fat loss while preserving muscle when dieting. [9] And if you struggle to maintain your weight and find the scale creeping up over the course of the year, higher protein diets have also been found to help offset fat gain during periods where energy intake is increased. [10] Lastly, protein needs *increase* as you get older since the body becomes less responsive to the protein you consume as you age. [11] Thus, there may be occasions where, due to your individual circumstances or simply out of personal preference, you may benefit from going above the 0.72 g/lb. minimum threshold.

The best sources of protein tend to be from meat, fish, dairy, and eggs. These protein sources have great amino acid profiles, digest well, and have a high protein-to-calorie ratio. Non-animal sources, such as nuts and legumes, can also contribute to your protein intake, but they are not a good "first choice" option for protein—especially if calories are limited. A good rule of thumb is your protein source should have at least 1 g of protein per 10 calories. So, if you are eating 200 calories worth of a protein source, you should be getting a *minimum* of 20 g of protein from it. Many plant-based protein sources (peanut butter comes to mind) fail this test miserably.

It is a common misconception that vegans and vegetarians can't get enough protein to perform optimally. If you make smart food choices and have high energy requirements, it can usually be accomplished with some careful planning. That said, there *is* some evidence to suggest that plant-based sources of protein may need a higher dosage to achieve the same post-meal amino acid levels when compared with something like whey protein. [12] So rather than shooting for the minimum 0.72 g of protein per lb. of body weight, you may want to aim closer to 1 g/lb. if you're really concerned with maximizing muscle mass. If you find this difficult, it may be worth supplementing with a plant-based protein powder. Rice + pea blend powders have a similar amino acid profile to whey protein and can help boost your protein intake without adding a ton of calories to your diet.

HEALTH RISKS OF HIGH PROTEIN DIETS

One of the most persistent myths regarding a high protein diet is that it will be harmful to your kidneys. At this point, the research very clearly shows high protein diets do not adversely affect kidney function in healthy adults. [13] We do, however, need to pay some attention to the linkage of red meat consumption with cancer.

First, it's important to understand that much of the research that condemns meat consumption is correlational rather than causative. People who have higher intakes of meat also disproportionately engage in behaviors that negatively impact their health (higher BMIs, smoking, inactivity, lower vegetable intakes, etc.). These confounding variables make it difficult to tease out what is really causing the poor health outcomes. So, although there is a valid association between the consumption of highly processed red meats and cancer, [14–15] because the relative risk remains rather small, a 2019 review of the literature published by the *Annals of Internal Medicine* recommended that adults continue both processed and *unprocessed* red meat consumption because the desirable effects of reduced consumption probably do not outweigh the undesirable effects. [16] Thus, given the health-protective benefits of high activity levels and fruit and vegetable consumption, the occasional inclusion of some processed red meats should not be a major concern for the serious athlete who follows a well-balanced diet.

Still, I personally believe that a little mindful moderation of the more highly-processed red meats is warranted. I would also avoid frequently consuming heavily charred, blackened, and/or smoked meats. These seem to be the main things associated with poor health outcomes. You don't need to throw the baby out with the bathwater. There's a big difference between including high-quality cuts of meat like steak as part of a healthy, balanced diet and having most of your meat consumption come from hot dogs, bacon, and Slim Jims!

FAT

Dietary fat plays an essential role in the health of your body, assisting with hormone production, nutrient absorption, and supporting cell growth, to name just a few of its roles. With the rise in popularity of the ketogenic diet in recent years, dietary fat has successfully shed many of the negative connotations that plagued it in the past. Unfortunately, as these things often do, the pendulum has now swung too far in the other direction, with people making claims like "butter is a superfood" and that becoming "fat adapted" will turn your body into a fat burning furnace. In this section, I will cut through the hype and give you some simple recommendations and tips based on the latest evidence.

SETTING YOUR TOTAL FAT INTAKE FOR THE DAY

A minimum threshold of dietary fat should be met on a daily basis to ensure enough essential fats are consumed and hormone production can be supported. Sports scientists tend to agree on around 0.3 g per lb. of body weight daily as being a good minimum target for general health. To give a general idea of what it would take to hit this minimum, a 180-lb. (82 kg) man would need to consume at least 54 g of fat per day. This could easily be accomplished by having two eggs for breakfast, a couple ounces of nuts with lunch, and a salmon fillet with dinner. This isn't even counting incidental fats from other foods that would also contribute to your intake for the day.

Put in terms of a percentage of total calories, about 15%–35% of your total calories daily should come from fat, provided you are still hitting the minimum of 0.3 g per lb. of body weight. Within this range, fat intake can be set based on personal preference, though there is some rationale to stay closer to the bottom end of the range because fat does not have as direct an impact on performance and recovery as protein and carbs do. For this reason, a moderate-to-low-fat diet may be preferable for those involved in hard training. In keeping your dietary fat on the lower side, you free up space for more carbs to be eaten. There is also some evidence that consuming a high fat diet (40% or more of total calories coming from fat) may negatively impact diversity in the gut microbiome. [17]

With those considerations in mind, 20%–30% of total calories coming from fat seems to be a good sweet spot for most athletes.

This is high enough to allow for some enjoyable foods (which can assist with adherence to the diet) while being low enough to allow for enough carbs to fuel training.

The Low Down on "Good" Versus "Bad" Fats

There are four main types of fats: polyunsaturated, monounsaturated, saturated fats, and trans fats. With the exception of trans fats, which should generally be avoided, the remaining fats can all contribute positively to your health in varying ways. I find it useful to split dietary fats into three categories in order to ensure a proper balance: fats to purposefully include, fats to potentially moderate, and fats to avoid.

FATS TO PURPOSEFULLY INCLUDE

→ Fatty fish
→ Olive oil
→ Nuts

→ Seeds
→ Nut butters
→ Avocados
→ *Some* fattier cuts of red meat, full/partial fat dairy, and/or eggs

The foods in this category should be purposefully included as a first choice in your daily diet. These fats impart health benefits that go beyond merely fulfilling your body's base requirements for dietary fat. Monounsaturated fats found in foods such as olive oil and nuts have been linked with better cardiovascular health, [18] and avocados have been shown to have a positive impact on health as well. [19] The real show stealer, however, are polyunsaturated fats, specifically the omega-3 fatty acids. Here's a quick rundown of some of the health-promoting effects associated with them:

→ Improved body composition and maximal strength. [20]
→ Improved anabolic signaling and satellite cell activity. [22]
→ Reduced symptoms of depression. [22]
→ Decreased risk of cardiac death. [23]
→ Decreased blood pressure. [24]
→ Decreased waist circumference. [25]
→ Reduced inflammation. [26]

Many of the effects listed above are fairly modest in practical terms, but taken together, it is clear there are a host of potential benefits to including fatty fish in your diet. Because of this, I typically recommend athletes supplement with fish oil if they are unable to eat fatty fish two to three times per week.

*For the hard-training athlete, I also recommend purposefully including some fattier cuts of red meat, full or partial fat dairy, and eggs in the diet. Although these foods are higher in saturated fat, they are also very nutrient-dense and bring other health benefits to the table.

It is a myth that including some saturated fat in your diet will "clog your arteries" and lead to cardiovascular disease. There are some links between saturated fat and heart disease *risk factors*, but multiple meta-analyses of the data show no significant association between the consumption of saturated fats and the risk of heart disease itself. [27–28]

Still, that doesn't mean it's wise or even beneficial to start dumping butter and coconut oil into your morning coffee. While the research regarding the health effects of saturated fats is mixed, there is a *wealth* of evidence showing the positive health effects of polyunsaturated and monounsaturated fats. If your intake of saturated fats gets too high, you run the risk of using up your dietary fat "budget" on saturated fats and missing out on the proven health-promoting effects of polyunsaturated and monounsaturated fats. Thus, when you *do* consume saturated fats, it pays to do so in the form of nutrient-dense foods such as eggs, dairy, and meat.

The fact that these foods are also high in cholesterol may raise a few eyebrows, but like saturated fat, dietary cholesterol doesn't deserve the bad rap it gets. For the typical person, the amount of dietary cholesterol consumed does not have a significant impact on the amount of cholesterol that ends up in the blood. [29] Because you need cholesterol to help make hormones and assist with organ function, its levels are tightly controlled by the body.

Nutrition researcher, Menno Henselmans, also points to some interesting research [30–32] linking cholesterol to increased muscle growth:

> The available research indicates a high cholesterol diet may be advantageous for muscle growth and strength development by increasing muscle cell integrity and signaling for muscle growth. The beneficial cholesterol intake seems to be at least 7.2 mg dietary cholesterol per kg of lean body mass and more than 400 mg in men.

To wrap this section up, the majority of your fat intake should be coming from the standard "healthy fats," with a smaller relative percentage coming from saturated fat sources high in cholesterol. Unless you have a specific reason designated by your doctor, attempting to "play it safe" by completely avoiding the saturated fat and cholesterol found in meat, dairy, and eggs is misguided and may cause you to miss out on the health and performance benefits those foods have to offer.

FATTY FOODS TO POTENTIALLY MODERATE

→ Butter
→ Vegetable oils
→ Coconut oil
→ Grapeseed oil
→ Fattier cuts of highly processed red meat, full/partial fat dairy, and/or eggs

The butter and oils listed in this section should not be viewed as "bad" *per se*; they simply don't have much to offer except to help you reach your dietary fat intake for the day. As mentioned previously, since your saturated fat intake should make up a smaller relative percentage of your total fat intake, I recommend getting your saturated fat mainly from sources such as meat, eggs, and dairy as they are far more nutrient-dense. Still, even with these foods, most will need to exercise at least some level of moderation in order to maintain an optimally balanced diet. One reason for this is so a higher protein intake can be reached without exceeding your fat target for the day. This is why I recommend mostly aiming for leaner protein sources. This will ensure protein needs can be met while leaving sufficient room in the diet for carbs.

FATTY FOODS TO AVOID

→ Foods containing trans fats

Thanks to near universal recommendations from national and global public health authorities, trans fats have been eliminated from many food products available today. Studies show that the policies seem to have been largely effective in reducing consumption of trans fatty acids and seem to have had a net positive effect on public health. [33]

It's still a good idea to check the labels of the foods you consume to look for trans fats and check for partially hydrogenated oils in the ingredients list. Be wary of baked goods and things that are breaded and deep fried. As with most things, a little trans fat isn't going to kill you, but you're better off avoiding them to the extent you can.

CARBOHYDRATES

Along with protein, carbs have the most direct impact on your body composition, performance, and recovery. Because carbs are your body's preferred source of fuel, having too low of an intake can negatively affect athletic performance. [34–40]. For this reason, most athletes will find it advantageous to arrange the diet in a way that allows for plenty of carbs to be eaten.

There are three main categories of carbs: monosaccharides (glucose, fructose, galactose), disaccharides (sucrose, lactose, maltose), and polysaccharides (starch, cellulose, glycogen), but in common parlance, carbs are more typically described as either *simple* or *complex*, with simple carbs often being viewed as "bad" and complex carbs viewed as "good." As usual, there's a little more nuance than that, so let's take a more in-depth look.

SIMPLE VERSUS COMPLEX CARBS: NOT SO SIMPLE...

The *simple* vs. *complex* categorization of carbs is based on the carb's chemical structure and its effect on blood sugar levels, or its *glycemic response*. This response is measured by the glycemic index (GI), which ranks foods on a scale from zero to 100. A score of 55 or less is considered low, and a score of 70 or more is considered high. There are issues with attempting to categorize carbs in this way, however. A banana is primarily composed of fructose and sucrose. Many would consider this a simple carb, but if we look at its GI, it only scores a 51. Meanwhile, a baked sweet potato, which is a complex carb, clocks in at 94 on the GI.

Furthermore, because the GI of a food is determined by eating said food in *isolation* after an overnight fast, it doesn't account for the impact of other nutrients that will be present when the carb is eaten as part of a mixed meal. Nutrients such as fiber, fat, and protein will greatly reduce the speed at which the meal is digested—lowering the GI of the meal as a whole. To muddy the waters even further, there is evidence that shows a high variability in the GI response to identical meals between individuals. [42]

Thus, for general health and body composition goals, it's much more important to pay attention to your total energy intake and your carb intake *in relation to* protein, fats, and fiber, than it is to nit-pick carb choices using the GI. There are specific situations, however, in which the GI can become a useful tool for sports performance. If you need quick energy during an intense training session/tournament, or you need to quickly replenish glycogen levels when training multiple times per day, preferentially choosing high GI carbs will be your best option. This will be elaborated on further in the "Peri-Workout Nutrition" section.

DETERMINING YOUR TOTAL CARB INTAKE

Having chosen your optimal protein and fat intake already, we can simply use a bit of math to find out how many calories are left for carbohydrates: subtract the calories from protein and fats from your TDEE and the balance can be spent on carbs.

Taking a 200 lb (90 kg) man with a TDEE of 3,000 calories, we would get the following daily targets:

→ **Protein**: 144 g (200 x 0.72) per day. Protein has 4 calories per gram, so 576 total calories come from protein.
→ **Fat**: 83 g (3,000 x 25%, divided by 9). Fat has 9 calories per gram, so 747 total calories come from fat.
→ **Carbs**: 419 g (3,000 - 576 - 747, divided by 4). Carbs have 4 calories per gram, so 1,677 total calories come from carbs.

In terms of what specific types of carbs you should be eating daily, use the following hierarchy to inform your decisions:

The Athlete's Carb Pyramid

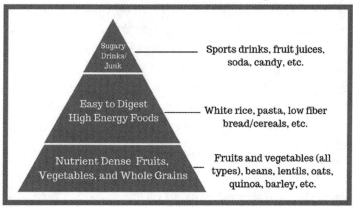

As you can see, you should first prioritize fulfilling nutrient needs by ensuring you include plenty of nutrient-dense fruits, vegetables, and whole grains in your diet. Five or more combined servings of fruits and vegetables per day is a good base target to fulfill nutrient requirements, and has been shown as a bottom-threshold intake to lower the risk of all-cause mortality.[42] For whole grains, around three servings per day is a reasonable target and has also been associated with a lower risk of all-cause mortality. [43]

Despite the scare-mongering around grains causing inflammation, the literature suggests the opposite occurs, with whole grains generally having a positive impact on systemic inflammation. [44–46] That said, more is not necessarily better. If your carb intake is particularly high, you may find consuming large quantities of whole grains on top of your fruit/veggie intake to be tough on your stomach. That's a lot of fiber to process! If that's the case, shift to the second level of the pyramid and utilize easier to digest carb sources such as white rice, pasta, white bread, and/or low fiber cereals.

Finally, for the hard-training athlete, there is typically room for some sugary beverages and/or junky sweets to help with enjoyment and adherence to the diet, as well as filling in that last 10% or so of calories from carbs. This is where sports drinks, fruit juices, and even the occasional soda and/or candy can have a place in your diet. Yes, even *sugar* can be part of a healthy diet! Sugar is often claimed to be "bad" for you regardless of the context. It's been called "toxic," as "addictive as cocaine," and is widely cited as the cause of the obesity epidemic. The truth is, well-controlled studies have shown that reasonable sugar consumption is not a significant health risk if you're following a well-balanced diet. [47]

FIBER GUIDELINES

Most people get around half the recommended amount of fiber per day. There is strong evidence supporting the health benefits of a high fiber intake, [48] so make sure you take the time to track your intake every now and again. General guidelines for fiber intake from various health organizations tend to converge around 14 g of fiber per 1,000 calories consumed.

Getting your daily servings of fruits, vegetables, and whole grains will probably get you about 80% of the way there, but you may need to intentionally include more high-fiber foods in order to get the recommended amounts. Legumes are all-stars in this area, so making them a regular part of your diet can help in that regard.

CHAPTER SUMMARY:

→ All three macronutrients play vital roles in your diet.
→ Balancing them in the correct proportions will have a significant impact on your performance and health.
→ As long as the majority of your calories are coming from whole, nutrient-dense foods, there is nothing wrong with occasionally enjoying traditionally unhealthy treats in moderation.
→ A daily target of 0.72–1.2g per lb. of body weight (1.6–2.6 g/kg) is optimal for protein.
→ About 20%–30% of total calories from fat is a good range for most athletes. Don't go below 0.3 g of fat per lb. of body weight.
→ Set your carb intake based on how many calories are left over after calculating protein and fat.
→ Aim for around 14 g of fiber per 1,000 calories consumed.

LEVEL THREE: MICRONUTRIENT AND WATER INTAKE

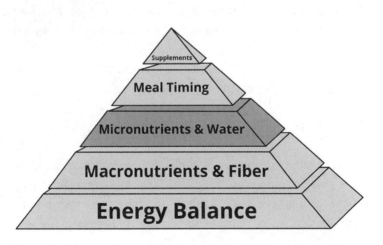

If you read through the previous chapter carefully, you will likely have noticed I made several specific recommendations regarding the types of foods to eat in order to meet each macronutrient requirement. This was to help ensure you put yourself in a good position to meet micronutrient needs while still meeting base energy requirements. In this chapter, I summarize the recommended intakes to help meet nutrient needs and highlight some specific micronutrient concerns faced by athletes.

Summary Recommendations:

→ Meet protein needs mostly through a variety of lean, whole food options such as lean meats, fish, and low-fat dairy.

→ Meet base fat requirements with a special focus on including fatty fish, olive oil, avocados, and nuts.

→ Bridge the gap of remaining fat and protein requirements with fattier cuts of red meat, eggs, and/or full fat dairy.

→ Meet carbohydrate needs first with five or more combined servings of nutrient-dense fruits and vegetables, and around three servings of whole grains per day.

→ If additional carbs are required, supplement with easy-to-digest, high-energy foods, such as white rice, pasta, and low fiber bread/cereals.

→ Aim for around 14 g of fiber per 1,000 calories consumed.

Assuming sufficient variety in your diet, the above recommendations are a great starting place for most. There are several nutritional deficiencies that are more common in athletes, so taking some proactive measures to "shore up" these potential weaknesses is wise.[14]

---

14   The calorie tracking app Cronometer has a feature that automatically tracks your micronutrient status based on the foods you eat. If you want a quick snapshot of your levels, you can track your typical diet for 1–2 weeks in the app.

The first micronutrient to be aware of is vitamin D. The rates of vitamin D deficiency are surprisingly high among American adults. [1] Even if one is *not* deficient in this vitamin, much like with protein, there is a gap between the amount required to prevent deficiency and the *optimal* dose of vitamin D. [2] Furthermore, since table tennis is an indoor sport and vitamin D is received mostly through sunlight, as table tennis players, we don't get the same exposure as outdoor athletes do.

Fatty fish, such as salmon, or fortified dairy/cereal products are good whole-food sources of vitamin D, but aiming for regular sun exposure (20–30 minutes of midday sun at least several times per week) should be your first line of defense. Depending on your schedule and the weather in your area, this may not be possible. Thus, you may need to supplement with vitamin D3 to help ensure optimal levels. 2,000 IU per day is a common daily dose.

Besides vitamin D, athletes may be at risk of deficiency in iron, calcium, magnesium, zinc and vitamin B12, particularly if calorie intake is low. [3] To help prevent deficiency in these vitamins and minerals, look to the following foods:

→ **Iron:** red meat, clams, mussels, oysters, chicken, spinach, beans, and lentils.
→ **Calcium:** dairy products, fortified cereals/juices, sardines, and dark leafy greens.
→ **Magnesium:** pumpkin seeds, almonds, whole wheat, dark chocolate, cashews, peanuts, avocado, and spinach.
→ **Zinc:** oysters, red meat, poultry, crab, lobster, and fortified cereals.
→ **Vitamin B12:** Beef, liver, chicken, fish, eggs, and dairy.

I will now take a moment to go over some slightly controversial and/or misunderstood topics. Most of the things on this list have an undeserved bad rap. By taking the time to clear up these misconceptions, I hope to provide you with more flexibility in how you go about meeting nutrient needs. There is a lot of fear-based marketing that goes on in the nutritional world. Arm yourself with the facts so you can make an informed decision!

NUTRITIONAL MYTHS AND FALLACIES

ARTIFICIAL SWEETENERS

Artificial sweeteners (also called non-nutritive sweeteners) are food additives that mimic the sweet taste of sugar but provide little to no calories and have no nutritional benefit. One important thing to consider when evaluating the safety of non-nutritive sweeteners is that the term itself is an umbrella term—there are *many* distinct types and they each need to be evaluated on an individual basis. For the sake of time, I will not be going into great depth over each individual non-nutritive sweetener. Instead, I'll zero in on aspartame as that seems to be the one that is most maligned and misunderstood.

In short, aspartame is one of the safest and well-studied food additives *ever*. Here is the conclusion from a 2002 review of the literature: [4]

> The aspartame safety data have been evaluated and found satisfactory by regulatory scientists in all major regulatory agencies and expert committees, including the U.S. Food and Drug Administration (FDA), the EU Scientific Committee for Food (SCF), and the Joint FAO/WHO Expert Committee

on Food Additives (JECFA). Further, aspartame has been approved for human consumption by regulatory agencies in more than 100 countries and received wide consumer acceptance with consumption by hundreds of millions of people over the past 20 years, representing billions of man-years of safe exposure. [4]

Amazingly, despite the *staggering* amount of evidence demonstrating the safety of aspartame, it's still incredibly common for people to make dramatic claims about its effects on health. The most common concerns point to one or more of the following:

→ Links with cancer.
→ Effects on insulin.
→ Effects on appetite and/or weight gain.
→ Acute side effects (headaches, nausea, etc.).
→ Effects on gut health.

The link to cancer stems from studies on rats and mice that show a dose-dependent increase in various cancers when they are given aspartame—usually in absurdly high doses. Fortunately, humans are not mice! There are important metabolic differences between us and mice that allow humans to process aspartame just fine. You cannot blindly apply animal research to humans. If that were the case, studies on dogs would suggest that chocolate is extremely toxic—and what a terrible world that would be to live in!

To be clear, there are *no* human trials that show a causative link between cancer (or other health conditions such as stroke, dementia, etc.) and aspartame. What the media typically reports on are studies that show *associations* between artificial sweeteners and poor health outcomes, but these are all from observational studies that cannot establish causation.[15] All these studies do is point out that unhealthy people often consume artificial sweeteners. This is almost certainly a case of reverse causation: overweight individuals (who are far more likely to be in poor health) tend to drink diet sodas in an attempt to cut down on sugar consumption and reduce their weight. The diet sodas are not *causing* the health conditions, they are just a behavioral symptom.

Are there dosages at which deleterious effects on health can appear? Sure. But that's true of anything—even *water* can kill you if you consume too much, too quickly! The dose makes the poison. The thing that really helps to put this into perspective is examining how the FDA sets the "acceptable daily intake" (ADI) for aspartame.

The ADI refers to how much aspartame you can consume every day for your *entire life* with no negative health effects. Currently, it stands at 50 mg/kg of body weight. To arrive at this number, they first figured out the dosage at which no observable adverse health effects are shown. They then divide that number by one hundred and set *that* as the ADI. So, they've already built in a hundred-fold safety factor just in case! And even with this safety factor, an average person would need to drink something like 18+ cans of diet soda every day just to exceed the ADI.

I know plenty of people who are fine with consuming a couple glasses of wine per night "for the antioxidants," but won't touch anything with aspartame. Yet alcohol is far more toxic than aspartame and is a known carcinogen. [5] It's a lot like the irrational fear many of us have regarding flying on a plane vs. driving in a car.

---

15   And correlation does *not* equal causation. If you want to have a bit of fun, google "spurious correlations" to see how common it is for completely unrelated phenomena to be strongly correlated.

The data is crystal clear that you are far safer in a plane, nonetheless, most fear flying more.

To briefly address the other concerns regarding aspartame: No, it won't spike your insulin and trick your body into gaining weight or craving sugar. This was shown in a 2019 systematic review and meta-analysis. [6] And no, you probably don't have short-term side effects (headaches, nausea, etc.) from aspartame either. There's a very strong chance you're simply experiencing those things due to a nocebo effect. [7] There is some emerging evidence suggesting that aspartame may reduce the diversity of the gut microbiome, but as you'll see in the "Gut Health" section later, there is simply not enough research in this area to draw definitive conclusions yet.

At the end of the day, whether you choose to consume artificial sweeteners, such as aspartame, is totally up to you. I have no dog in this fight. I do take issue, however, with those who make strong claims about artificial sweeteners that are not based on facts. This only serves to spread fear and misinformation. I've worked with plenty of people for whom the occasional diet soda helped keep them sane and adhere to their diet better. Dieting is tough enough as it is. Let's not needlessly take away options that can help!

ORGANIC FOODS

If I had to guess, I'd say at least eight out of 10 people would expect me to universally recommend consuming mostly organic foods in this book. This is because the organic food industry has done a *fantastic* job at marketing. The average person assumes that organic foods are more nutritious than conventionally grown foods, don't contain toxic chemicals, and are more environmentally friendly. The truth is, organic foods have no special nutritional benefit compared with non-organic foods, [8] and organic foods are *not* pesticide-free. [9] The main difference is that organic farming uses natural pesticides as opposed to synthetic. But the fact that something is "natural" has no bearing on whether it is safe for human consumption.[16]

Most people consume organic foods because they want to reduce their exposure to chemicals, but it is fallacious to call man-made things "chemicals" as if chemicals are automatically bad and must be manufactured. *Everything* is made up of chemicals! Dihydrogen monoxide sounds pretty scary until you realize it's just the chemical name for water. And did you know you're already consuming non-lethal doses of toxic chemicals every day? Pears contain formaldehyde. Apples have cyanide in them. These are naturally occurring chemicals that we consume with no problem because *the dose makes the poison.*

You may have heard of the infamous "Dirty Dozen." This is a list of foods shown to contain the highest levels of pesticide residue when taken from your average grocery store. Here's the problem though, even if you took the *worst* offender from this list, you'd have to consume an impossibly high amount of that food in a single day to even come close to reaching dangerous levels of exposure. The latest USDA and FDA reports show that pesticide residue on food is well below the safety levels set by the EPA. [10] To add yet another wrinkle, it is not entirely clear whether organic farming is better for the environment because it requires far more land to produce the same yield as conventionally grown crops [11].

---

16   The idea that natural things are inherently better and/or safer than man-made things is a logical error called the "appeal to nature" fallacy. You should take little comfort in something being natural—most of nature is trying to kill you!

The most important take-away is this: Do not let your fear of pesticides (or the exorbitant prices of organic foods) discourage you from eating plenty of fruits and vegetables! You can choose to eat organic if you like, but it should not be a major concern for you if you don't.

GENETICALLY MODIFIED ORGANISMS (GMOS)

Genetically modified foods are foods that are produced from organisms or microorganisms whose genetic material has been altered through genetic engineering. It is very common to see products proudly label themselves as "GMO Free" as if GMOs are somehow dangerous or unhealthy.[17] The truth is, there is no real evidence to suggest genetically modified foods are something we should worry about.

I understand the knee-jerk reaction against the idea of genetically modifying foods. One might picture a mad scientist stitching together horrible "frankenfoods" that were never meant to exist.

What could happen?! Could there be some hidden health risks lurking beneath the surface?

But farmers have been genetically modifying crops for thousands of years. By selecting the best plants with the most desirable traits and preferentially planting and cross-breeding them, farmers have drastically altered the foods we all know and love today. Modern GMO science is simply the natural progression of this ancient practice.

---

17 It's especially funny to see this label on foods for which there are no genes to even modify. Believe it or not, you can buy "GMO Free" salt. This is akin to selling "fat-free" sugar.

If you're still unsure, consider this: modern GMO foods have been exposed to *decades* of research and thousands of studies, and have been shown to be absolutely safe and beneficial for human consumption. In a major meta-analysis from 2018, 6,000 studies were analyzed from over 20 years of data on GMO corn. It was found to both increase crop yields and be safer than non-GMO corn due to the reduction of various toxins (mycotoxins, fumonisins, and thricotecens). [12]

"TOXINS" AND THE NEED TO "DETOX"

Speaking of toxins, there are countless "detox" kits, teas, pills, and programs available that promise to get rid of some vaguely mysterious toxins that are supposedly accumulating in your body and ruining your health. These things are nothing more than scams designed to prey on your fears and take your money. In a 2014 critical review of the evidence, [13] the authors couldn't find a single randomized controlled trial that assessed the effectiveness of commercial detox diets. They concluded the following:

> At present, there is no compelling evidence to support the use of detox diets for weight management or toxin elimination. Considering the financial cost to consumers, unsubstantiated claims, and potential health risks of detox products, they should be discouraged by health professionals and subject to independent regulatory review and monitoring.

The body does take in certain amounts of noxious elements (heavy metals, etc.), but we have built-in systems for handling these things (liver, kidneys, etc.). And if you've reached levels of acute toxicity, that's something handled by a doctor, not by a supplement sold to you by someone who looks like they just walked off the set of *Portlandia*.

DAIRY

Dairy is another category of foods that is unfairly demonized. In a major review of the literature, [14] researchers performed an in-depth assessment of the totality of scientific evidence regarding dairy and its effects on health. Here is what they found:

> *The totality of available scientific evidence supports that intake of milk and dairy products contribute to meet nutrient recommendations, and may protect against the most prevalent chronic diseases, whereas very few adverse effects have been reported.*

Among other things, dairy intake was associated with reduced risk of certain cancers, higher muscle mass, lower body fat percentage, and improved bone density. So, if you can tolerate it, making dairy a regular part of your diet is not a bad idea. Even those with lactose intolerance can generally consume dairy products with no symptoms if they are mindful of the amount of lactose in the foods they eat. [15] For those who are sensitive to lactose, foods such as hard cheeses, yogurt, and kefir are good low-lactose dairy sources.

GUT HEALTH

The impact the gut microbiome has on health and performance is an exciting new area of research. Unfortunately, as the science is relatively young at this point, it is difficult to make definitive recommendations. There is simply too much that is unknown.

The gut microbiome is an incredibly complex ecosystem, and improving it is a little more complicated than indiscriminately throwing as much "good bacteria" at it as possible. Probiotic supplementation is a perfect example of this. While it may help with certain gastrointestinal problems, [16] it has also been shown to *delay* gut healing when taken after antibiotics. [17] So, beware of internet "gut gurus" who make wild claims about transforming your health by healing your gut with their probiotics and digestive enzymes (the latter of which will simply be destroyed by your stomach acid). If the leading scientists and experts in the field of gut health are still unsure on these matters, you should pause before going all in on the advice from "Gut_Health_Mama_82" on Instagram.

Just getting yourself to a healthy body weight, staying active, and following a well-balanced diet full of a variety of high fiber foods is more than sufficient to maintain a healthy gut for most. If you still have digestive issues, see a qualified specialist.

SODIUM

Sodium gets a bad rap because of the long-held belief that it causes high blood pressure, increases the risk of heart disease, and because changes in sodium intake can cause you to temporarily hold some water weight, making it appear like you've gained fat. The truth is, if you have normal blood pressure and follow a healthy lifestyle (eat mostly unprocessed foods, drink lots of water, stay active, etc.), then you probably don't need to go out of your way to excessively restrict your salt intake. This is especially true for highly active individuals who sweat a lot as they will lose electrolytes like sodium at a higher rate than the average person.

Meta-analytic data from a study published in the *American Journal of Hypertension* suggests that a range of 2,645–4,945 mg per day is acceptable for most people. [18] This is much more reasonable than the 2,000 mg/day cutoff reflected on nutrition labels—especially for athletes. Like many things in nutrition, both too much sodium and *too little* appear to be suboptimal for health. There are some individuals who suffer from high blood pressure who may be salt sensitive. If that is the case for you, consult with your doctor to find a suitable sodium intake.

Pro Tip: If you find you do have salt-sensitive hypertension but struggle with keeping your salt intake low enough, you can increase the amount of potassium-rich foods in your diet to attack the problem from another angle. People tend to get plenty of sodium while not getting enough potassium, and it's actually the *ratio* of these two minerals that has the most effect on blood pressure. To up your potassium intake, try to regularly include foods such as yogurt, broccoli, baked potatoes, leafy greens, white mushrooms, and bananas.

BRAIN BOOSTING FOODS FOR THE TOP BRAIN SPORT

As a table tennis player, you should already know how important it is to stay sharp mentally in order to stay competitive. Fortunately, just by playing table tennis you are already giving your mind quite a workout, but is there anything else you can do to gain an edge? Well, here's some *literal* food for thought...

Research shows including foods such as blueberries, [19] leafy greens, [20] fatty fish, [21] dark chocolate, [22] and coffee/tea (caffeine) [23] in your diet may have neurocognitive benefits. Since most of these foods are beneficial to your health in other ways as well, this should make including them as a regular part of your diet a no brainer!

HOW TO INCREASE PERFORMANCE WITH STRATEGIC VEGETABLE CONSUMPTION

If I can't sell you on the importance of eating your veggies for general health reasons, consider this: with the right combination of vegetables each day, it's not too difficult to reach ergogenic levels of nitrate in the body. [24] You only need around 400–800 mg of nitrates per day (split across multiple meals) to see a beneficial effect on exercise performance. Consume three to four medium-sized beets, plus a salad or two, and you could easily find yourself within the performance-enhancing range.[18]

Here's a short-list of high-nitrate foods:

→ Beets[19]
→ Leafy greens
→ Radishes
→ Turnips
→ Garlic
→ Watercress
→ Celery

---

18 If you plan on supplementing with nitrates, you shouldn't use mouthwash as it will blunt the effects. Turns out, we need oral bacteria to convert the nitrate to nitrite!

19 Eat enough beets and your pee turns pinkish red. Don't worry, you're not dying, you've just been *dyed*!

It's also possible to hit ergogenic levels of betaine through your diet with the strategic consumption of things like wheat bran, wheat germ, spinach, and beets. Research suggests that a daily dose of 2.5 g of betaine per day may improve body composition when combined with resistance training, [25] and it's quite possible to hit that number through diet alone with a little planning.

Full credit goes to Dr. Eric Trexler for putting these two strategies on my radar via the *Monthly Applications in Strength Sport (MASS)* research review. [25a] Although nitrates and betaine have some emerging evidence that shows performance-enhancing effects, the base of support is nowhere near as strong as with supplements such as creatine and caffeine. But since you need to eat fruits and veggies anyway, *and* it's feasible to reach ergogenic doses through your diet (which isn't true for something like creatine), there is little harm in giving it a shot to see if you notice a benefit.

WATER INTAKE

Even though hydration is vitally important for survival, it falls on the third level of the pyramid because your body's natural thirst mechanism does a pretty good job of automatically getting you in the right ballpark. Once you are mindful of it, it is fairly easy to remain well hydrated (with one notable exception), so this is an area that does not require quite as much focus as other aspects of your diet.

A good ballpark figure for your fluid intake is about two-thirds of your body weight in fluid ounces per day. This can include water, coffee, tea, soda, and juice. Essentially, any liquid except alcohol can count toward reaching this target. Another good measure of proper hydration is at least five of your daily urinations should be clear.

FLUID INTAKE WHEN TRAINING

The "notable exception" I mentioned earlier comes into play once you start training or participating in sports. You cannot trust your natural thirst instinct when it comes to hydrating during athletic performance. If you simply consume liquids at will based on thirst, then you won't adequately replace fluids lost through sweat. This is referred to as *voluntary dehydration*. You will need to increase the amount of water you drink on days when you will be training heavily, especially if it is in a hot or humid environment. Even a small (2%) loss of body weight due to dehydration can cause significant performance reductions. [26]

The amount of water you'll need to drink will vary based on the intensity and duration of your training as well as the temperature of the training facility. Use common sense and scale your water intake accordingly. The "Intra-Workout Nutrition" section will contain more detailed recommendations regarding fluid replacement during activity.

SUPERCHARGE YOUR WATER!

Rather than drinking just plain water, consider strategically adding a couple cups of decaffeinated green tea to your daily fluid intake. As nutrition researcher Kamal Patel puts it, green tea *"has been implicated in benefiting almost every organ system in the body. It is cardioprotective, neuroprotective, anti-obesity, anti-carcinogenic, anti-diabetic, anti-artherogenic, liver protective and beneficial for blood vessel health."* [27]

Why decaf? Personally, I prefer to have a cup or two of coffee in the morning. Since I'm looking to limit my total caffeine intake for the day, I drink decaf tea so I can "spend" my remaining caffeine before training. This may be different for you, but you should be aware of your total caffeine consumption before adding caffeine-containing drinks willy-nilly.

Decaf green tea (with no cream/sugar) is virtually calorie-free and can easily fit into nearly any diet. It's no magic elixir, but when added to an already well-constructed diet, it's one more way to stack the nutritional deck in your favor!

CHAPTER SUMMARY:

→ Aim for five or more combined servings of fruits/vegetables, three servings of whole grains, and 14 g of fiber per 1,000 calories consumed per day.

→ The more active you are, the more important it is to pay attention to micronutrient intake—we're interested in optimal amounts, not just the minimum!

→ Athletes may be at risk for deficiency in vitamin D, zinc, magnesium, calcium, iron, and B12.

→ Do not spend a lot of time worrying about artificial sweeteners, GMOs, buying organic, detoxes, etc. Instead focus on what research consistently shows to matter—adequate consumption of fruits and vegetables and appropriate energy intake.

→ Including foods such as blueberries, leafy greens, dark chocolate, fatty fish, and coffee/tea may impart some neurocognitive benefits.

→ Performance-enhancing effects can be obtained from a diet high in nitrates and/or betaine.

→ Drink at least two-thirds of your body weight in fluid ounces daily.

→ Scale water intake upwards if training intensely and/or in hot temperatures.

→ At least five of your daily urinations should be clear.

LEVEL FOUR: NUTRIENT TIMING AND MEAL FREQUENCY

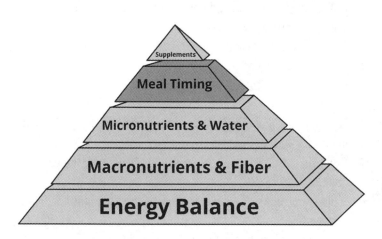

Even though energy balance, proper macronutrient ratios, and adequate micronutrient intake are far and away the most important factors for dietary success, nutrient timing and meal frequency tend to steal the spotlight. This is especially true in recent years where fasting has become mainstream. To clear up the confusion, this chapter will first dispel some common misconceptions regarding meal timing, and then will outline the cases in which meal timing *does* impart a special benefit.

COMMON MISCONCEPTIONS

SIX SMALL MEALS A DAY

Thanks to the rise in popularity of various fasting protocols in recent years, this myth isn't as ubiquitous as it once was. The idea behind eating smaller, more frequent meals was that it would boost your metabolism more frequently and thus increase energy expenditure. Studies have repeatedly shown, however, that when caloric intake is static, there is no difference between eating larger, more infrequent meals and smaller, more frequent meals. [1–2]

FASTING WILL IMPART AMAZING HEALTH BENEFITS

At the other end of the spectrum, we have people claiming that fasting protocols will impart uniquely beneficial health improvements through increases in growth hormone and autophagy (cellular cleansing). Claims of anti-cancer and life extension effects are also common. Unfortunately, although there is some element of truth to these claims, it's mostly hype with little to no substance.

It is true that fasting increases growth hormone, but it's only a modest increase which won't translate into greater fat loss or anabolism. When pitted against a standard caloric deficit with a distributed meal pattern, fasting provides equivalent but not superior results. [3] And while fasting *does* increase autophagy, so does a normal caloric deficit and exercise; this isn't something unique to fasting. Finally, claims of life extension and anti-cancer effects are based on animal research that has not yet been demonstrated in humans. So, while fasting may be a valid way to help achieve a caloric deficit, it's not magic and it's likely *not* the ideal way to maximize performance and body composition—depending on how it's implemented.

YOU MUST EAT PROTEIN FREQUENTLY TO AVOID GOING CATABOLIC

You may have heard that it's important to eat some protein every 2–3 hours so that your muscles have a constant supply of amino acids. In fact, it used to be a fairly common recommendation for fitness enthusiasts to wake up in the middle of the night so they could have a protein shake! The truth is, it can easily take 5 hours or more for your body to fully digest and absorb the nutrients from a normal meal, [4] so there's no need to cram in extra protein every couple of hours.

That said, there is some evidence showing a benefit to spreading your protein intake out somewhat over the course of the day. [5–6] Eating at least four protein-rich meals (each with a minimum of 0.18 g of protein per lb of body weight) spread throughout the day may be optimal for maximizing muscle protein synthesis rates. This is something to consider if you are attempting to gain strength and muscle at optimal rates. If you are more concerned with muscle maintenance (like during a dieting phase), then a lower meal frequency of 2–3 meals is just fine, provided you get sufficient protein by the end of the day.

BREAKFAST IS THE MOST IMPORTANT MEAL OF THE DAY

Ever notice how often this piece of advice is offered by companies who happen to sell breakfast food? The problem with saying "breakfast is the most important meal of the day" is that it places it up on a pedestal and ignores context. In truth, if you are meeting your caloric and macro/micro nutritional needs, then eating (or not eating) breakfast is not going to have a significant impact on your results. Most claims that tout the benefits of eating a large breakfast are generally based on observational studies which confuse correlation with causation. [7]

With that in mind, it seems that having a larger breakfast and avoiding eating a large meal right before bed may help to entrain the circadian rhythm and improve sleep quality. [8] There is also some evidence that shifting a larger proportion of your calories toward breakfast may improve your energy levels, reduce cravings, and potentially increase your energy expenditure. [9]

Still, remember that meal timing falls on the *fourth* level of the pyramid. These small advantages will be completely washed out if your personal preference, schedule, and lifestyle make routinely eating a large breakfast problematic. Get the first three levels sorted out first and then experiment with shifting more calories toward breakfast. If it works out, great. If not, don't worry about it!

EATING MEALS LATE AT NIGHT WILL CAUSE YOU TO GAIN WEIGHT

Seems to make sense, right? Eating a large meal and going to sleep soon after. . . surely your body is going to store all that energy as fat! Fortunately, unless those calories consumed at night put you in a caloric surplus (which they won't if you are aware of your caloric intake), they are no more likely to be stored as fat as calories eaten at any other time of day. [10–11] You may, however, experience some sleep disruption if you eat a huge meal within a close proximity of your bedtime.

YOU MUST CONSUME PROTEIN WITHIN 30 MINUTES OF WORKING OUT

Ah, the greatly feared and respected "anabolic window." When I was a teenager, I was convinced I needed to drink a protein shake within 10–30 minutes of working out or else the whole session would be wasted. I only lived 10 minutes from the gym, but I'd still be sure to pack a protein shaker cup and choke down a room temperature protein shake immediately after training "just in case."

To be fair, there is some scientific evidence that suggests some benefits to utilizing peri-workout nutrition protocols, but this "window" is nowhere near as rigid and narrow as most people think. Researchers Alan Aragon and Brad Schoenfeld did an excellent job of reviewing the current literature and have proposed a much more reasonable set of guidelines:

> *Due to the transient anabolic impact of a protein-rich meal and its potential synergy with the trained state, pre- and post-exercise meals should not be separated by more than*

approximately 3–4 hours, given a typical resistance training bout lasting 45–90 minutes. If protein is delivered within particularly large mixed-meals (which are inherently more anticatabolic), a case can be made for lengthening the interval to 5–6 hours. This strategy covers the hypothetical timing benefits while allowing significant flexibility in the length of the feeding windows before and after training. [12]

For serious athletes, nutrient timing *does* play a slightly more important role because multiple training sessions in the same day and/or particularly long training sessions require extra care and consideration in order to ensure optimal performance. The following sections will outline how to properly time your nutrition around training.

PERI-WORKOUT NUTRITION: WHAT TO EAT BEFORE TRAINING

Peri-workout nutrition refers to the timing of meals you eat before and after training. Although recent studies have shown this to be less important than previously thought, the research is not clear enough to *totally* discount the potential benefits of properly timed pre- and post-workout nutrition. While the benefit may be small, it's not insignificant.

The easiest most "common sense" recommendation is to eat a meal containing a decent amount of protein and carbohydrates 1–2 hours before training and within 1–2 hours after training. This protocol can be used both for table tennis and resistance training.

In your pre-workout meal, you want to make sure to choose foods that are well-tolerated by your stomach and will have time to digest before training. Heavy meals high in fat and fiber will slow down the digestion of your food and may cause some gastric distress during your training session. So, consider keeping things light.

Studies show that to ensure maximal muscle protein synthesis, you should aim for at least 0.18 g of protein per lb. of body weight (0.4 g/kg) in this pre-workout meal. [13] So a 170-lb. (77 kg) man would need to consume around 30 g of high-quality protein to achieve this. The amount of carbohydrates you consume will depend on several factors: If it's been 24 hours or more since you've last trained, you've most likely already replenished your muscle glycogen stores through your normal meals. If this is the case, a small serving of fruit may be sufficient to help "top off" liver glycogen stores and assist with energy levels before training. Or, you may be fine with a protein-only meal if that simplifies things for you.

If you've already trained once that day, or perhaps you had a late session the day prior and are training relatively early the next morning, you may need to up the carb content of your pre-workout meal to ensure your glycogen stores are fully replenished. In this situation, opting for high glycemic, fast-digesting carbs is ideal. Be careful with consuming *too* many carbs pre-training, however. It's possible to experience reactive hypoglycemia after a high carb meal, which could result in your blood sugar levels dropping during your training session. If this is the case for you, choosing more complex carb choices with a bit of fiber to help slow digestion may reduce the likelihood of this occurring.

If you need to eat a meal within an hour or less of training, you should consider taking in liquid calories and simple carbs to maximize the speed of digestion and minimize the amount of food in your stomach.

As you can see, besides hitting your minimum protein target, there are no hard and fast rules for exactly what your pre-training meal should contain. The best thing to do is to experiment with various combinations of foods until you find something that consistently results in good performance.

INTRA-WORKOUT NUTRITION

Intra-workout nutrition refers to any food or drink you take *during* exercise.

For a typical resistance training session lasting 60–90 minutes, the only intra-workout nutrition you should be concerned with is drinking enough water.

If you follow the peri-workout nutrition protocol listed above, your body will still be processing and utilizing the nutrients from your pre-workout meal. To ensure you are well-hydrated, start drinking water at the beginning of the session (before feeling thirsty) and continue to drink at regular intervals throughout your training session.

TABLE TENNIS SPECIFIC RECOMMENDATIONS

HYDRATION

A common mistake that athletes make is showing up to practice partially dehydrated. This is like starting the race 10 m back! To ensure you are fully hydrated, make sure you've had at least 24 oz of fluid spread out over the 2–3 hours before training. Once you start training, you will need to hydrate at regular intervals to ensure you are replacing the fluids lost through sweat. As mentioned previously, our natural thirst instinct is not a reliable measure to adequately replace said losses, so you need to stay on top of taking those water breaks. Something like 4–6 oz (2–4 large gulps) every 15–20 minutes is a good starting place.

Since people sweat at different rates, a tailored hydration plan is necessary to ensure you are getting enough fluids and optimally maintaining your performance. [16] The best way to determine whether you are adequately hydrating during training is to weigh yourself before and after your session. If you are *heavier*, you are overhydrating. If you have lost weight (appx. 2% or more of your total body weight), then you aren't hydrating enough. To rehydrate after training, drink 16–20 oz for every pound lost and eat some food as well.

For hard training that pushes past the 60–90-minute range, you will also need to replace the electrolytes lost through sweat—particularly sodium. This can be achieved by sipping on a carbohydrate-electrolyte sports drink (like Gatorade). Some people are "salty sweaters" and may need to add a pinch of salt to their sports drink. This also may be required if your session pushes past the 2–3-hour mark. If you are feeling symptoms of dehydration despite adequate water intake, then you may need to tinker with adding additional electrolytes to the fluids you drink.

CARB REQUIREMENTS

Because exact carbohydrate requirements will vary depending on factors such as your level of play, your particular style of play, and the intensity and duration of the match, it is difficult to predict exactly when intra-workout carbohydrate supplementation becomes beneficial. There is evidence that shows ingesting carbohydrates before and after training can directly increase anaerobic and aerobic exercise capacity in table tennis players who train daily, [15] but the point at which carbohydrate supplementation within the session itself becomes necessary is less clear.

For a typical casual night of play at your local club where your games will be interspersed with periods of rest and your total time spent at the club is around 2 hours, you'll probably be fine eating nothing and just drinking water. If you anticipate 2 or more hours of near continuous, moderate-to-high-intensity play, then taking approximately 30–60 g of easy-to-digest carbohydrates may help delay the onset of fatigue. This is most easily achieved through a carbohydrate-electrolyte sports drink, which can be sipped periodically in-between games.

The benefits of carbohydrate ingestion before and during a match tend to have the greatest impact on performance toward the end of the match. [16] And since it can be difficult to anticipate how long matches will go (will it be 3–0 or will it go to five games with every game going to deuce?), it may be wise to adopt a "better safe than sorry" approach and get in the habit of drinking some liquid carbs when playing, even if they may be unnecessary in some cases. Evidence from similar sports, such as badminton, suggests that ingesting a carbohydrate beverage when in a fatigued state may be able to increase serving accuracy, [17] so it's worth experimenting with.

If you are playing several events in a tournament and will be playing many matches in a 2–4-hour time period, then packing some non-perishable, easy-to-digest snacks will help stave off hunger and should not significantly interfere with match play. These snacks should be relatively high in carbs and low in fat/fiber. Foods such as bagels, cooked rice/pasta, yogurt, and fruit are popular options. Do not experiment with new foods or special "power gels" on the day of a competition. Use your *training sessions* to experiment and stick with food that you know your body tolerates well.

PERI-WORKOUT NUTRITION: WHAT TO EAT AFTER TRAINING

The urgency of consuming your post-training meal will vary based upon how long it's been since you've last eaten. Generally speaking, you want to sandwich your training session between two meals separated by no more than 3–4 hours. If you trained completely fasted, or it's been 5 or more hours since your last meal, it becomes slightly more important to consume some protein relatively soon after training. Much like your pre-training meal, your priority with this feeding is to get sufficient protein to maximally stimulate muscle protein synthesis. The same guidelines apply for dosing: 0.18 g per lb of body weight (0.5 g/kg).

Whether you need to consume carbs along with the protein depends on the proximity of your next training session. If you are training more than once a day, then getting some high GI carbs in quickly is important so you can maximize muscle glycogen replenishment before your next session. Here is a relevant quote with more specific guidelines from an excellent review on the fundamentals of glycogen metabolism:

> *The consumption of high-glycemic carbohydrates soon after exercise can maximize and sustain the rate of glycogen synthesis to help speed glycogen restoration on days that*

require >1 session of hard exercise. When rapid glycogen resynthesis is required, consuming 0.5–0.6 g/kg BW of high-glycemic carbohydrates every 30 minutes (0.23–0.28 g/lb BW/30 min) for 2–4 hours (or until the next full meal) will sustain high rates of muscle glycogen synthesis. When 24 hours or more are available for glycogen restoration, the frequency of carbohydrate intake is less important than the total amounts of carbohydrates and energy consumed. [18]

So, if your next session is 24 hours away, your normal meals will typically contain enough carbohydrate to fully replenish muscle glycogen stores. Thus, consuming a protein-only post-training meal could be perfectly fine. If you will be training hard again soon—within that same day or early the next morning after a late session—you should include some carbs with your post-training meal as per the recommendations in the quote above.

There is also a bit of evidence that suggests combining fructose along with glucose (as opposed to just glucose) may help accelerate post-exercise glycogen replenishment and help lower gastrointestinal distress if large quantities of carbohydrates must be ingested after training. [19] This can easily be accomplished by including some fruit or fruit juice in your post workout meals.

DETERMINING OPTIMAL MEAL FREQUENCY AND TIMING (WHEN DOES IT MATTER?)

Personal preference and common sense will go a long way toward determining the best meal frequency for you. I've generally found around four to five meals a day to be the sweet spot for most athletes. This could be as simple as three to four solid meals plus one protein shake after training. This minimizes hassle and eliminates the constant need to prep meals and tote around Tupperware everywhere you go.

If your goal is to lose weight, you may want to experiment with larger, more infrequent meals with little to no snacking. Something along the lines of three or four meals per day. . . There is some evidence that suggests that lower meal frequency can have a greater effect on satiety [20] and my anecdotal experience confirms this as well. If you need to eat 2,000 calories or fewer per day in order to lose weight, splitting those calories into six small meals of around 300 calories each is going to make it difficult to feel satisfied. If you ate only three meals instead, each meal can be slightly larger and more satisfying.

Conversely, if you are trying to gain weight and must consume 3,000 calories a day, then a higher meal frequency of five to six meals may work better. Trying to cram 3,000 calories into one or two meals can be fun on occasion, but it's a slippery slope: This type of eating pattern almost requires you to eat excessive amounts of junk to hit your calories. If this comes at the expense of your fruit/veggies, then you have made a poor trade-off. Whatever frequency you decide upon, it's best to be consistent. The body thrives on routine, so try to keep your meal timing fairly static day-to-day.

CHAPTER SUMMARY:

→ As long as you are controlling your caloric intake and hitting your macronutrient targets, meal timing is a relatively minor concern.

→ Use personal preference to decide how to structure your meals, but getting roughly four or more protein feedings spread throughout the day may be slightly superior when aiming to optimally stimulate muscle protein synthesis.

→ Do not worry about the mythic "anabolic window" of 30 minutes; instead, sandwich your training between two protein/carbohydrate-containing meals that are roughly 3–4 hours apart.

→ Make sure you show up to training adequately hydrated and continue to drink at regular intervals throughout your session.

→ Weighing yourself before and after training is an effective way to assess whether you're drinking enough.

→ If you anticipate 2 hours or more of near continuous, moderate-to-high-intensity exercise, then taking approximately 30–60 g of an easy-to-digest carbohydrate-electrolyte beverage may help delay the onset of fatigue and improve performance.

→ If you are training twice in the same day, ingesting 0.23–0.28 g/lb. of body weight of high-glycemic carbohydrates every 30 minutes (0.5–0.6 g/kg/30 min) for 2–4 hours will help you recover fully for your next session.

→ On average, lower meal frequencies tend to be better for weight loss and higher meal frequencies tend to be better for weight gain.

LEVEL FIVE: SUPPLEMENTATION

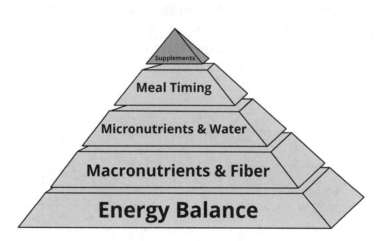

Finally, we reach the top of the pyramid. Supplements have their place, but there is a reason they are last on the list: any small beneficial effect of supplementation will be completely washed out if you don't have the foundational levels of the pyramid in place first. Furthermore, at their worst, supplements aren't merely a waste of money, they can actually *harm* your performance and health if used incorrectly. Despite this, many athletes put a lot of faith in supplements, often without proper guidance. Amazingly, in one study on table tennis players, 90% of the athletes surveyed did not rely on their coach's and/or physician's opinions regarding nutritional supplements. [1] As this is a topic that is rife with misinformation, that is *not* a good sign.

You will see a few other supplements mentioned elsewhere in this book. These supplements tend to be either less strongly supported by the literature or only conditionally useful. I have reserved this chapter for the supplements with more universal application and a stronger base of support. I've split the supplements up by type. We'll start with the exciting stuff, the performance enhancers!

Don't get too excited, though—the list is short!

PERFORMANCE ENHANCERS

TIER ONE

The supplements in tier one have an extremely broad base of support regarding their efficacy. These can be recommended on a near universal basis to enhance performance.

CREATINE

Creatine is very well-researched, safe, and effective. So much so, in fact, that it stands in a class of its own in terms of effectiveness and potency. With the possible exception of caffeine, no other supplement comes close. Creatine can improve your strength [2–3], power output [4], *and* your memory/cognitive functioning. [5] And as it happens, creatine is very cheap and can be bought in bulk for as little as ten cents per serving. For creatine supplementation to be effective, you must take it daily and allow time for full saturation of muscles. Simply taking 5 g of plain, creatine monohydrate every day is the easiest, most fail-proof protocol. There are no acute effects, so your daily dose of creatine can be taken any time of day.

CAFFEINE

Caffeine is an extremely effective energy booster, which has been shown to improve your strength and power, [6] endurance, [7] cognition, [8] and your reaction time, [9–10] so it's a supplement well worth considering for the serious athlete. People's tolerance to caffeine varies, but 2–4 mg/kg of body weight taken 30–60 minutes before hard training is a good place to start in terms of dosing. The research demonstrating performance enhancing effects tends to use higher doses in the 3–6 mg/kg range, but I highly recommend starting well below that to assess tolerance before going that high.

Despite the common perception, moderate caffeine consumption is generally associated with health *benefits*. Research shows that up to five cups of coffee a day is associated with a probable decreased risk for breast, colorectal, colon, endometrial, and prostate cancers; cardiovascular disease and mortality; Parkinson's disease; and type 2 diabetes. [11] Still, it is clear that *too much* caffeine consumption can cause problems too, particularly if it disrupts your sleep. Thus, if you are interested in maximizing both the health *and* performance benefits of caffeine, it is best to strategically plan out your intake.

If you typically enjoy a couple of cups of coffee a day, then consider limiting your pre-training caffeine to days when you feel particularly lethargic or before especially intense training sessions. Taking caffeine "as needed" is a great way to help ensure you stay within that moderate consumption range, which demonstrates health benefits while still being caffeine-"naive" enough to see acute performance improvements.

TIER TWO

Tier two supplements have enough evidence to warrant considering, but may be only conditionally useful and/or have a smaller magnitude of effect. If you have money to spare and like experimenting, these may be worth a look.

DIETARY NITRATE

I mentioned dietary nitrates in the micronutrient section because I personally like to achieve performance-enhancing levels of nitrate through the diet, but if you feel the need to supplement, that can be an effective route as well. Nitrate supplementation through beetroot juice has been shown to increase endurance [12] and power, and strength endurance [13]. Most research shows the efficacious dose to be in the range of 400–800 mg. It also seems that keeping your intake in this range daily is likely to be more beneficial than a single pre-exercise dose.

BETA-ALANINE

Beta-alanine supplementation can result in a small increase in muscular endurance. Notably, performance only seems to improve during extended sets in the 60–240-second range. [14] Thus, while it may be useful for higher rep (20+ reps) bodybuilding style training or during intense extended training drills where having a physiological buffer against acidity may help you extend performance, for most strength work, it is not likely to have an impact.

Most of the research showing benefits to beta-alanine supplementation uses a daily dose between 3–6.4 grams per day. New research suggests, however, that this may be *undershooting* the potential benefits of beta-alanine because this dosage range is likely not high enough to fully saturate muscle carnosine stores. [14a] It's possible doses higher than 6.4 grams per day may provide slightly better results, though this must be weighed carefully against potential side effects—typically paresthesia (a harmless tingling sensation commonly felt when supplementing with beta-alanine) and headaches. Splitting the dose up into two to four smaller doses seems to help mitigate these side effects. Like with creatine, the timing of your dosage doesn't matter—take when convenient. Allow four to eight weeks for full saturation.

CITRULLINE MALATE

Citrulline Malate (CM) has been shown to potentially improve both strength endurance and power endurance. [15] You may also note an improved "pump" when supplementing with CM as it increases blood circulation. This does not have a direct benefit to performance but is a side effect that most enjoy.

CM should be taken 30–60 minutes pre-training. The minimum effective dose (6 g) is often quite a bit more than the amount you'll find in most pre-workout formulas. Therefore, I recommend buying in bulk and mixing it yourself to ensure you're getting an effective dose.

Note: CM has a sour taste, so if you mix it into your drink, it will increase the "tartness" of the flavor.

WHY NO BCAAs?

Branched Chain Amino Acids (BCAAs) are a popular supplement, but there is no strong evidence to show they are anything more than a waste of money for those who already consume adequate protein in the diet. If you already consume sufficient daily protein, taking BCAAs is akin to running your sprinklers when it's raining out.

GENERAL HEALTH/WELL-BEING

Your first line of defense against micronutrient deficiency should be your diet, but even the best of diets can still lack certain vitamins and minerals. To determine whether this is the case for you, I suggest carefully following the recommendations outlined in the chapters from the second and third levels of the pyramid for several months. Once you've been consistently providing your body with a nutrient-dense, whole foods diet, get some blood work done and see if there are any areas of need. I know this may seem like a hassle, but if you are truly interested in improving your health and optimizing performance, getting regular blood work should be a no-brainer. You check the oil in your car, right? Why not pay the same courtesy to your own body?

As outlined in the micronutrient section, you may find it difficult to achieve sufficient levels of iron, calcium, magnesium, zinc, and/or vitamin B12. If you don't eat fatty fish, then getting sufficient omega-3s could also be difficult. The following list outlines effective daily dosages for some of these common deficiencies:

→ **Vitamin D3**: 2,000–4,000 IU of vitamin D3.
→ **Zinc**: 10–30 mg.
→ **Iron**: Around 150–200 mg per day is common. Take with some vitamin C to increase absorption. It is possible to overdose on iron, so do not take this without consulting with your doctor and getting the requisite bloodwork done.
→ **Vitamin B12**: 1,000 mcg (or 1 mg).
→ **Magnesium**: 200–400 mg.
→ **Calcium**: 500–750 mg.
→ **Fish Oil**: 1–2 g combined EPA/DHA.

WHY NOT JUST TAKE A MULTIVITAMIN?

Taking a basic multivitamin is an option and is probably better than nothing—especially if you are eating at a deficit and struggle with variety in your diet. Unfortunately, while being great in concept, multivitamins tend to fall short in their effectiveness. They often lack efficacious doses of the key vitamins and minerals listed above, while including too much of other vitamins that aren't really needed. As long as you are hitting your macronutrient targets and getting your daily servings of fruits/veggies, I find it better to examine your diet and individually target specific vitamins/minerals that are lacking.

WHAT ABOUT POTASSIUM?

While it is true that maintaining optimal levels of potassium is important for athletes, taking potassium in the form of a supplement is something that should be approved and supervised by a doctor. Very high doses of potassium can lead to severe heart problems. Fortunately, it's fairly easy to get the appropriate amounts of potassium just by eating a healthy diet. Foods such as potatoes, bananas, nuts, avocados, milk, and leafy greens are all great sources. Taking a few bananas as a snack to a tournament is a popular way to get some potassium and quick-to-digest carbs to help fuel performance.

SPECIAL CONSIDERATIONS FOR VEGETARIANS/VEGANS

If you are following a plant-based diet, you may need to rely a little more heavily on supplementation than an athlete who also eats animal products. Vitamin B12, for example, is only found naturally in animal products, so deficiency is inevitable without supplementation. Things like calcium, iron, and zinc can be found in plant-based foods, but they are poorly absorbed. Additionally, vegans may need to supplement with iodine as they have been identified as a population that is at risk of deficiency. [16] Vitamin D3 and EPH/DHA levels also tend to be lower in non-meat eaters.

This is *not* to say you can't be successful as a vegan or vegetarian. You can absolutely be a high-performing athlete while following such a diet. What you must be cautious about, however, is the "health halo" effect that accompanies plant-based diets. Simply switching to a plant-based diet is no panacea. Any time you cut out large food groups, you have potentially thrown some babies out with the bathwater. I recommend getting blood work done to get to the bottom of any potential issues and supplementing accordingly.

THE "LOOPER" FORMULA: BOTTLING THAT "IN THE ZONE" FEELING

I love caffeine, but it can be a double-edged sword, particularly for table tennis players. If I have some caffeine in my system, I generally feel more energetic, productive, creative, and more focused on the task at hand. I also get slightly jittery and sometimes feel a bit nervous or over-stimulated. This isn't a problem if I'm just writing or trying to power through a tough workout, but for table tennis it can be a disaster! Table tennis requires such fine motor control that any amount of jitteriness can really impact performance—serves especially seem to suffer.

But although caffeine can impair motor function if it results in over-stimulation, [17] it's also true that mental fatigue (something that caffeine can help attenuate) will negatively affect both the speed and accuracy of the ball in table tennis. [18] So how do we find a balance between the potential benefits of caffeine supplementation while avoiding the side effects?

That's where the Looper formula comes in. By pairing caffeine with some synergistic ingredients, you can increase the potency while *reducing* jitters and overstimulation. After much experimentation, I have settled on a simple three-ingredient formula as an effective way to reliably increase energy and focus without feeling overstimulated:

→ Caffeine: 100 mg
→ L-theanine: 100 mg
→ L-tyrosine: 1 g

Taking some L-theanine alongside caffeine will drastically reduce most of the negative side effects of caffeine (jitters, excitability, nervousness, etc.) while enhancing the positive effects. The two work synergistically to provide a noticeable increase in energy and focus. [19–21]. Taking L-theanine with caffeine in a 1:1 ratio is ideal if you are somewhat tolerant to caffeine. If you are more caffeine sensitive, a 1:2 ratio in favor of L-theanine may work better.

L-tyrosine is an amino acid that produces noradrenaline and dopamine. There is some interesting research that shows it can improve cognition [21] and working memory. [22] Its effect seems to manifest particularly in stressful situations. [23] There is also a theoretical rationale for a synergistic effect between caffeine and L-tyrosine as it provides the building blocks to "fuel" the increase in catecholamine release that occurs from the caffeine. Anecdotally, 1 g of L-tyrosine for every 100 mg of caffeine seems to be a good ratio.

These ingredients have some research backing them individually, but there is also evidence they work well in combination—particularly for a sport such as table tennis. A 2019 study from the *Journal of the International Society of Sports Nutrition* concluded the following:

> *A combination of a low-dose of caffeine with theanine and tyrosine may improve athletes' movement accuracy surrounding bouts of exhaustive exercise without altering subjective mental states. Based on this finding, supplementation with caffeine, theanine and tyrosine could potentially hold ergogenic value for athletes in sports requiring rapid accurate movements. [24]*

I will typically take this Looper stack on days when I feel a little run-down physically and/or "scattered" mentally. After about 30 minutes, I feel energetic, focused, and "in the zone." Should you need to adjust this formula based on your own tolerance to caffeine, simply maintain the ratios of the ingredients and you should be able to scale the potency up or down. Personally, I take 200 mg of caffeine, 200 mg of L-theanine, and 2 g of L-tyrosine.

THE "BLACK MARKET" COGNITIVE ENHANCER

I've gone back and forth over whether to include this supplement in the book, but after carefully reviewing the research and weighing the pros and cons, I've decided to include it. I will trust you, the reader, to assess your own risk tolerance, consult with your doctor, and make an adult decision as to whether you wish to experiment with using nicotine for the purpose of performance enhancement. Currently, the World Anti-Doping Agency (WADA) has not placed nicotine on its prohibited substances list, though it *is* on the "monitoring program" alongside other drugs such as caffeine. Furthermore, nicotine use among athletes is already fairly common and may be increasing. [24a] Consequently, I felt the inclusion of the section was warranted—both to properly set expectations regarding the performance effects and to outline some of the risks.

There is a reasonable body of evidence that suggests nicotine supplementation can have a nootropic effect, potentially improving motor abilities, attention, and memory. [25] In terms of direct ergogenic effects on performance, the evidence is more mixed, with most studies showing no effect on muscular endurance or high-intensity exercise performance. [24a] Nicotine has strong negative sentiments surrounding it because of its association with smoking, but when nicotine is studied in isolation, it has not been shown to carry the same health risks as tobacco-containing products.

In fact, meta-analytic data, as well as the position stands from authoritative bodies such as the Royal College of Physicians, the US Surgeon General, and the FDA, all converge on the conclusion that nicotine poses few serious health risks, particularly with short-term and/or intermittent use. [26] Youth[20] and pregnant or breastfeeding women should not use nicotine-containing products as these populations have been identified as potentially being at risk for negative health effects. It's also important to remember that nicotine can be highly addictive, so if you are the type who is prone to addiction and has difficulty with self-control, I strongly recommend giving it a pass.

With that said, it seems that the risk of nicotine dependency depends greatly upon the method of delivery, with nicotine patches and chewing gum presenting a relatively lower risk of addiction. [27] Furthermore, there happens to be an interesting body of evidence that demonstrates improvements in sustained attention and focus simply from the act of chewing *normal* gum. [28–30]

With all of this in mind, taking 1–2 mg of nicotine via nicotine gum during a match could be used as a potential delivery method to both maximize performance benefits (both from the gum chewing and the nicotine) while minimizing the risk of dependency. Because this will elevate your heart rate and increase levels of arousal, it's important to experiment with this before implementing it in an actual tournament. You may find the effect too potent. Much like caffeine, you should start with a low dose (1 mg) and thoroughly assess your reaction to it under a variety of conditions.

---

20 As per the FDA, adolescents appear to be more prone to addiction than adults are. Furthermore, adolescents who are exposed to nicotine may experience disruptions to their brain development, resulting in long-term impacts to their health.

Nicotine can be taken alongside the Looper stack for an extremely potent boost in energy and focus. Personally, I have found this combination provides a reliable shortcut to that much desired "flow state," but it's easy to overdo it. If you notice side effects such as a pounding heart and/or hand tremors, you should reduce the dose or simply eliminate it. Finally, because there is a lack of research on the long-term use of nicotine, it may be wise to cycle on and off it rather than taking it year-round.

CONCLUDING THOUGHTS ON SUPPLEMENTATION

These are what I consider to be the most well-researched and effective supplements available on the market today. Whether or not you need to take any of them is totally dependent on your health, medical history, goals, and amount of disposable income. You should not blindly take every supplement listed in this book; instead, you should examine your diet, talk to your doctor, consider your goals, and supplement accordingly.

CHAPTER SUMMARY:

→ Supplements are the least important part of your diet. They should only be used to fill in some of the holes that your diet can't address.
→ There are some well-researched, safe, and effective performance-enhancing supplements. Whether or not you use them will have little impact on your progress long term, but many people do note a modest benefit when supplementing with them.

→ Multivitamins are a great idea in theory but fail to deliver; instead, target the nutrients that your diet lacks individually with effective doses.

→ If caffeine gives you the jitters, try taking the Looper stack for a smoother energy source with enhanced focus.

→ Nicotine gum can be used to enhance the potency of the Looper stack, but one must weigh the pros and cons and consult with their doctor before deciding to experiment with it.

PUTTING IT ALL TOGETHER: PRACTICAL IMPLEMENTATION, DIETARY HEURISTICS, KITCHEN GADGETS, AND SAMPLE MEAL PLANS

Okay, so I know that was a lot to take in (I did warn you!), but you now have all the tools you need to create a diet that is flexible and sustainable while still promoting high performance. The degree to which you need to monitor your caloric and nutritional intake will depend on several factors, but if you're looking a short list of "common sense take-aways," here's a distillation of what we've covered so far:

→ Calories count—you must take in the correct amount of energy to maintain, gain, or lose weight.

→ A total of 80%–90% of your diet should be composed of whole, minimally processed foods that are nutritionally dense.

→ Around 10%–20% of your remaining calories can be used flexibly to include more enjoyable foods (highly processed foods, sweets, etc.).

→ Do not villainize single macronutrients—they each have a role to play.

→ A daily target of 0.72–1.2 g per lb of body weight (1.6–2.6 g/kg) is an optimal protein intake.

→ Mindfully include fats in your diet—mostly unprocessed fats from whole food sources. Aim for a minimum of 0.3 g per lb or 20%–30% of total calories.

→ Scale carbohydrate intake based on activity level and ensure that you are adequately replenishing glycogen stores.

→ Try to get five or more servings of fruits and veggies per day.

→ Aim for three or more servings of whole grains per day.

→ Drink water! At least five of your daily urinations should be clear.

→ Meal timing and frequency should be determined mostly by personal preference.

→ Having at least four protein feedings spread throughout the day may help body composition goals.

→ Having a protein-containing meal 1–2 hours before and after training will assist with recovery from and adaptation to training.

→ Supplements can be used to support a healthy diet but will not fix a bad one.

Doing the above-listed things will go a long way toward ensuring that you are meeting your energy and micronutrient needs as an athlete while still providing a great deal of flexibility regarding food choices. There are people who live successful, healthy lives following all sorts of different dietary approaches—many of which directly contradict each other. What does this mean? There is no *one* way. You must choose what works best for you, and now you have the means to do so.

In the next section, I will provide some dietary heuristics that you can use to quickly get yourself in the right ballpark with some of these guidelines. If weighing out your food and tracking your calories is a bridge too far for you right now, you'll find this next section extremely useful.

DIETARY HEURISTICS: THE "RULE OF TWO"

No, I'm not talking about the Sith philosophy created by Darth Bane that states there can only be two Sith at one time—a master and an apprentice. The "rule of two" is something I developed after working closely with scores of people and carefully analyzing the commonalities between the ones who had the best fat loss transformations. I then took the next step and compared those commonalities with what scientific research says about effective fat loss strategies and found the following key habits:

→ Establish a regular, daily structure and meal schedule. [1]
→ Use single-ingredient food items. [1]
→ Have protein with each meal. [2]
→ Have fruit/veggies with each meal. [3]
→ Drink a glass of water before each meal. [4]

So, put simply, the rule of two is this—each meal is composed of only two things:

→ A high-quality protein source.
→ A fruit OR vegetable source.

And you will then follow these additional guidelines:

→ Drink a full glass of water before each meal (and continue to drink as you normally would throughout the meal as well).
→ Eat as many portions of your single protein source, and fruit or vegetables as needed until you begin to feel satisfied but *not* overly full.

The "rule of two" is something you can follow if you're going through a dieting phase and would like to try eating intuitively rather than tracking your calories to the gram. There are a couple things going on behind the scenes that make this rule effective: For one, it helps ensure that you get the most essential parts of the diet in—protein, fruits, and veggies. It also prevents the "buffet effect" where high food variety and palatability inadvertently cause you to eat more than you intended. In limiting the intra-meal variety, each individual food portion can be bigger. And, since you're eating more of the same food, you reach *sensory-specific satiation* more quickly.

Here are some example pairings you might go with. . .

→ Grilled chicken breast and watermelon.
→ Salmon and sweet potato.
→ Lean ground beef patties and broccoli.
→ Greek yogurt and blueberries.
→ Tuna and celery.
→ Cottage cheese and strawberries.
→ Protein shake and a banana (great as a pre- or post-workout meal).
→ Egg white scramble with avocado.

If you were going with the first pairing for lunch, you'd simply take a serving or two of grilled chicken breast and a serving or two of watermelon and eat them after having drunk a full glass of water. Still hungry? Have a little more chicken, or a little more watermelon.

Eat until you *just* begin to feel satisfied and stop there. These meals might feel a little boring. That's okay! In fact, it's kind of the point. . .

Simple meals, made up of single-ingredient food items, repeated often, on a consistent schedule.

This is the basic formula for success.

THE DINNER EXCEPTION

The rule of two works great for keeping 1–2 of your meals each day on track, but following it for every meal may be a little unrealistic. I often recommend following the rule of two for breakfast and lunch, and having a normal mixed meal for dinner. This provides an opportunity to flexibly fit in some of your typical family foods and recipes while keeping the majority of your diet on track.

DIETARY HEURISTICS: ESTIMATING PORTIONS

No matter *what* diet you're on, portion sizes matter. It doesn't matter how "healthy" the foods are, if you don't get your energy intake in the right ballpark, progress will not be made. A handy way to get a rough estimate of portion sizes is to use your *hand* as a guide:

→ **Meat/Protein:** One portion = the size of the palm of your hand; or, roughly *20 g* of protein (the macronutrient) from a relatively lean source (protein powder, egg whites, non-fat Greek yogurt, protein bar, etc.).

- Good protein sources should have around 10–18 g of protein per 100 calories.

→ **Vegetables**: One portion = the size of your fist.

→ **Fruit**: One portion = one piece, or one cupped handful.

→ **Starches**: One portion = one cupped handful.

→ **Fats:** One portion = one "thumb's worth" (an amount equal to the size of your thumb).

By having a rough idea of how many portions you are consuming of these various food types, you can make adjustments when your progress stalls. Let's say you are consuming six cupped handfuls worth of starches per day across all your meals. If your weight loss has stalled, you can start to reduce this number to get things moving again. This works far better than trying to just eyeball things with no metric by which you can quantify your intake.

DIETARY HEURISTICS: THE MINIMALIST TRACKING METHOD

If you've paid attention as we've worked our way through the five levels of the pyramid, you may have noticed something. There is a *lot* of flexibility in how you design your diet, save two areas—your energy intake and your protein intake. For many, without special care, these two areas are easy to mess up as there's some specific numbers you need to hit in order to stay in the realm of "optimal." The three primary concerns with these two components of your diet are as follows:

1. Energy intake must be in line with your goals by the end of the day—you need to maintain an energy deficit if you're looking

to lose weight and an energy surplus if you're looking to gain weight.

2. Protein intake must reach optimal levels by the end of the day—around 0.72–1.2 g per lb. of body weight—and should be spread relatively evenly across at least 3–5 meals a day.

3. Resistance training bouts should have protein-containing meals (of at least 0.18 g of protein per lb. of body weight) within 1–2 hours before and after training.

Outside of those three things, most other areas in your diet can fall in line naturally just by making health-conscious decisions and having a peripheral awareness of them. An easy way to ensure you have these three items checked off is to track two things: your weight and your protein intake.

If you track your body weight using a 7-day weighted average, you can use the changes you see on the scale week-to-week as a proxy for your energy intake. If the scale is moving up consistently over a period of several weeks, you're likely in an energy surplus.[21] If it's moving down, you're in a deficit. Staying the same? Maintenance. You can then use your natural hunger and satiety cues as well as some strategic food choices in order to adjust your energy intake up or down.

To track your protein, either keep a running tally each day by looking at labels and nutritional databases, or use the following "quick and dirty" formula:

---

21   Females may need to wait up to four weeks to accurately gauge body weight changes on the scale due to the hormonal fluctuations and water retention associated with the menstrual cycle.

Target body weight x 0.8 / 20 = Minimum number of protein
servings[22] per day.

So, if your ultimate goal is to weigh 150 lb., you'd shoot for a
minimum of six servings of protein per day (150 x 0.8 = 120. 120/20
= 6). Since most servings from high-quality protein sources should
equate to appx. 20 g of protein, that would put you right around 120
g total for the day.

This can also be useful for ensuring your pre- and post-workout
meals have enough protein. For most, around 25–35 g of high-
quality protein will be enough to maximally stimulate muscle protein
synthesis. Knowing this, you could aim to consume at least a palm
and a half worth of protein before and after training as this will
provide around 30 g.

USEFUL KITCHEN GADGETS

Unless you're rich enough to hire a personal chef and/or have all
your meals pre-prepared and delivered, all the nutrition knowledge
in the world won't help you if you can't cook a decent meal. I'm
no chef, but I do all the cooking for my household of five and I
know how tough it is to stay on top of cooking healthy meals on a
consistent basis. Fortunately, there are some useful tools you can use
to make cooking easier, faster, and tastier. I'm going to start with a
few obvious ones and then move onto some you may not have used
before.[23]

---

22 Each serving needs to match the guidelines provided in the "Estimating Portions"
     section.

23 To see a list of the exact products I use and recommend, head to
     peakperformancetabletennis.com/resources.

MICROWAVE OVEN (SERIOUSLY)

Trust me, when I set out to write this book, I had no idea I would be delving into how to obtain peak performance out of your microwave, but here we are. I'm starting here because while everyone has a microwave, most people don't use it well.

Here are a few simple tips to improve your microwaving:

- → Use the "reheat" function for leftovers rather than just blasting your food at full power. This will cycle the power level on and off and help to keep your food from overcooking.
- → Spread the food out. Reheat your food on a flat dish when possible so everything isn't piled up.
- → Make a donut. Put a hole in the middle of your food so it forms a ring. This will help it to reheat more evenly.
- → Cover your food! The inside of your microwave should not look like a crime scene!
- → Stir at least once. Rather than cooking the food for 2 minutes, cook for 1 minute and then stir it up and cook for another minute.

Follow these steps and your food will be heated evenly throughout and won't have the consistency of one of your old sheets of Tenergy.

A GOOD BLENDER

Shakes and smoothies are one of the most versatile ways to fill in holes in your diet. But the first step to being able to make a decent smoothie is making sure you have a blender that can handle harder ingredients like ice or nuts. Nothing is worse than trying to make a smoothie and ending up with a bunch of misshapen icy lumps bouncing around like ping pong balls that never seem to go away no matter how long you blend. A good blender should be easy to use and easy to clean. Be careful about the "single serving" blenders that don't have a big capacity. I find them to be too limiting when trying to make larger volume shakes.

Here are three basic templates for your shakes:

→ **Basic protein shake:** Milk or water plus protein powder. Maximum convenience. Usually used as a placeholder until you can get a bigger meal or to supplement a meal that's low in protein. You don't need a blender for these, just use a shaker cup.
→ **Green Smoothie:** Fruit juice (or water/almond milk), baby spinach/kale, cucumber, fruit (I like frozen bananas and mangos). Use to help get micronutrients in if you haven't had many fruits/veggies that day. High in carbs and nutrients. Can be high in protein as well if Greek yogurt and/or protein powder are included.
→ **Gainer Shake:** Milk, protein powder, oats, honey, peanut butter, banana. These shakes are high in calories and can fill in for one of your meals. Very useful if you're the type who struggles to put on weight.

As mentioned, shakes are a great way to fill the holes in your diet and fix a poorly planned day. If you get to the end of the day and you're super short on calories, fix up a gainer shake. If you realize you haven't eaten any fruits/veggies and the thought of eating a steaming bowl of broccoli is turning your stomach, whip up a green smoothie. If you just finished working out and realize you won't be able to get a decent meal in for another three hours, grab a protein shake. These are all very common situations that you will encounter and having the materials for shakes handy makes for an easy solution!

DIGITAL MEAT THERMOMETER

Meat thermometers are cheap, easy to use, and will help ensure you've cooked your meat to a safe temperature without *overcooking* it. This makes a HUGE difference in the texture and taste of your food! Having a meat thermometer when grilling is like having Superman's x-ray vision. Get one if you haven't already.

Boneless, skinless chicken breasts are a staple for athletes, but they are notoriously hard to cook. An easy way to make them juicer and more flavorful is to brine them before cooking. Just submerge the meat in a saltwater solution (one tablespoon of salt per cup of water), cover it, and refrigerate for 30–60 minutes (longer if it's something like a whole chicken). This will cause the meat to absorb some of the brine, which will begin to break down the muscle fibers within, making the meat more tender.

DIGITAL FOOD SCALE

A digital food scale is another must have—especially if you need to go through a phase where you want to accurately track your calories. Here's a fun experiment: Go ahead and scoop yourself 2 tablespoons of peanut butter using a normal tablespoon—that's one serving, right? Now use your digital food scale and *weigh out* a 33 g serving.

Odds are, the serving that you weighed out will be significantly smaller than the portion you measured using the tablespoon. This is the primary benefit to using a scale when tracking your food intake. You'll learn what proper serving sizes *actually* look like. You can then phase out the weighing once you've developed the ability to accurately eyeball your portions.

Food scales are also handy for measuring ingredients accurately for recipes, so I would pick one up even if you don't plan to go down the calorie counting route.

SLOW COOKER AND/OR INSTANT POT (PRESSURE COOKER)

Slow cookers (or crock pots) are a near foolproof way to easily cook up large batches of food. You can literally just dump some raw chicken in there along with a jar of pre-made salsa and come back 8 hours later to a delicious meal. I used to use a crockpot all the time, but for the past few years I've been using an Instant Pot pressure cooker instead. These have a slow cooker function, but can also serve as a rice cooker, steamer, yogurt maker, and more. It can cook foods incredibly quickly when needed—you can throw in *frozen* chicken breasts and have them cooked up and ready to eat within 20–25 minutes without having to worry about defrosting them first.

One of the best things about slow cookers/Instant Pots is the "set it and forget it" aspect to them. This allows you to front-load the time and effort of cooking during a time of day that is convenient for you and then walk away. You can leave the food in there and it will be kept warm and ready to eat hours later. This is invaluable if you're busy (and especially if you have kids). There is nothing better than coming home at the end of a tough training session knowing that dinner is hot and ready with no extra work.

JAPAN'S BEST KEPT SECRET

There's a little trick you can use to make an easy meal using a rice cooker or Instant Pot and some KFC chicken. This was Japan's best kept secret until the recipe went viral on Twitter toward the end of 2019.

Just put the uncooked rice in as usual, and add chicken stock instead of water. Toss in a tablespoon or two of soy sauce and a few pieces of KFC chicken on top of the rice. Then close the lid and cook the rice as you normally would. Once cooked, shred the chicken, and mix into the rice. You end up with some super savory and flavorful rice with chicken. This meal is cheap to make and strangely addicting. It's also a great way to rehabilitate leftover fried chicken.

Rumor has it, this is the secret to Jun Mizutani's success. . .

AIR FRYER

An air fryer is a countertop convection oven that cooks by circulating hot air around the food. I never paid much attention to air fryers since I never really fry food at home, but once I got one, my eyes were opened. I now use mine pretty much every day. First things first, if you like french fries, chicken tenders, or wings, an air fryer will be your best friend. Not only does the air fryer cook things up more quickly than an oven does, the food comes out *way* crispier.

On a healthier note, if you're the type who struggles to eat enough veggies, you can make some amazing homemade sweet potato fries, kale chips, or even beet chips in an air fryer. A big benefit of the air fryer is that you don't need to use much oil at all to get a nice crunchy texture. This saves a lot of calories and lets you control the macronutrient intake of your foods better.

SOUS VIDE

The latest gadget I've fiddled around with is an "immersion circulator" for sous vide style cooking. Essentially, this device heats and circulates water to a precise temperature. You can then seal some meat in a plastic bag and cook it in the water bath. The meat will slowly rise to the temperature of the water and stay there for *hours* without overcooking. All you need to finish it off is a quick sear on a cast iron skillet or grill for a nice crust and you're good to go! This method of cooking is nearly foolproof and is another "set it and forget" method that's great if you have kids. This will produce restaurant-quality steaks that are perfectly cooked throughout every time.

One drawback is that it's not as easy to cook up large quantities of food unless you have very large sealable bags and a large tub to put the water in. If you're just cooking for two to four people, however, it's hard to beat sous vide.

FUN FACT

If you are sous vide cooking something like a roast where it may be sitting in the water bath for 12–24+ hours, the water will start to evaporate causing the water level to become too low. To prevent this, you can grab a couple dozen of your favorite training balls and float them on the surface. They will conform to whatever shape your container is, and won't be bothered by the protruding immersion circulator that makes using a normal lid impossible. In addition to catching the steam, they will also help to insulate the water bath. Beautiful!

SAMPLE MEAL PLANS

I will now provide some sample meal plans so you can see how some of these nutritional principles can be applied in a real-world setting. Keep in mind, these plans are just sample days meant to show you one possible way to design a high-performance diet. It is *not* meant for you to copy blindly and use for yourself.

SAMPLE DAY OF EATING—WEIGHT LOSS

TARGETS PER DAY:
→ 1,950–2,050 calories
→ 140+ g protein
→ Carbs/fats (flux)
→ 28+ g of fiber

DAY ONE

MEAL ONE: 7:30 AM
→ Egg white scramble (1 egg, 4 egg whites, 1 cup spinach, 1 cup peppers)
→ Low-fat mozzarella cheese stick
→ 1 orange
Macros: 450 calories | 30 g protein | 9 g fat | 30 g carbs | 7 g fiber

---

MEAL TWO: 12:30 PM
→ 8 oz grilled chicken breast
→ 1 cup broccoli
→ 1 piece of whole grain toast

→ 1 oz almonds
→ 1 apple
Macros: 600 calories | 58 g protein | 20 g fat | 60 g carbs | 10 g fiber

---

MEAL THREE: 6:30 PM
→ 8 oz flank steak
→ 8 spears of asparagus
→ 1 medium sweet potato
→ 1 cup lentils
→ 1 cup low-fat ice cream
Macros: 950 calories | 77 g protein | 24 g fat | 110 g carbs | 21 g fiber

---

TOTALS FOR THE DAY:
2,000 calories | 166 g protein | 53 g fat | 200 g carbs | 38 g fiber

DAY TWO

MEAL ONE: 7:30 AM
→ Strawberry Greek yogurt (two containers)
→ 1 banana
→ 1 oz pistachios
Macros: 500 calories | 30 g protein | 13 g fat | 71 g carbs | 8 g fiber

---

MEAL TWO: 12:30 PM
→ 2 cups vegetable soup

➔ 4 oz 90% lean ground beef
➔ 1 pear

Macros: 480 calories | 30 g protein | 11 g fat | 67 g carbs | 12 g fiber

RESISTANCE TRAINING SESSION: 2:30 PM

MEAL THREE: 4:30 PM

➔ 1.5 scoops whey protein (mixed in water)

Macros: 180 calories | 36 g protein | 2 g fat | 5 g carbs | 0 g fiber

MEAL FOUR: 6:30 PM

➔ 6 oz grilled salmon
➔ 2 cups white rice
➔ 1 cup strawberries
➔ 2 cups air popped popcorn

Macros: 780 calories | 45 g protein | 23 g fat | 97 g carbs | 8 g fiber

TOTALS FOR THE DAY:

1,950 calories | 142 g protein | 49 g fat | 240 g carbs | 28 g fiber

RATIONALE

The first day has three meals spaced relatively evenly throughout the day. Fiber and protein are kept high to ensure each meal is sufficiently filling. The majority of foods are single-item ingredient, whole foods.

To help combat evening hunger, most of the calories for the day are saved for dinner. This gives the dieter something to look forward to and tends to be a little more flexible from a social standpoint since most people like to unwind and eat in the evenings. Because smart food choices were made during the day, there is room in the numbers for a little ice cream as a bedtime treat.

The second day utilizes the same basic structure, but includes a protein shake post-training to ensure that some protein is ingested within 1–2 hours before and after training. Neither day hits all the numbers "on the nose." Instead, they fall within a range that is totally acceptable.

There is no such thing as a "perfect" day nutritionally. Instead, you should be looking to hit basic targets within a certain range and include some degree of variety (don't eat the exact same fruits and veggies every day).

SAMPLE DAYS OF EATING—WEIGHT GAIN

TARGETS PER DAY:
→ 2,950–3,050 calories
→ 140+ g protein
→ Carbs/fats (flux)
→ 38+ g of fiber

DAY ONE

MEAL ONE: 7:30 AM
→ 3 hardboiled eggs
→ 1 oz sharp cheddar cheese

→ Green smoothie (8 oz juice, 1 frozen banana, 140 g frozen mango, 50 g baby spinach)

Macros: 650 calories | 25 g protein | 9 g fat | 81 g carbs | 8 g fiber

---

MEAL TWO: 11:00 AM

→ Grilled chicken sandwich (2 slices whole grain bread, 4 oz grilled chicken, lettuce, tomato)

→ 3 oz baby carrots

→ 1 oz peanuts

Macros: 550 calories | 39 g protein | 20 g fat | 60 g carbs | 11 g fiber

---

MEAL THREE: 1:30 PM

→ 2 containers Greek yogurt

→ 1 cinnamon raisin bagel

Macros: 520 calories | 39 g protein | 2 g fat | 84 g carbs | 15 g fiber

RESISTANCE TRAINING SESSION: 3:00 PM

MEAL FOUR: 6:30 PM

→ 6 oz shrimp

→ 2.5 cups white rice

→ 1 cup blueberries

→ 1 medium sweet potato

→ 1 chocolate chip cookie

→ 1.5 oz dark chocolate

Macros: 1,200 calories | 53 g protein | 29 g fat | 182 g carbs | 17 g fiber

---

TOTALS FOR THE DAY:
2,920 calories | 160 g protein | 76 g fat | 407 g carbs | 50 g fiber

DAY TWO

MEAL ONE: 7:00 AM
→ Protein oatmeal (1 cup oats, 30 g peanut butter, 0.5 scoop whey)
→ 1 medium grapefruit
Macros: 590 calories | 30 g protein | 23 g fat | 73 g carbs | 11 g fiber

---

MEAL TWO: 11:00 AM
→ 4 oz grilled chicken
→ 1 cup broccoli
→ 1 apple
→ 1.5 oz almonds
Macros: 550 calories | 39 g protein | 20 g fat | 60 g carbs | 11 g fiber

---

MEAL THREE: 1:00 PM
→ 2 containers Greek yogurt
→ 1 cinnamon raisin bagel
→ 1 banana
Macros: 625 calories | 40 g protein | 2 g fat | 111 g carbs | 18 g fiber

RESISTANCE TRAINING SESSION: 3:00 PM

MEAL FOUR: 4:30–5:30 PM
→ Whey protein shake (1 cup skim milk, ½ scoop whey)

→ 2 cups watermelon
→ 2 bowls of cornflakes w/ skim milk
Macros: 510 calories | 34 g protein | 1 g fat | 95 g carbs | 3 g fiber

TABLE TENNIS SESSION: 6:30

MEAL FIVE: 9:30 PM
→ 2 cups pasta
→ ½ cup spaghetti sauce
→ 2 slices sourdough bread
→ 1.5 tbsp olive oil
Macros: 830 calories | 21 g protein | 35 g fat | 133 g carbs | 8 g fiber

TOTALS FOR THE DAY:
3,015 calories | 159 g protein | 74 g fat | 453 g carbs | 50 g fiber

RATIONALE
Compared with the dieting days, you'll notice a higher meal frequency as well as more liquid calories. Both strategies will make it easier to reach the higher calorie target. The second day outlines a potential strategy for when you have multiple training sessions on the same day. Notice the meal following the first training session contains a fair amount of high GI carbs, a moderate amount of protein, and almost no fat/fiber. This meal can be split into two "mini meals" to maximize glycogen replenishment rates so that you are fully recovered for the table tennis session that night.

SAMPLE DAY OF EATING—IN-SEASON MAINTENANCE

Here is an example of an "in-season" day of eating on a day where the player will be competing in a round robin style tournament. Note the inclusion of dietary nitrates and strategic supplementation around the tournament.

TARGETS PER DAY:

→ 2,700–2,800 calories
→ 140+ g protein
→ Carbs/fats (flux)
→ 35+ g of fiber

MEAL ONE: 7:00 AM

→ Nitrate Smoothie (beet juice, baby spinach, banana, mango, celery)
→ 2 slices "ancient grain" toast
→ 2 eggs
→ 1 cup black coffee
Macros: 670 calories | 25 g protein | 14 g fat | 112 g carbs | 12 g fiber

MEAL TWO: 11:00 AM

→ Nitrate Salad: (arugula, butter lettuce, garlic, 6 oz grilled chicken, balsamic vinaigrette)
→ 1 plain bagel
Macros: 530 calories | 46 g protein | 12 g fat | 62 g carbs | 3 g fiber

12:00: Looper Stack w/ 5 g creatine + 30-minute power nap

ROUND ROBIN TOURNAMENT 1:00–5:00 P.M.

TOURNAMENT SNACKS:

→ 20 oz G2 Gatorade
→ 1 banana
→ 1 rice cake

Macros: 200 calories | 2 g protein | 0 g fat | 50 g carbs | 3 g fiber

MEAL THREE: 5:00 PM

→ 1 oz almonds
→ 2 squares dark chocolate

Macros: 284 calories | 8 g protein | 26 g fat | 14 g carbs | 7 g fiber

MEAL FOUR: 6:30 PM

→ 2 cups white rice
→ 6 oz grilled chicken breast
→ ½ cup steamed broccoli
→ 1 dinner roll with a pat of butter
→ 3 cookies

Macros: 1,040 calories | 46 g protein | 31 g fat | 144 g carbs | 5 g fiber

TOTALS FOR THE DAY:

2,725 calories | 131 g protein | 83 g fat | 382 g carbs | 30 g fiber

RATIONALE

This player's maintenance calories are around 2,750, and the macronutrients are balanced at 55% carbs, 25% fats, and 20% protein. After some experimentation, this player has found he feels and plays better without a whole lot of food in his system, so his pre-tournament meal is kept rather light. He has also noticed a difference since including high nitrate foods as a regular part of his diet, so his first two meals strategically include them.

Right before leaving for the tournament, he takes a dose of the Looper stack (along with some creatine) and takes a 30-minute power nap. As he wakes up from his nap, the caffeine has just started to kick in and he feels energized and ready to go.

At the tournament, he has some high glycemic carbs handy as snacks. He stays on top of his hydration and plays to the best of his abilities. On the way home, he snacks on some almonds and dark chocolate. He fills in his remaining macros with a large dinner, even including a few cookies.

CHAPTER SUMMARY:

→ Sports nutrition can be overwhelming, but focusing on the "big picture" principles will get you 90% of the way there.

→ Dietary heuristics and "set it and forget it" kitchen gadgets can make all that tracking and food prepping a lot easier.

SECTION V
PHYSICAL TRAINING

SECTION OVERVIEW

At last, we reach the final component to peak performance—physical training. As I stated in the introduction, since the adoption of the plastic ball, table tennis has become a more physical sport. As with most sports, this trend is only likely to continue. In this section, I will provide a basic overview of the key guiding principles for setting up an effective routine, I will debunk some common myths regarding physical training for table tennis, and I will outline a detailed *holistic* periodization model that covers an entire year of training and ties all the preceding sections together.

PHYSICAL TRAINING: MYTHS, MISTAKES, AND GENERAL GUIDELINES

Before diving into the nitty gritty of the training programs I've designed for this book, I'd like to take a little time to go over some basic terminology and give an overview of how to train for various athletic attributes such as strength, power, hypertrophy, speed, and endurance. This will give you the knowledge to better understand what is going on "behind the scenes" in the training routines presented in the next chapter. It will also help you to audit your own training programs to make sure what you're doing matches your goals. After going over the general guidelines, I will take some time to dispel common myths regarding physical training for table tennis.

THE ANATOMY OF A ROUTINE: BASIC TERMS, PRINCIPLES, AND GUIDELINES

There is no such thing as a "one size fits all" program. The routines I have included in this book are a good starting place for the average athlete with some prior training experience, but they may need to be tailored and tweaked somewhat for them to be maximally effective for you.[24] To facilitate this process, I have provided a basic rundown of terms and principles so you can get a general idea of how you may adjust your training to better suit your goals.

TRAINING VOLUME

Training volume refers to the total amount of work performed each workout and cumulatively throughout the week for a given muscle group. The most popular way to quantify volume is by the number of "hard sets per week" for each muscle. If you performed three sets of push-ups twice per week with no other exercises for your chest, for example, your weekly training volume for the chest would be six.

It's valuable to be able to quantify your training volume because it allows you to troubleshoot your training in a more precise way: If you notice a particular muscle is not recovering well enough between bouts, you can adjust the volume down to compensate. Then, when the time comes to switch to a new program, you have a quantifiable way of comparing the two programs and deciding whether the total amount of "work" matches your ability to recover.

---

24   For fully bespoke programming that is tailored to meet your precise needs, head to peakperformancetabletennis.com/coaching.

INTENSITY OF EFFORT

So how do you determine what counts as a "hard set"? Well, that's where *intensity of effort* comes in. Intensity of effort is how hard you push yourself in a given set. This can be measured by determining how close you come to reaching technical failure (being unable to perform another rep with proper form) in a set. An easy way to track this is using the "repetitions in reserve" (RIR) method. When tracking your RIR, simply note the number of reps left "in the tank" at the end of each set and jot down that number. If you perform a set of eight repetitions on the bench press, but you could have done *10* if you went all out (gun to the head effort), then that would count as an RIR of two because you had two repetitions in reserve at the end of your set.

Quantifying your effort in this way allows you to track your progress in a more granular manner and can let you train effectively while minimizing injury risk and excessive fatigue. Many people erroneously think that to get stronger one must keep lifting a weight to the point of failure and sometimes even beyond with the help of a spotter. This type of training may provide good footage for Instagram videos, but it is not necessary for an athlete looking to maximize performance. In fact, research shows there doesn't appear to be a significant difference in terms of strength [1] or hypertrophy [2–4] in failure vs. non-failure training.

The appropriate proximity to failure *does* shift depending on the rep range, however. The heavier the weight, the further you can be from failure while still receiving full motor unit recruitment. Conversely, the lighter the weight, the *closer* to failure you need to come to fully recruit those higher threshold motor units. This makes intuitive sense if you think about it. A super heavy weight is tough, pretty much from the start. A lighter weight only starts to burn during those last few reps.

Here are some general recommendations for reference:

Repetitions in Reserve Reference Chart	
Repetition Range	Recommended Reps in Reserve
1–6 reps	2–5 RIR
6–10 reps	2–4 RIR
10–15 reps	1–3 RIR
15–20 reps	1–2 RIR
20–30 reps	0–1 RIR

Trained lifters tend to be fairly accurate in gauging RIR, [5] but if you are new to training, you will need to practice training to failure (with proper form and the help of a spotter) so you can learn what it feels like. Once you have a bit of practice, you should be able to gauge your RIR accurately in the manner described above.

INTENSITY OF LOAD

Unless otherwise specified, training intensity, when expressed as a percentage, refers to the *intensity of load*, i.e., how much weight is on the bar compared with your one rep maximum. So, if your one rep max was 100 lb for the bench press and you were told to train for three sets of five at 80% intensity, you should load the bar with 80 lb for those three sets. It does *not* mean 80% effort.

TRAINING FREQUENCY

Frequency refers to the number of times a week a muscle is trained. Many popular bodybuilding-style workouts involve hitting each muscle group only once a week: Monday is chest day, Tuesday is back day, Wednesday is legs, etc. This is referred to colloquially as the "bro split." Interestingly, data shows that even when volume is matched, hitting a muscle at least *two times* a week is better for both strength [6] and hypertrophy. [7]

Another benefit of spreading out your training volume over the week is it provides more opportunities to practice each lift, potentially increasing neuromuscular efficiency. Furthermore, since your training volume is spread out across the week, you provide an opportunity for the "repeated bout effect" to protect you against excessive muscle damage.

REST PERIODS

Using insufficient rest periods is one of the most common training mistakes I see both trainers *and* athletes make. Research tends to show that longer rest intervals between sets result in better outcomes for both strength and hypertrophy. [8] Longer rest intervals are also critical when training to improve maximal speed. A good rule of thumb is to rest between 3–5 minutes between heavy sets of major compound movements. For more moderate rep compounds, 2–3 minutes can be sufficient. Finally, for high rep accessory work, you can shorten your rest periods to 1–2 minutes on average. As you gain experience, you can auto-regulate your rest periods, but always ensure you are recovered well enough that the *target muscle* becomes the limiting factor during the set rather than cardiovascular fatigue.

Need to catch your breath? Research shows that leaning forward and putting your hands on your knees results in appx. 10%–20% more oxygen uptake compared with standing upright with your hands on your head. [9]

TEMPO/CADENCE

Your tempo, or cadence, refers to how quickly you move the weight during the concentric (lifting) and eccentric (lowering) portions of the lift. Unless otherwise stated, you should always attempt to move the concentric portion of the lift as quickly as possible while still maintaining control. During the eccentric, you should focus on lowering the load under control without allowing gravity to let the weight just fall. This will help maximize muscle activation and will result in greater performance gains compared with lifting at a deliberately slower pace. [10]

EXERCISE SELECTION

In these programs, we will be placing a dedicated focus on getting stronger in basic, compound movements. Building a base of strength will have a positive, trickle-down effect on other aspects of athleticism we find desirable as table tennis players—namely, power and speed.

The best way to increase strength is to focus on progressively getting stronger on compound movements, which are exercises that utilize two or more joints through a given range of motion. Examples include squats, deadlifts, bench press, pull-ups, leg presses and pushups. Compound movements provide the best bang for your buck and are ideal for rapidly improving full body strength.

Although I have prescribed specific exercises in the routines in this book, the truth is, there is no single "best" exercise for a given muscle. Rather than putting specific movements up on a pedestal, you should carefully evaluate each exercise and make sure it's a good fit for *you*. If it's not, swap it out.

This should be your thought process behind exercise selection:

1. Is this swap a roughly equivalent exchange? Replacing a squat with another compound movement, such as a leg press, is fine, but you shouldn't swap it with something like a leg extension, which is a single-joint exercise.

2. Can I perform the exercise pain-free with good form and full range of motion?

3. Can I gradually increase the load in small increments so that I can continue to make progress?

If you can answer *yes* to all three questions, you can make the switch!

PROGRESSION (PROGRESSIVE OVERLOAD)

Progressive overload is the gradual increase in training stress placed on the body through training. There are many ways to achieve progressive overload, but the two most common ways are by incrementally increasing the load and/or reps performed for a given movement, workout to workout. If you constantly do the same workouts and never increase the demands you place on your body, you will quickly adapt, and no new muscle/strength gains will occur. To ensure progressive overload is occurring, it is vital you track your training by recording your performance each session. The goal should always be to "beat the logbook" while maintaining proper form.

DELOADS AND TAPERS

A deload is a planned reduction in training volume and intensity of one or more of your training sessions in order to drop fatigue, provide psychological relief, and allow for active recovery to occur. This is usually achieved by some combination of the following:

→ A reduction in the number of training sessions in the week.
→ A reduction in the total number of working sets per session and across the week.
→ Reduced intensity of effort (staying farther from failure each set).
→ Reduced intensity of load (lowering the weight on the bar).

A good deload will cause you to break a sweat but will not feel very challenging beyond that. Typically, deloads last one week and occur once every 4–6 weeks or so. If you find yourself needing to deload more often than that, consider it a red flag. This is likely an indication that you're training beyond your abilities to recover. Likewise, if you can train for months and months on end without feeling like you need a week to recover, you may not be pushing yourself hard enough!

Here's a sample deload protocol:

→ Reduce set count by one for all movements.
→ Take 10–15% off the load on the bar.
→ Increase the RIR by 1–2 each set.

A taper is very similar to a deload. The primary difference between them is a taper is used to "peak" an athlete before a specific competition or performance test. Tapers can be very individual and require some experimentation to find what works best. One key distinction between a taper and a deload is that tapers usually involve keeping the *intensity of load* relatively high in order to maintain the maximum adaptations from the training cycle. Fatigue is primarily dropped by a reduction in total training volume (by up to appx. 30%–60%) and/or through a reduction in training frequency.

Here is a sample taper:

→ Cut total weekly volume by 40%–50%.
→ Maintain load on testing lifts, but increase RIR by two to four each set.
→ Reduce load of accessory lifts by 10% and increase RIR by two.
→ Take 1–3 days off before the test/competition.

PERIODIZATION

It's tempting to go for an "everything but the kitchen sink" approach when it comes to improving as an athlete, but this type of training pulls your body in too many directions at once, hampering overall progress. He who chases two rabbits catches none! It is much more beneficial to break your training up into sessions and cycles that have a specific focus. This purposeful manipulation of training variables over time is called *periodization*. Periodization is important because many of the key performance variables required for peak performance *feed into* one another. This results in a "phase potentiation" effect that occurs when you transition from one training block to another.[25]

25   This graphic is inspired by a conceptualization created by Eric Cressey.

Strength - Speed Continuum

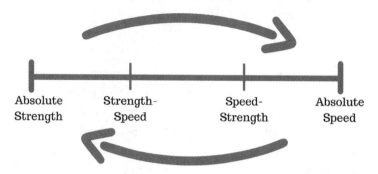

Absolute Strength	Strength-Speed	Speed-Strength	Absolute Speed

Properly periodized training programs recognize the fact that the training that will cause you to perform your best next week is *not* the same as the training that will cause you to perform your best next month or next year. So even though table tennis athletes are primarily interested in speed and agility, dedicating some time to building absolute strength will ultimately result in greater top-end speeds. You may have to become a little slower before you can be truly fast!

A *holistic* periodization model goes a step beyond the typical training plan and recognizes the interplay between physical training, nutrition, recovery, psychology, social-emotional health, and sports-specific practice.[26] In methodically planning the training of these various domains, an athlete can put himself or herself in the best position possible to achieve peak performance on game day.

---

26   I first came across this form of periodization from the integrated periodization model outlined by Tudor Bompa and colleagues in *Integrated Periodization in Sports Training & Athletic Development.*

HOW TO TRAIN FOR KEY ATHLETIC ATTRIBUTES

With all the above in mind, I want to take a moment to give some general guidelines for how to train for the various athletic qualities we value as athletes. A critical error I see athletes make is failing to understand that you must meet specific criteria in order to achieve certain outcomes when training.[27] One of the most common ways this error manifests itself is in workouts that attempt to do *too much* with too little rest. Here's an example of what I mean.

Circuit Style "Functional" and "Sport-Specific" Training Workout:

→ Burpees
→ 10-meter sprint
→ Box jumps
→ Agility ladder
→ Clapping push-ups
→ Kipping pull-ups
→ BOSU ball squats loaded with kettlebell
→ Dumbbell shadow strokes
→ Rest then repeat

This workout seems to have it all, right? It appears to target speed, power, strength, balance, agility, and endurance all within the same session. It even has some "sport specific" overloading with the dumbbell shadow strokes. Forget killing two birds with one stone, this nails *seven*. Unfortunately, while this workout would get a lot of likes on social media, it's not accomplishing much other than

---

27   The technical term for this concept is the S.A.I.D. principle: Specific Adaptations to Imposed Demands.

raising your heart rate and improving your muscular endurance a bit. This is because athletic attributes such as speed, strength, and power typically do not "get along" well with endurance/conditioning work. Remember, different athletic attributes have specific training parameters that must be met for them to result in the desired adaptations. If you fail to meet those requirements, you will get either suboptimal results, or worse, no results at all.

Here's a quick analogy: I recently discovered there is a "4-in-1" shampoo, conditioner, body wash, and face wash product available for men (women would never go for such a product). As a guy, this appealed tremendously to me. How practical! Unfortunately, my wife splashed cold water on the idea. Apparently, the shampoo and the conditioner are trying to do different things to my hair—the shampoo is meant to wash things out, while the conditioner is leaving chemicals *in* to soften/moisturize the hair. Their purposes are at odds with each other, so what you end up with is a product that does *neither* very well.

This is exactly the problem with the workout above. There's a lot "on the label" but the end result is not very good. To avoid making this same mistake in your training, you must carefully design your program so that it adheres to the training parameters required to result in the adaptations you need. It doesn't mean you can't target more than one outcome. You just need to make sure the pieces fit together in a logical way—much like a puzzle. With that firmly in mind, here is a brief rundown of how to train for the basic athletic qualities we desire as table tennis players.

Note: Do not take the ranges listed in these tables below as "absolutes." These are just general guidelines meant to put you in the right ballpark. There are plenty of exceptions and circumstances where some of these specific numbers may not apply, but for the average table tennis athlete, these guidelines should serve as a valid reference point.

STRENGTH

Volume	Intensity / Rep Ranges	RIR	Frequency	Rest Periods	Tempo
8–15 sets per muscle, per week	80%–95% 1RM[28] 1–8 reps	0–4	2+ / week	ALAN[29] 2–5 minutes	Control down, explode up

When training for strength, you should use compound exercises with a weight that is heavy enough that you can only get around one to eight repetitions with it. This will typically fall in the 80%–95% intensity range. Your primary focus should be to get progressively stronger through incremental increases in load within this rep range. This is the most efficient way to gain *maximal* strength. In terms of volume, meta-analytic data shows around 10 sets per week to be a good minimum threshold for developing strength at optimal rates. [11] You should split this volume over a frequency of at least two sessions per week as this has been shown to be superior when compared with lower frequencies.

It is possible to gain strength with much lower volumes, however. One study [12] showed that even doing a *single set* of 6–12 reps, 2–3 times per week over a period of 8–12 weeks was enough to see "suboptimal yet significant" gains in squat and bench press one rep

---

28   1RM = One rep maximum

29   ALAN = As Long As Necessary.

max strength in resistance-trained men! So, a little can go a long way in terms of strength training if you're really pressed for time.

For those who are wary of training heavy, keep in mind, you can gain strength very effectively *without* training to failure. A 2016 systematic review and meta-analysis [1] found it unnecessary to perform failure training to maximize muscular strength gains. On average, leaving anywhere from 1–4 "reps in reserve" can allow you to still build strength while reducing the risk of injury, excessive fatigue, and soreness.

Rest periods should be as long as necessary to ensure full recovery between sets—2–5 minutes is a good general range. Finally, when considering the tempo of each rep, you should focus on controlling the eccentric while aiming to move the concentric portion of the lift as quickly as possible. Since the load will be heavy, the bar speed will be slow, but your *intent* should be to move the weight quickly.

POWER

Volume	Intensity / Rep Ranges	RIR	Frequency	Rest Periods	Tempo
6–12 sets per muscle, per week	80%–90% for 1–2 reps or 75%–85% for 3–5 reps	3–5	2+ / week	ALAN 1.5–4 minutes	Max velocity & intent while maintaining control

Power is the ability to produce or generate force quickly. It is a marriage of *strength* and *speed*. To effectively train for power, you must be able to put forth a maximal effort while simultaneously having the presence of mind to *terminate* the set when your reps are no longer explosive. Slow and grindy reps are okay for strength training but should be avoided when training for power. Notably, when training for power at higher intensities, the bar speed may be *slow,* but you are still attempting to move the load as quickly as possible. If you notice the bar speed slowing significantly in comparison with previous reps, you've taken the set a bit too far.

The guidelines listed in the chart above are for barbell-based movements, but power can (and should) be trained through plyometrics (jump training) and with ballistic implements, such as medicine balls, as well. In these cases, the general principles still apply: aim for max velocity each rep, keep technique crisp, and ensure you rest long enough between attempts so you can apply maximal effort.

HYPERTROPHY

Volume	Intensity / Rep Ranges	RIR	Frequency	Rest Periods	Tempo
10–20 sets per muscle, per week	30%–85% 1RM 6–30 reps	0–4	2+ / week	ALAN 1.5–3 minutes	Control down, explode up

Hypertrophy training is training that focuses primarily on building muscle. One of the more useful things about training for hypertrophy is that you have an incredible amount of flexibility in how you go about doing so. If you perform enough volume and put forth enough effort each set, research shows that you can build muscle equally well using both high reps [13] and low reps. [14] Technically speaking, anywhere from 6–30 reps per set can be equally effective for building muscle, but if I had to narrow it down, I'd say sets of 6–15 reps should represent the lion's share of your training if hypertrophy is the main goal.

Here's two reasons why:

→ **Time Efficiency:** Because training with fewer than six repetitions stimulates hypertrophy less on a per set basis, you need to do *more* sets to get an equivalent stimulus. And since you need to rest longer in between heavier sets, this can take up a lot of time. In the low-rep study mentioned above, the volume-equated lower-rep workouts took one hour to perform while the moderate-rep workout only took 17 minutes!

→ **Training Comfort:** On the other end of the spectrum, for high-rep training in the 15–30 rep range to be maximally effective, you need to take the sets to failure (or at least very close). This is so you can fully recruit the higher threshold motor units required to optimally stimulate and challenge the muscle. For something like bicep curls, this isn't too big of a deal, but if you give this a try with squats, you'll quickly discover how tortuous it is. In the high-rep study, many of the participants ended up vomiting due to the intensity of the extended sets. There's a reason they call 20-rep squat programs "widow-makers"!

So, exclusively using low reps to build muscle isn't very time efficient, and exclusively using high-rep training is difficult because the sets need to be taken very close to failure. The 6–15-rep range is a nice sweet spot between the two. It's light enough to allow for slightly shorter rest periods so you can get sufficient volume in, but heavy enough to get a solid stimulus, even with a few reps left in reserve at the end of each set.

When training for maximal hypertrophy, 10–20 hard sets per muscle split over a frequency of at least two sessions per week is the most cited range for volume and frequency. Hypertrophy is more tightly correlated with training volume when compared with strength. Research shows there is a "dose response" relationship between the two where (up to a point) more volume usually results in more muscle growth. [15] This doesn't mean more is always better though! You must take into account your ability to recover. Furthermore, as an athlete, there is an opportunity cost as well—performing extremely high-volume programs for marginal increases in progress may not be the best use of your time!

Beginners should generally stick to the lower end of the volume spectrum, while more trained lifters may need more volume in order to achieve sufficient stimulus. Finally, while some bodybuilders are a fan of using a partial range of motion to achieve "constant tension" on the muscle, the research leans in favor of full range of motion training for superior muscle growth. [16]

MUSCULAR ENDURANCE

Volume	Intensity / Rep Ranges	RIR	Frequency	Rest Periods	Tempo
6–12 sets per muscle, per week	30%–67+% 1RM 12–30+ reps	0–3	2+ / week	10–90 seconds	Smooth and controlled cadence

When you train for muscular endurance, you are aiming to improve a muscle's ability to sustain repeated contractions against some form of resistance (even if it's just body weight) for an extended period. This is an important attribute for table tennis players, but it's also one that can be trained fairly well through sport-specific practice. Utilizing multi-ball and/or training sessions with a robot is a particularly effective way to accomplish this. Thus, for most, it doesn't make a lot of sense to set aside large chunks of time during physical training sessions for the sole purpose of improving muscular endurance. Instead, you can kill two birds with one stone by improving your muscular endurance during hypertrophy-focused periods of training. Notice how much overlap there is between training for hypertrophy and training for muscular endurance! Doing a few hard sets of 20–30 reps a couple of times a week can effectively stimulate both hypertrophy and muscular endurance. You can then allow sport-specific practice to "pick up the change" to get in additional work in at lower intensities.

MAX SPEED (SPRINTING)

Volume	Intensity / Rep Ranges	Effort	Frequency	Rest Periods	Tempo
50–200 meters per session	10–40 meters (acceleration) 10–30 meters with flying start (max speed)	90%–100% Max Speed	1–3 sessions week	appx. 1 minute per 10 meters sprinted, 48–72 hours between sessions	Max velocity and intent with no form breakdown

To truly train for speed it is not enough for you to run "hard." You need to come fairly close to your *maximal* speed levels in order to generate the adaptations needed to improve. This means you should be fresh and well rested between bouts so you can run hard enough to get close to (or beat) your previous times.

If your old high school coach had you run "suicides" at the end of practice, they may have been super hard, but they are *not* speed work. They can build grit, but they won't build speed! You should perform speed work first in a session, or on a separate day, so you are fresh enough to run fast. Effective speed work tends to be low volume and high quality. You may not feel totally run down from these session like you would during an extended bout of aerobic conditioning.

One reason sprinting (and plyometric exercise) is valuable to table tennis players is because it is a great way to build up "stiffness" in the lower leg. In this context, stiffness does not mean "limited range of motion," it refers to the muscle/tendon's ability to "harden up" in anticipation of impact and efficiently transfer the elastic energy created by the stretch-shortening cycle. Imagine the difference between a table tennis rubber with an ultra-soft sponge compared with a rubber with a much harder sponge. Which will have greater top end speeds? The harder sponge! In the same way, an athlete with greater ability to produce stiffness in the ankles will be able to maximize reactive strength and *minimize* power leakage when changing direction.

As you will see in later sections, sprinting is not something that should be undertaken lightly. While people tend to overestimate injury risk from resistance training, they *underestimate* the injury risks present when sprinting. It's just running, right? Kids run! Don't fall into that trap. Be conservative with speed work at first and build up slowly. Always warm-up thoroughly and don't push yourself to the point where form breaks down. Your hamstrings will thank you!

AEROBIC ENDURANCE

Volume	Intensity / Rep Ranges	Effort	Frequency	Rest Periods	Tempo
30–45 minutes per session	Zone 3: 70%–80% max HR	Moderate Effort	2–3+ sessions week	24–48 hours between sessions	Steady and even

My standard recommendation to table tennis players is to allow sport-specific practice to do the heavy lifting when it comes to building aerobic endurance. If you find you still need to supplement your training with a little roadwork, focusing on zone 3 (70%–80% max heart rate) is a good way to build aerobic endurance efficiently without cutting into your recovery too much. If you are unable to sustain zone 3 training for 30–45 minutes, use an interval training approach to build up:

→ Zone 3: 10 minutes
→ Recovery (brisk walk/slower pace jog): 5 minutes
→ Zone 3: 10 minutes
→ Recovery: 5 minutes
→ Zone 3: 10 minutes
→ Cool-down (5–10 minutes)

Lower-intensity cardio sessions (50–60% max heart rate) can be used strategically as part of a warm-up or on a recovery day to get the blood pumping without wearing you down. They can also be a good way to provide some extra calorie burn during fat-loss phases. If running does not agree well with you, lower impact options such as cycling and/or elliptical machines can be a good alternative.

FLEXIBILITY

Volume	Intensity / Rep Ranges	Effort	Frequency	Rest Periods	Tempo
60-120 total seconds per muscle, per session	15–30 seconds per stretch	To the point of slight discomfort	2–4+ sessions week	24–48 hours between sessions	Steady and even

If you want to increase your flexibility with a minimal time investment, here is a good protocol to follow based on the recommendations from the American College of Sports Medicine:

→ Stretch each muscle two to three times per week, holding for 10–30 seconds to the point of slight discomfort.
→ Perform as many sets as needed until you accumulate 60 seconds per muscle.

This will be enough to improve flexibility a bit, and you might notice mild benefits to strength training performance as well. [17]

Remember, don't perform this routine directly before training. This is not a "warm-up." Long-duration static stretching is best placed at the end of a session or as a short session of its own. It can be a great way to unwind at the end of the day, so try doing some light stretching at night while watching TV or listening to a podcast.

AGILITY

Volume	Intensity / Rep Ranges	Effort	Frequency	Rest Periods	Tempo
2–4 drills per session, 5–20 total minutes per session	5–12 seconds per rep or set of a drill	90%–100% effort	2–5 sessions per week	Auto-regulate for full to near-full recovery between attempts	Max speed

Agility is your ability to move quickly and easily. An agile athlete can change direction on a dime and react more quickly to the movements of their opponent. Agility is a complex motor ability, underpinned by other athletic attributes such as relative strength, speed, and power. There is also a perceptual, "decision making" component that pays a key role in agility—if you are able to "read" your opponent and recognize patterns during a game, you will be able to start moving sooner and react more quickly.

Thus, to some extent, just improving your game and increasing your athletic qualities across the board can result in better agility as it is the summation of those factors. Even so, research shows that adding some targeted agility work on top of your other training sessions can help speed things along. Fortunately, a little goes a long way here. In one study, a mere 15 minutes a day of agility training over three weeks was enough to result in significant improvements. [18] And another study [19] showed that agility training performed twice a week as part of the warm-up was enough to improve agility in elite soccer players.

Much as with speed work, when training for agility think *quality* over quantity. Hit it hard and rest enough so you can maintain a high level of performance each rep of the drill. For examples of when and how to perform agility work, see *Phase IB* in the next chapter.

CLOSING THOUGHTS ON TRAINING FOR SPECIFIC ATHLETIC QUALITIES

Many athletes have a very high work ethic. Like moths to a flame, we are drawn to pursue physical training regimens that place an undue focus on training "hard" and reaching fatigue—short rest periods, grinding out reps, pushing to complete failure, etc.

If you are serious about reaching peak performance, however, you must learn to give your body what it *needs*, not what it wants. Use the guidelines listed above to help ensure you are doing so!

Training Parameters Summary Table

Attribute	Volume	Intensity / Rep Ranges	RIR / Effort	Frequency	Rest Periods	Tempo
Strength	8–15 sets per muscle, per week	80%–95% 1RM / 1–8 reps	0–4 RIR	2+ / week	ALAN 2–5 minutes	Control down, explode up
Power	6–12 sets per muscle, per week	80%–90% for 1–2 reps / 75%–85% for 3–5 reps	3–5 RIR	2+ / week	ALAN 1.5–4 minutes	Max velocity & intent while maintaining control
Hypertrophy	10–20 sets per muscle, per week	30%–85% 1RM 6–30 reps	0–4 RIR	2+ / week	ALAN 1.5–3 minutes	Control down, explode up
Muscular Endurance	6–12 sets per muscle, per week	30%–67+% 1RM 12–30+ reps	0–3 RIR	2+ / week	10–90 seconds	Smooth and controlled cadence

(continued)

(continued)

Attribute	Volume	Intensity / Rep Ranges	RIR / Effort	Frequency	Rest Periods	Tempo
Max Speed (Sprinting)	50–200 meters per session	10–40 meters (acceleration) 10–30 meter with flying start (max speed)	90%–100% Max Speed	1–3 sessions week	1 minute per 10 meters 48–72 hours between sessions	Max velocity and intent with no form breakdown
Aerobic Endurance	30–45 minutes per session	Zone 3: 70%–80% max HR	Moderate Effort	2+ sessions / week	24–48 hours between sessions	Steady and even
Flexibility	60–120 total seconds per muscle, per session	15–30 seconds per stretch	To the point of slight discomfort	2–4+ sessions / week	24–48 hours between sessions	Steady and even
Agility	2–4 drills per session, 5–20 total minutes per session	5–12 seconds per rep or set of a drill	90%–100% effort	2–5 sessions / week	Autoregulate for full to near-full recovery between attempts	Max velocity and intent with no form breakdown

PHYSICAL TRAINING MYTHS

Now that we've established the proper way to train for various athletic outcomes, I'd like to close out this chapter by debunking some common myths and misconceptions regarding physical training and table tennis. Most of these myths are things I've heard repeated many times on internet forums, but they have also made their way into interviews with players/coaches and in certain popular table tennis books, so I think it's worth taking the time to discuss them!

1. RESISTANCE TRAINING WITH HEAVY WEIGHTS WILL MAKE ME BIG AND BULKY, SLOWING ME DOWN.

This myth used to be tossed around a lot more frequently, but in the past few years it seems to finally be losing some steam. This is a good thing because it represents a fundamental misunderstanding of how the training process works.

First, you can make dramatic increases in physical strength *without* significant increases in total body weight. You don't necessarily have to get "big" to get a lot stronger. Secondly, even if you *were* trying to build a significant amount of muscle, it is not so easy to do! Muscle gain is a slow process. A novice male trainee doing everything he can to grow should only expect to put on around 1–2 lb. of muscle per *month*. Females can expect about half that number. Thinking you can unintentionally become too big from resistance training is akin to thinking if you buy a basketball hoop for your driveway, you might accidently end up in the NBA.

Thinking of strength may conjure images of overweight powerlifters and strongmen—big lumbering fellows who bear little resemblance to the quick and snappy table tennis player. But the fact is, all the key elements of athleticism—balance, coordination, speed, power—are dependent on a certain baseline level of strength. Strength is the attribute that allows us to *express* those other traits.

Fast, powerful, and agile athletes tend to be muscular. Why is that? Because in order to achieve maximal speed and agility, one must be able to rapidly accelerate, decelerate, brake, and transition from one position to another. This precise control over your body requires a high degree of *relative strength*. In fact, when young, developing athletes are studied, strength is shown to be a key determinant for change-of-direction ability. [20] Still don't believe me? Go ahead and google "Fan Zhendong + legs" and take a gander. At the time of writing this, Fan just won his fourth World Cup and those massive quads didn't seem to slow him down one bit!

2. TRAINING WITH WEIGHTS WILL GET ME INJURED.

Compared with other physical activities, resistance training has a relatively low injury rate. [21] With proper form, training volume, and intensity of effort, your chances of injury are very low! You should be far more worried about getting injured playing a pickup game of soccer or basketball than you should during resistance training.

3. SPENDING EXTRA TIME IN THE GYM WILL INTERFERE TOO MUCH WITH MY TABLE TENNIS TRAINING.

The idea that lifting weights a few times a week will ruin your table tennis game due to excessive fatigue and soreness is simply not true. I could point to personal anecdotes of both myself and other table tennis players that I have trained who have successfully integrated resistance training with table tennis, but there's actually some direct research on this. In a 2016 study [22], researchers took 30 elite table tennis players and randomly split them into two groups: a control group and an experimental group. The experimental group was given a weight-training routine to follow for 6 weeks during their competitive season. They trained three times per week. By the end of the study, the group that trained with weights significantly improved maximal strength, vertical jump, sprint performance, and agility compared with the group that did not. There were no reports of the weight-training protocol interfering with the participants' normal table tennis training and competition.

These results are mirrored by research in other sports as well. One study [23] showed that indoor soccer players who added lower body resistance training on top of 13 hours of sport-specific training per week (plus one official match) were able to increase their jump and sprint performance without negatively affecting their training. Another study [24] found football players were able to participate in practice, and even compete in a match, a mere *24 hours* following a strength training session with no ill effects. Similar results were found in tennis where they successfully increased the agility, speed, and strength of competitive junior tennis players through a six-week training program with no injuries or overuse syndromes. [25] So, not only will resistance training give you a more athletic, healthy, and injury-resistant body, it can also fit seamlessly into your current table tennis training regime without interfering with your performance. How's that for a win-win?

Amazingly, despite all the benefits outlined above, proper strength training is often ignored by coaches. In a review of the physiological demands of table tennis, the authors interviewed coaches from all over the world and found many of them didn't pay much attention to physical training, strength training or otherwise. [26] As a reader of this book, you should take this as good news as it means you will now have an edge over much of your competition!

4. GETTING REALLY SORE IS A GOOD INDICATOR OF AN EFFECTIVE TRAINING SESSION.

Although delayed onset muscle soreness intuitively seems like it should be palpable "proof" that your training session was productive, it's a bit more complicated than that. Of the three proposed mechanisms of muscle growth (mechanical tension, metabolic stress, and muscle damage), muscle damage is likely the least important and may even *inhibit* progress if it is excessive. [27] It is normal to get a bit sore from time to time, but if you consistently get extremely sore from training, your body is forced to devote the lion's share of its resources to repairing the damaged tissue rather than building *new* tissue. When you apply the principles outlined in this book—a graded prescription of volume, higher training frequencies, controlled proximity to failure, etc.—you can minimize soreness to a great degree while still getting optimal results.

5. "FUNCTIONAL TRAINING" IS SUPERIOR TO STANDARD EXERCISES WHEN YOUR AIM IS TO BECOME A BETTER ATHLETE.

Functional training is a term that's a bit nebulous and hard to pin down. If by "functional" you mean training with a specific purpose and creating a well-balanced routine that results in the adaptations you need for your sport, then functional training is great. But if you think functional training means taking tried and true exercises and endlessly modifying them in ways that provide additional challenges to your balance, core stability, and/or coordination, then we start to have a problem.

There *is* a kernel of truth in thinking that working your stabilizer muscles and balance can be a good thing for an athlete: All else being equal, I do like to see most athletes progress to using free-weight exercises over just machines. And I think including unilateral movements that require a little more stabilization and control is good for mobility, proprioception, and balance. But it's easy to take this line of thinking too far. There's a big difference between including some rear-foot elevated squats in your program and loading up a barbell to squat on a BOSU ball. The former is a challenging but doable exercise that can be overloaded well and performed safely. The latter is a "circus act" movement that confuses *difficulty* with effectiveness.

At the end of the day, your priority in the gym should be overloading your muscles in a safe and effective manner. For that, traditional, "bread and butter" movements are just fine.

6. IT'S IMPORTANT TO TRAIN SPECIFICALLY TO IMPROVE BALANCE—ESPECIALLY BY USING UNSTABLE SURFACES.

Speaking of BOSU balls, I do not recommend dedicating a lot of time for the sole purpose of training your balance. Sport-specific practice, resistance training, plyometrics, and agility work will provide plenty of opportunities for challenging your balance in a variety of positions. You don't need to learn how to walk a tightrope to become a good table tennis player! Odds are, it is not your balance that is bottlenecking performance. If you still feel the need to improve your balance, I suggest doing so on a stable surface using single-leg exercises and plyometrics rather than using devices such as BOSU balls. Outside of specific rehabilitative conditions, the use of unstable surface training does not appear to be very effective: A 2015 systematic review and meta-analysis concluded that for young and healthy athletes, the use of unstable surfaces to train is not recommended if the goal is to enhance performance on *stable* surfaces. [28] This makes sense when you think about it. After all, we play table tennis on solid ground, not on trampolines!

7. A TABLE TENNIS BALL WEIGHS LESS THAN 3 G. PHYSICAL STRENGTH IS NOT IMPORTANT FOR TABLE TENNIS PLAYERS!

If we set aside all the health benefits associated with strength training and take the injury-preventing effects off the table as well, how important *is* physical strength for table tennis? I'd argue it's more important than you might think, but not for the reasons you might expect. . .

It's true that simply becoming stronger is not likely to have much direct carryover to your table tennis performance—at least in the short term. This is especially true if you only focus on strengthening individual muscles while failing to practice translating that strength into greater power. In one study for example, a group of table tennis players strengthened their wrists through flexion and extension activities, but failed to see any noticeable improvements over the control group in terms of their table tennis performance. [29]

Besides the fact that it's questionable how much of a role wrist strength plays in increasing the power of your shots, this study highlights the importance of including *some* degree of sport-specific training into your strength and conditioning program. In doing so, you will not only better target the specific muscles most relevant to increasing performance (hint: not your wrists), you will also engage in the intermediary steps necessary to bridge the divide between strength and performance. The key mindset shift when considering strength and table tennis is this: you are not merely attempting to accelerate your racket to hit a 3 g plastic ball, you must accelerate *yourself* in order to get to the ball in the first place! And I'm willing to wager you probably weigh a fair bit more than 3 g.

Thus, becoming strong and powerful for table tennis is less about directly using your muscles to apply more force to the ball and more about gaining the requisite strength to quickly accelerate and decelerate your *body* so you can move into position to hit the ball well. Once in position, your timing and technique will have the largest impact on the power of your stroke. Gold Medalist Ryu Seung-Min refers to this as being able to *"send the ball to 100 even if you use 50 power."* [30] You don't need to "muscle" the ball in table tennis; excessive force applied inefficiently is just wasted energy. In Korean, this is called *no ga da*—physically demanding and inefficient. You *do* need to "muscle" yourself a bit though!

8. SWINGING A WEIGHTED PADDLE OR DUMBBELL IS A GOOD "SPORT-SPECIFIC" WAY TO GET STRONGER FOR TABLE TENNIS.

I often hear players suggest swinging a weighted paddle or using a dumbbell (or some other implement) to mimic table tennis strokes in order to increase power and hand speed. I've softened my position on this *slightly* after consulting with a few other coaches and trainers, but I still do not recommend this as a primary means of increasing speed and power. Table tennis is a sport of precision that requires a great deal of accuracy. Because of this, it is important to maintain the integrity of your stroke when training. I'd particularly recommend against using a weighted paddle as part of a warm-up directly before playing. Two studies performed on baseball players shed some light on this.

In one study, [31] researchers found that because a weighted bat has a different "moment of inertia," it altered the swing mechanics enough to decrease performance with the normal-weight bat. Another study [32] found the same with the additional wrinkle that although the athlete *perceived* swing velocity to be faster after using the weighted bat, the first swing post-weighted condition was significantly slower. The book *Periodization Training for Sports* offers some additional insight. The authors caution against using wrist weights or weighted implements to increase speed as they "disrupt the motor pattern because their force vector (gravity) is perpendicular to the resulting force vector of the offensive action which has a forward, not downward, direction." [33]

So, what's the alternative? Research shows that advanced players can generate higher levels of spin and speed because they can accelerate the racket in less time compared with lower-level players. [34] When viewed carefully with high-speed video cameras, the researchers found that the higher racket speeds were attained by generating power from the *lower trunk* through *axial rotation*. Thus, a good "sport-specific" movement for table tennis players would be one that focuses specifically on developing rotary power by producing force through the more powerful lower body and core muscles. Think about the difference between simply swinging your arm to hit the ball versus performing a proper loop by rotating your body, transferring your weight, and accelerating through the ball.

The routines included in this book will address this through the inclusion of exercises that increase *rotational* strength and power— something that is generally lacking from run-of-the-mill strength-training programs. In the later phases of this plan, you will see medicine ball throws become a more prominent part of the training. This is because research shows they are a superior way to build torso rotational strength and power compared with traditional resistance training alone. [35] *That* is what proper sports-specific training is, not swinging a dumbbell around pretending to do table tennis strokes.

So, to tie all the above together, rather than using a dumbbell to perform a bastardized loop that neither perfectly mimics the stroke used in actual play, nor challenges the proper muscles with a sufficient degree of intensity, a better alternative is to strategically train the musculature used in the loop separately for both *strength* and *power*. In doing so, you will elicit the strongest adaptations and see the biggest payoff in terms of sport-specific speed.

Here is one way to do so:

→ Train the muscles of the lower body and core using bread and butter strength-building exercises (squats, lunges, planks, etc.) and perform *rotational strength* exercises, such as woodchoppers as well.
→ Increase the rate of force development by using medicine ball throws, plyometrics, and lower body power exercises.
→ During table tennis training, include drills specifically devoted to evaluating your stroke and ensuring you are using the muscles of your lower body and core to generate power for your loops.

Improving your strength and power while matching the *motor patterns* used in the sport is more than sufficient to see direct carryover to performance.

9. BECOMING EXTREMELY FLEXIBLE WILL REDUCE MY INJURY RATE AND IMPROVE MY PERFORMANCE.

Beware of falling into the trap of thinking the answer to better movement quality and athleticism is simply becoming more and more flexible. The likelihood that flexibility is the true limiting factor in your ability to execute high-level table tennis strokes is low. Furthermore, excess flexibility, particularly without the strength to control those end ranges of motion, can actually *increase* your chance of injury. [36]

For these reasons, I usually advise against investing a significant portion of time working on flexibility—especially if it comes at the expense of resistance training. Contrary to popular belief, rather than making you "muscle bound," performing full range of motion resistance training will help *increase* your flexibility. [37] When you combine resistance training with the mobility drills included in the warm-ups, most will find themselves plenty limber from those two things alone. There's nothing wrong with working on your flexibility if you have time to do so. It just shouldn't be done at the expense of more high-priority training.

10. DISTANCE RUNNING IS A GOOD WAY TO BUILD UP MY LEGS AND CONDITION MYSELF FOR TABLE TENNIS.

There is a strong tradition in athletics for coaches to use distance running as the go-to method of building endurance and strengthening/conditioning the legs, but this is rarely the best approach for table tennis athletes. Prominent strength and conditioning coach Eric Cressey likens using distance running to build up your legs to "changing the tires on a car with no engine, or studying for the wrong test." This sentiment is echoed in *Periodization Training for Sports* as well:

> *Athletes in racket sports respond best when aerobic training is not planned in the traditional form of long, easy, distance runs. These sports require interval training repetitions in general preparation and specific high-intensity tactical drills in the second part of the preparatory phase. [33]*

There is a place for long duration, steady-state cardio—particularly in the early off-season, but it should be a relatively minor part of your physical training regimen. Most of your endurance for table tennis should be built by playing table tennis. Your physical training routine should focus on building up the athletic qualities that table tennis can't develop as effectively—namely strength, power, and speed.

11. IT'S GOOD TO "CONFUSE THE MUSCLES" BY SWITCHING UP EXERCISES FREQUENTLY.

Constantly changing exercises workout to workout is a good way to keep your training interesting and fresh, but it is *not* a good way to make progress. The idea behind muscle confusion is correct: your muscles will not continue to adapt if they receive the same stimulus repeatedly. The mistake people make is thinking the ideal way to change the stimulus is through constant exercise variation.

It's true, your muscles *do* get "confused" to an extent when you change exercises. Ironically, it has the exact opposite effect that proponents of muscle confusion desire. When given an unfamiliar movement, you will experience a degree of neuromuscular inefficiency for the first couple of weeks. This means your muscles will not be able to produce as much force as they are capable of because they are still "learning" the movement. So instead of "shocking" your muscles you are artificially handicapping them! Exercise variation has its place, but, generally speaking, you should stick with movements for the duration of a training cycle so you can nail down the form and accurately track your progress.

Remember, muscles respond to tension. They don't care which exercise is providing it! The way to force a muscle to keep growing is through progressive overload—gradually increasing the training stress, usually through increases in the load and/or reps over time. Constantly switching exercises makes tracking your progress very difficult. Ten reps with 150 lb. on the squat is *not* the same stimulus as 10 reps with 150 lb. on a leg press. If you constantly switch exercises each workout, you can't be sure you're actually increasing the training stress.

HOLISTIC PERIODIZATION MODEL FOR TABLE TENNIS: AN ANNUAL PLAN

In this chapter, I will present a holistic periodization model that takes into account many of the elements mentioned previously in this book and provides a basic overview of how to harmonize those variables over the course of a year. Keep in mind, although I have done my best to lay things out clearly, I have also intentionally made this model rather complex. There's a *lot* going on here! If you're more of a casual player, you may not be in the position to dedicate this much time to your development as an athlete (and that's fine). Look for the principles I discussed in the previous chapter and draw them out so you can pick and choose what you see here and adapt it to your specific situation. What follows is merely a template.

PHASE I: THE OFF-SEASON PREPARATORY PERIOD (10–16 WEEKS)

The off-season is a good time to make body composition changes and establish a base level of conditioning and strength. This will lay the groundwork for the more intense and sport-specific training coming in later training cycles. It's worth noting, as a table tennis athlete, you may not have a true "off season." When developing your yearly plan, you should choose the tournaments that are most important to you (ideally within the same 2- to 3-month period) and plan to peak around those. Minor tournaments during other parts of the year may not warrant a full peak and can be handled by a quick taper/deload the week of the tournament.

The preparatory phase will be split into two subphases: an anatomical adaptation +hypertrophy/muscular endurance phase and a maximal strength phase. Here is a basic overview of what we are looking to accomplish in the first subphase:

RESISTANCE TRAINING: ANATOMICAL ADAPTATION, HYPERTROPHY, AND MUSCULAR ENDURANCE

To prepare the body for the more intense exercises used in later phases, time must be taken to build the strength of the more passive structures of the body (tendons, ligaments, connective tissue, etc.). This can be accomplished through graded exposure to a simple full body resistance training routine with a focus on moderate-to-high reps. This will establish a base of muscular endurance and will provide the athlete with an opportunity to familiarize him- or herself with the core resistance training movements.

This is also a good time to build a little muscle if that is determined to be an area of need. The slightly higher volume and moderate-to-high rep ranges will provide a potent stimulant for growth.

ENERGY SYSTEM TRAINING: BUILDING AN AEROBIC BASE

The focus of the energy systems training in this phase is building the endurance necessary to prevent fatigue from becoming a limiting factor in matches and tournaments. Most of this work can be accomplished through technical and tactical drills used during sport-specific practice. If additional endurance is needed, a cardiovascular conditioning protocol can be used in addition to the resistance training and sport-specific practice. This will build a strong aerobic base, which can later be maintained at a lower frequency and volume.

NUTRITIONAL PROTOCOL: OPTIMIZING BODY COMPOSITION

Reference the chapters on nutrition and make a judgment call as to whether your performance may benefit from actively changing your body composition. If you determine that you need to gain or lose weight in order to get into optimal shape, you should follow the rates of weight gain/loss outlined in the nutrition section. These changes to your body weight should be made well in advance of your competitive season so you have the time for your body to calibrate to the changes. Just like driving a new car, it will take some practice before you are able to get optimal performance out of it!

PSYCHOLOGICAL AND SOCIAL/EMOTIONAL SKILLS PROTOCOL

The preparatory phase is an excellent time to start building some of the skills and habits that will provide you with the mental and emotional fortitude needed in your competitive season. Pick a few high priority areas in this domain to focus on and work on making them habitual. From there, you can begin to create a system.

PHASE IA: RESISTANCE TRAINING PROTOCOL: ANATOMICAL ADAPTATION, HYPERTROPHY, AND MUSCULAR ENDURANCE (4–8 WEEKS)

The farther away you are from your competitive season, the less need there is for specificity of training. These early phases are about building a foundation from which you can take your performance to new heights. If you are new to progressive resistance training, it is particularly important to complete this introductory phase before diving into the more intense phases that follow. If you are already experienced in the gym and have built a strong foundation, you may benefit from a program that is a little higher in volume.[30]

Day 1	
Exercise[31]	Sets x Reps
Bench Press	4 x 12–15 (1–2 RIR)
Dumbbell Row	4 x 12–15 (1–2 RIR)
High Bar Back Squat	3 x 12–15 (1–2 RIR)
Standing Calf Raise	3 x 15–20 (0–1 RIR)
Plank	3 x ALAP[32]

Day 2	
Exercise	Sets x Reps
Trap Bar Deadlift[33]	3 x 6–8 (1–2 RIR)
Dumbbell Shoulder Press	3 x 10–15 (1–2 RIR)
Pull-ups[34]	3 x 10–15 (1–2 RIR)
Face Pulls	3 x 15–20 (1–2 RIR)
Split Squat	3 x 15–20 (0–1 RIR)

Day 3	
Exercise	Sets x Reps
High Bar Back Squat	4 x 8–10 (1–2 RIR)
Bench Press	4 x 8–10 (1–2 RIR)
Inverted Row	4 x 8–10 (1–2 RIR)
Seated Leg Curl	3 x 10–15 (1–2 RIR)
Pallof Press	3 x 10–15 (1–2 RIR)

---

30   For a personalized needs-analysis and performance assessment, contact me through the application page at peakperformancetabletennis.com/coaching.

31   For access to a video database with each of these exercises, head to peakperformancetabletennis.com/resources.

32   ALAP = As long as possible.

33   If no trap bar is available, do a conventional or sumo deadlift.

34   If you aren't strong enough to do pull-ups in this rep range, you can do assisted pull-ups using a band or use a lat pulldown machine.

RAMP UP PROTOCOL

If you are brand new to resistance training, or are coming off an extended lay-off, I recommend a ramp-up period of 1–3 weeks where you build from 1–2 sets of each exercise up to the prescribed amount. Ramping up in this way will engage the repeated bout effect and help prevent excessive soreness while still providing enough of a stimulus for improvement.

If you are familiar with resistance training and have already built up a decent work capacity, treat the first week as an "intro week" and simply reduce each set count by one. Depending on your level of advancement, the volume for this intro block may need to be adjusted up or down.

PROGRESSION SCHEME

To get the most out of this routine, you must achieve *progressive overload* over the long term. The most straightforward way of accomplishing this is to focus on adding weight to the bar and/or increasing the number of repetitions performed in a set.

A complete beginner should be able to see improvements each workout. An intermediate trainee may only see improvements on a weekly or monthly basis. Regardless, the goal of each session should be to "beat the logbook" and improve in some small way. For the routines listed in this book, we will be using a *double progression model* to achieve progressive overload.

Here's how it works:

1 First let's look at the notation and get some terms out of the way. If you see the following:

3 x 6–8 (1–2 RIR)

That means you are to perform 3 total sets and aim for 6–8 repetitions in each set with an average of 1–2 RIR.

To ensure you fall within the proper repetition range, you need to select a weight that is heavy enough to feel challenging in the prescribed rep range, but not so heavy that you fatigue early and fall out of the rep range.

If you are relatively new to lifting, I recommend starting with a weight you can easily lift with *perfect form*, at the upper end of the rep range, for all the prescribed sets. This allows you to build up a little momentum before the weights start feeling challenging and provides an opportunity to dial in your form.

If you were trying to knock over a wall, would you rather start from one inch away or give yourself enough room for a running start? That is the rationale behind starting with weights that are a little too easy. Give yourself a runway.

2 Put forth your best effort in each set but do not exceed the prescribed rep range. If you are going for 6–8 reps, you may find you are able to perform 9 reps in the first set because you are completely fresh. Don't go for that ninth rep. Instead, stop at 8 and save that energy for sets 2 and 3.

Furthermore, you should pay attention to the prescribed RIR and leave the corresponding number of reps "in the tank" for each set you perform. As you lift the weight, note when the bar speed begins to slow and gauge your levels of fatigue. When you get to the point where you think you could only do *one more rep* with good form, stop the set.

Let's say you are going for 8 reps with an RIR of 1–2. If an all-out, gun-to-the-head effort would result in you just barely getting 8 reps, you would end the set 1–2 reps short of that—in this case 6–7 reps.

3 Once you can hit the top end of the prescribed rep range with good form in all three sets, increase the weight by the smallest increment possible in your next workout. If you hit all your reps *again* the next workout, increase the weight again. If you miss a few reps on the later sets (you get 8 reps, then 7, then 6), keep the weight the same for the next workout and concentrate on completing additional repetitions in the next workout. Eventually you won't be able to make every session. That's okay! In that case, focus on biweekly or monthly progress.

Here's what all the above might look like over the course of a month:

Session One:

→ Set 1: 100 x 8 (could have done 11 if putting forth max effort)
→ Set 2: 100 x 8
→ Set 3: 100 x 8

Session Two:

→ Set 1: 105 x 8 (could have done appx. 10 if putting forth max effort)
→ Set 2: 105 x 8
→ Set 3: 105 x 8

Session Three:

→ Set 1: 110 x 8 (could have done 9 if putting forth max effort)
→ Set 2: 110 x 7 (could have done 8 if putting forth max effort)
→ Set 3: 110 x 6 (could have done 7 if putting forth max effort)

At this point, since 8 reps were not achieved in all three sets, the weight will remain the same and you should attempt to perform additional reps.

Session Four:

→ Set 1: 110 x 8 (could have done 10 if putting forth max effort)
→ Set 2: 110 x 8 (could have done 9 if putting forth max effort)
→ Set 3: 110 x 7 (could have done 8 if putting forth max effort)

In the above session, progressive overload was achieved because you picked up an extra rep in the second and third sets. The next workout would likely result in reaching 8 reps in all three sets, allowing for another increase in weight.

GENERAL TRAINING GUIDELINES

Now that you know how to progress with each exercise, we can discuss the particulars of this routine. This section will outline your basic, "need to know" information regarding how to perform this routine. Unless otherwise stated, these guidelines will apply to all the other phases as well, so refer to this section as needed.

WHEN TO PERFORM THIS ROUTINE

In this routine you will be performing three full body workouts, three times a week, on non-consecutive days (Monday/Wednesday/Friday is a common choice).

WARM-UP SETS

Just as you need to do a general warm-up before lifting, you need to do a *specific* warm-up before you perform the working sets for your primary compound movements. The warm-up sets are not listed. They should not be challenging: their only purpose is to groove your technique and prime your nervous system for heavy lifting. Take squats for example.

Let's say over time you've worked your way up to doing 3 sets of 6–8 reps with 225 lb (102 kg). You don't simply walk up to the bar, throw two 45 lb (20 kg) plates on each side and have at it! You need to work your way up so your body can acclimate to the heavy load. Here's a basic way to structure it.

Sample Warm-Up for reps in the 2–8 range:

→ Warm-up Set 1: 50% of working weight for 5 reps. 1 minute rest.
→ Warm-up Set 2: 70% of working weight for 3 reps. 1 minute rest.
→ Warm-up Set 3: 90% of working weight for 1 rep. 1–2 minutes rest.

Sample Warm-Up for reps in the 8–15+ range:

→ Warm-up Set 1: 50% of working weight for 8 reps. 1 minute rest.
→ Warm-up Set 2: 70% of working weight for 4 reps. 1 minute rest.
→ Warm-up Set 3: 90% of working weight for 2 reps. 1–2 minutes rest.

You only need to warm-up for the *first* compound movement for each muscle group. After you have performed your compound movements, you do not need to warm-up for your accessory work.

On Day 2 for example, you do not have to perform warm-up sets for the face pulls because the pull-ups have taken care of warming that area up.

BREATHING

Conventional wisdom is to breathe in on the easy part of the lift, exhale on the difficult part. It's important to pay attention to your breathing as you may inadvertently be holding your breath without realizing it during your set. This will hurt your performance unless it's done intentionally and in a methodical manner. When squatting and deadlifting for example, creating high amounts of intra-abdominal pressure will help protect your spine and allow for better performance.

Here's how to do it for the squat:

→ At the top of the squat, take a deep belly-breath.
→ Let the bar "settle" and hold your breath, bearing down.
→ Descend into the squat while holding the breath in your belly and bracing your core.
→ Once you've powered through the sticking point, exhale forcefully and begin the process again.

This is known as the Valsalva maneuver and it is a very effective way to brace your core and safely train with high loads.

REST PERIODS

Refer to the previous section for a more detailed explanation of the rationale regarding rest periods, but for reference:

→ Rest 2–3+ minutes between sets of the more fatiguing compound movements (squat, bench, deadlift).
→ Rest 1–2 minutes between sets of less fatiguing accessory work (calf raises, face pulls, leg curls, etc.).
→ Autoregulate rest periods as needed to ensure the target muscle is the limiting factor during your set rather than cardiovascular fatigue.

COOL-DOWN

When you finish training, taking 5–10 minutes to cool down can potentially help reduce post-workout soreness and improve recovery. Something like 10 minutes of low-impact, low-intensity cardio (brisk walking, cycling, etc.) is a good option. If you do this at all, make sure it's super light and easy. If you are *adding* training stress, then you have completely defeated the point!

PHASE IA: ENERGY SYSTEMS TRAINING PROTOCOL

Having a well-conditioned aerobic system is important both for your general health and your performance as an athlete. In a review of the physiological demands of table tennis, [1] the authors note "while the anaerobic alactic system is the most energetic system used during periods of exertion in a table tennis game, a strong capacity for *endurance* is what helps a player recover quicker for the following match and the next day of competition." So even though power, speed, and agility are the things that are most required during a rally, without a sufficient aerobic base, the athlete will be unable to recover sufficiently between points to *display* that power and agility.

Indeed, the review mentioned above notes the best players usually have higher levels of endurance.

With the above in mind, the table tennis athlete should first look to include endurance-enhancing drills (multi-ball, footwork drills, robot drills, etc.) during technical practice sessions. This is a far more efficient use of time than long duration steady-state, and it's more sport-specific as well. Research shows that multi-ball protocols used in table tennis training can effectively stimulate match conditions. [2] And since the off-season is also a great time to refine and perfect technique, repetitive drills that are longer in duration are the perfect means to both build endurance and improve technique.

If you consistently find yourself gassing out during matches despite including endurance-enhancing technical/tactical drills in your training, you can add 1–3 aerobic training sessions a week to help build your aerobic endurance. I recommend starting with a steady-state, low-impact protocol (cycling, elliptical, etc.) for 20–45 minutes 2–3 times per week. Once you can maintain 70–80% of your max heart rate[35] for the duration of the session, you can switch over to an interval training protocol.

High intensity interval training will more closely mimic the intermittent movement profile of table tennis, but it is also more taxing on the body and can be more challenging on your recovery. For this reason, I recommend limiting these sessions to 1–2 sessions per week in the 10–20-minute range.

In a study titled "Energetics of Table Tennis and Table Tennis-Specific Exercise Testing," the authors suggest an activity-to-rest ratio of 1:2–1:5

---

35   To get a rough estimate of your max heart rate use the following formula: 208 - (0.7 x age).

after carefully analyzing the typical duration of rallies and rest intervals most common in match play. [3] I recommend using low-impact machines that use both the upper and lower body (such as an elliptical machine) to mimic the upper body high-speed actions used in table tennis. Other options include using a "slideboard" (great for building the endurance needed for holding the ready position for extended periods of time), or "battle ropes" combined with quick lateral footwork.

Here's what a typical interval session might look like:

→ Warm-up: appx. 5 minutes at an easy pace/intensity.
→ 10 second "sprint" using max/near max effort.
→ 20–50 second active rest period at an easy pace.
→ 10 second "sprint" using max/near max effort.
→ 20–50 second active rest period at an easy pace.
→ Repeat until desired total time is reached.

Note: There is a documented "interference effect" between cardio—particularly moderate–intensity, steady-state cardio such as jogging—and strength, hypertrophy, and power outcomes. To minimize this effect, it's best to place the resistance training and cardio sessions on separate days, if possible. [4–5] If you are going to perform cardio on the same day, separating the sessions by at least 6 hours has been shown to be a potentially sufficient window of recovery to allow for the full adaptive response from concurrent training. [6] If you are going to perform the cardio within the same session as your resistance training, the cardio should always be placed last, at the *end* of the session.

PHASE IA: NUTRITIONAL PROTOCOL

As already mentioned, if you need to lose or gain some weight, now is the time to do so. Use the information from the nutrition section and start making the necessary changes to your diet to move your weight in the right direction.

PHASE IA: PSYCHOLOGICAL AND SOCIAL/EMOTIONAL SKILLS TRAINING PROTOCOL

Here are a few things you can begin to incorporate into your weekly schedule in this phase:

→ Take a guided course on meditation (via Headspace, Calm, Insight Timer, Waking Up, etc.).
→ Identify any ritualistic behaviors and flag for potential pre-performance routines.
→ Begin to build awareness of your emotional state during match play.
→ Read a book (or take a class) on improving social skills/relationships.[36]
→ Choose two steps from the "Building Robust Sports Confidence" graphic to work on.
→ Perform the goal setting and "Perfect Week" exercises outlined in the chapter on motivation.

TAPER/TRANSITION WEEK (1 WEEK)

Before transitioning to the max strength block, we will take a week to reduce training volume and perform some testing for your main lifts. This will allow you to drop some fatigue and get an idea of your current strength levels. Some of the progressions used in the strength

---

36 I highly recommend Dale Carnegie's *How to Win Friends and Influence People* for improving your social interactions. My copy is well-worn, copiously highlighted, and liberally underlined. I suppose I needed a lot of help in this area!

block require an estimate of your one rep maximum, so this data will be useful moving forward.

Here's how to perform the taper and test week:

→ **Day One:** Perform the workout as listed, but reduce each set count by one and take 10% off the load on the bar. Aim for the bottom end of each rep range.

→ **Day Two:** Perform a single AMRAP (as many reps as possible) set[37] of 3–6 reps for the trap bar deadlift. Deload all other exercises as described in Day One.

→ **Day Three:** Perform a single AMRAP set of 3–6 reps for the squat and bench press. Deload all other exercises as described in Day One.

It's important that you warm-up thoroughly and put forth your absolute best effort on the AMRAP sets. Don't compromise form and use a spotter! Once you have your estimated one rep maxes for the squat, bench press, and deadlift, you can proceed to the next phase.

PHASE IB: THE OFF-SEASON MAX STRENGTH BLOCK (6–8 WEEKS)

Now that we've established a base of muscular endurance and are familiar with the basic compound movements in the gym, it's time to shift the focus of training toward developing maximal strength.

---

37   If you have experience performing one-rep max tests and/or you are working with an experienced trainer, you can just go for a one rep max. Otherwise, you should perform an AMRAP set with a weight, which will allow you to get somewhere in the 3–6 rep range. You can then use a one rep max calculator (a simple Google search will pull up plenty) to get an estimate of your one rep maximum.

Strength - Speed Continuum

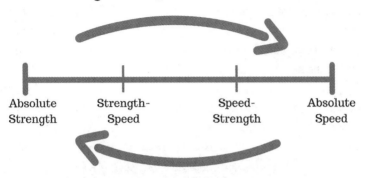

There is certainly a time and place for agility, speed, and power training, but starting with strength first will *potentiate* those qualities later.

Additionally, if you happen to be lagging disproportionately on one end of the strength-speed continuum, you can gain an *outsized* benefit from shoring up that weakness. This was demonstrated in a 2017 study [7] where researchers tested athletes to determine whether they were force deficient (lacking strength) or velocity deficient (lacking speed). The goal of the study was to determine the best way to improve power output, as measured by a jump height test. In the end, the participants who received a specialized training program that targeted their weakness outperformed the groups that received a well-balanced or non-optimized training program.

What does this mean for the table tennis player? Well, if I had to hazard a guess, I'd say that most table tennis players are much more likely to be force deficient than speed deficient. Many players, in a good faith effort to increase speed and agility, place a lot of focus on plyometrics, agility drills, and light body-weight movements aimed at increasing muscular endurance and foot speed. This will work well up to a point, but these athletes will eventually hit a ceiling as they max out the adaptations possible from that type of training. Dedicating some time to build a foundation of strength will *raise* that ceiling and allow for additional increases in speed and power to be made. That is the purpose of this block.

Formerly ranked number 1 in the world, Xu Xin, knows the importance of resistance training: "*I train my core a lot. That's important. Since all strokes involve the core. If you can be stable and strong, you can have a better quality in all your strokes.*" [8]

PHASE IB: RESISTANCE TRAINING PROTOCOL

In this phase, we will build a foundation of strength through bread-and-butter compound exercises that have stood the test of time. We will also be introducing some more sport-specific movements to build rotational strength. Use the training principles and guidelines outlined previously to complete the following 4-day split.

Day 1		
Order	Exercise	Sets x Reps
1	Rear-foot Elevated Split Squat	3 x 10–12 (1–2 RIR)
2A	Bench Press	3 x 10–12 (1–2 RIR)
2B	Split Stance Rotational Row	3 x 10–12 (1–2 RIR)
3A	Eccentric Overload Leg Curls	3 x 5–8 (2–3 RIR)
3B	Standing Calf Raise	3 x 10–15 (0–1 RIR)
3C	Half-kneeling In-line Stable Chop	2 x 8–12 (1–2 RIR)

Day 2		
Order	Exercise	Sets x Reps
1	Squat*	4 x 1–3 @ 80%–85% 1RM (4–6 RIR)
2	Bench Press*	4 x 1–3 @ 80%–85% 1RM (4–6 RIR)
3	Trap Bar Deadlift*	4 x 1–3 @ 80%–85% 1RM (4–6 RIR)
4	Band Resisted Broad Jumps*	2 x 5
5A	Single-leg Lateral Hops*	2 x 4 (each direction)
5B	Half-kneeling In-line Stable Lift	2 x 8–12 (1–2 RIR)

Day 3		
Order	Exercise	Sets x Reps
1	Squat	3 x 4–6 (2–3 RIR)
2A	Pull-ups	4 x 4–6 (2–3 RIR)
2B	Bench Press	3 x 6–8 (2–3 RIR)
3A	Half-kneeling, Side Twist Throw*	3 x 10
3B	Face Pulls	3 x 10–15 (1–2 RIR)

Day 4		
Order	Exercise	Sets x Reps
1	Trap Bar Deadlift	3 x 4–6 (2–3 RIR)
2A	Dumbbell Shoulder Press	3 x 10–12 (1–2 RIR)
2B	Inverted Row	3 x 10–12 (1–2 RIR)
3A	Landmine Lateral Squat	2 x 10–12 (1–2 RIR)
3B	Standing Cook Bar Hip Rotation	2 x 8–12 (1–2 RIR)
4	Medicine Ball Fake Throw	3 x 5

*Refer to the "Speed and Power Guidelines" section for these movements.

Schedule:

REST	Day 1	Day 2	REST	Day 3	REST	Day 4

WHAT'S NEW THIS BLOCK

There are a few changes to this block that require a bit of explanation. First, if you see exercises listed with an A, B, or C you will be performing them as paired sets or tri-sets.

To complete a paired set, perform one set of the first exercise, rest 30–60 seconds, and then perform the first set of the second exercise. Alternate back and forth this way until all the sets are completed for both movements. Performing agonist-antagonist paired sets is a great way to save some time without affecting performance. In fact, there is some evidence that performance may be *enhanced* when movements are paired this way. [9]

For the tri-sets, it's largely the same idea. Move from one exercise to the next with 30-60 seconds of rest in between. If you can't perform the sets this way because of logistical issues (crowded gym, etc.), use normal rest periods and perform the exercises in the order listed.

There are also some movements that are intended to develop explosive speed and power. These movements require a different frame of mind than the other exercises and should be progressed differently as well.

SPEED AND POWER GUIDELINES

Notice on Day 2 your first three movements are listed as 4 x 1–3 @ 80%–85% of your one rep max. Your aim for these sets is to work on explosiveness and crisp technique. These sets should not feel grindy or super difficult as you are purposely staying far from failure. Here's a quick example of how to perform these sets.

Let's say you completed your taper/testing week and found your squat one rep max to be 200 lb. (91 kg). If you plan on scheduling 6 weeks for the strength phase, here's how you could progress your power day for the squat:

→ Week 1: 4 x 3 with 160 lb. (80% of 1RM)
→ Week 2: 4 x 2 with 165 lb. (82.5% 1RM)
→ Week 3: 4 x 1 with 170 lb. (85% 1RM)
→ Week 4: 4 x 3 with 165 lb. (82.5% 1RM)

→ Week 5: 4 x 2 with 170 lb. (85% 1RM)
→ Week 6: 4 x 1 with 175 lb. (87.5% 1RM)

You should have anywhere from 3–6 reps left in the tank at the end of these sets. Your focus should be to keep form very tight, lower the bar under control, and *maximize* bar speed on the concentric portion of the lift. The purpose of these sets is multifold. First, they help to improve your technique under load. Second, since you will be staying far from failure, they provide some active recovery. And third, there is some evidence that this type of training can potentiate your strength performance up to 48 hours later, [10] making it the perfect prelude to your heavier strength days.

For plyometric movements such as the band-resisted broad jumps and lateral hops, once again, your focus should be on speed and explosiveness rather than fatiguing the muscles. These are *not* conditioning movements meant to elevate your heart rate and tire you out! Unlike the exercises that follow the double progression scheme, there is not a clean way to incrementally progress these movements week to week. Instead, focus on technique and execution. Work on your explosiveness, but just as importantly, work on controlling the landing and decelerating properly. Record yourself and aim to maintain an athletic position (chest up, knees bent, etc.) with a soft landing.

Finally, for ballistic movements such as the side twist throw, your focus should be 100% on maintaining the speed of the ball. Again, it's all about explosiveness not exhaustion. Start with a relatively light "wall ball" in the 2- to 10-lb. range. Terminate the set if the speed of the ball starts to drop off.

Here are some guidelines for choosing the correct weight ball based on your body weight:[38]

Athlete's Weight	Ball Weight (rotational)	Ball Weight (overhead)
100–135 lb.	4 lb. (2 kg.)	2 lb. (1 kg.)
135–175 lb.	6 lb. (3 kg.)	4 lb. (2 kg.)
175–200 lb.	8 lb. (4 kg.)	6 lb. (3 kg.)
200+ lb.	10 lb. (5 kg.)	8 lb. (4 kg.)

PHASE IB: ENERGY SYSTEMS TRAINING PROTOCOL

After the anatomical adaptation/endurance phase, you should now have a solid base from which you can build up the intensity of your table tennis drills so that they become more specific to in-game situations. This means incorporating drills that are equal to or *higher* in intensity than what you will experience during a typical match. As previously mentioned, one of the best ways to accomplish this is to incorporate multi-ball training, intense footwork drills, and "mock matches" that include an element of randomness.

Since the focus of this block is maximal strength, any cardio sessions outside sport-specific practice should be reduced to a maintenance level of 0–2 sessions per week to accommodate the additional time spent resistance training.

---

38   These guidelines are based on Michael Boyle's recommendations outlined in his book, *New Functional Training for Sports*.

PHASE IB: INTRODUCTION TO SPEED AND AGILITY TRAINING

During this phase, we will get your feet wet with one to two agility sessions a week as well as a bit of sprinting in the latter half of the block. We will be focusing more on power and agility in Phase II, but it pays to start planting some seeds now so you can start to get a feel for the form and mechanics of these drills. Remember *The Karate Kid*? These agility drills are like the famous "wax on, wax off" scene— you will be working on the raw fundamentals of movement, which can then be applied instinctively during sport-specific practice. Build those base patterns first and your table tennis training will absorb them.

AGILITY DRILLS

Agility work can be slotted in before your table tennis training. Do them after warming up, but before sport-specific practice begins. This will help "prime" your body for quick and explosive movement and will provide an opportunity for learning without tiring you out excessively. The aim is maximal intensity and speed—they are *not* meant to condition you like a cardio session would. The total time for each agility session might only be around five to ten minutes during this phase. Nothing too overwhelming, but you might be surprised at how effective some targeted agility work can be.

Include both open and closed agility drills throughout the week. A closed agility drill is one that requires the athlete to complete a pre-programmed set of movements, often using implements such as cones or ladders. An open drill requires the athlete to anticipate and respond to an environmental cue or stimuli of some sort and rapidly change direction in response (changing direction at the sound of a coach's whistle, for example). Starting with a closed drill, such as an agility ladder, is a great way to dynamically warm-up and "wake up" your body and mind. From there, you can move onto an open drill of some sort. After that, you could include one to two drills within your table tennis session that work on the same movement patterns practiced in the agility drill. This will help with transfer. Here are two sample sessions that include agility work as part of the general warm-up:

SESSION ONE (LINEAR FOCUS)

Warm-Up/Agility Work:

→ Table Tennis Ten: 5–10 minutes.
→ Falling Starts: 3–5 minutes.
  • Feet square and together.
  • Lean forward till you "fall" into a sprint.
  • Accelerate maximally for a short distance and terminate.
→ Ball Drops: 3–5 minutes.
  • Coach/partner stands a set distance in front of you and drops a ball.
  • You accelerate forward and catch ball before it bounces twice.
→ Red Light/Green Light:[39] 3–5 minutes.
  • Players line up on starting line.
  • When coach shouts "green light" everyone runs forward.
  • When coach shouts "red light" players must decelerate into the ready position.
  • Anyone who falls or takes an extra step must go back to the start.
  • First player across the court wins.

---

39 The use of games can be a powerful way to help build agility and speed while keeping things fun. This is especially true if you are working with younger athletes. Avoid drills that involve a lot of standing in line and waiting.

Table Tennis Drills:

→ "In and out" footwork drills.
→ General drill and practice.

SESSION TWO (LATERAL FOCUS)

Warm-up:

→ Table Tennis Ten: 5–10 minutes.
→ Lateral Cone Drill: 3–5 minutes.
→ Offensive/Defensive Catch/Dodge drills (alternate): 3–5 minutes.
   • Offensive: Move in the opposite direction in response to a signal or cue.
   • Coach throws a ball at you and you dodge.
   • Defensive drill: Move in the same direction as signal/cue.
   • Coach throws a ball away from you and you move to catch it.

Table Tennis Drills:

→ Falkenberg Drill.
→ Rapid-pace multi-ball feeding.
→ General drill and practice.

The above is just one possible example of what you might perform during a given week. There are literally *hundred*s of potential agility drills that could cover the same ground, but don't get overwhelmed. It's not about finding the perfect drill. The important thing is to cover the various planes of movement and to identify and correct movement inefficiencies as you see them. For more examples of potential agility drills, you can skip ahead to the agility section in Phase II.

SPEED WORK

During the last two weeks of this block, we will add two days of hill sprints to begin to condition your body for the speed work coming in the next phase. Sprints are an excellent way to improve speed, power, and athleticism, but they are also an excellent way to get injured if you're not careful. Starting with hill sprints is a good way to build up to sprinting on flat ground because hill sprints will limit your max speed and are a lower impact exercise.

Use the following protocol twice a week either *after* your resistance training or on a rest day:

→ General Warm-up:
   - Appx. 5–10 minutes light steady-state cardio (get warm).
   - Dynamic stretching/mobility as needed.
   - A-Marches – 10 meters down and back.
   - High Knees with Foreleg Extension – 10 meters down and back.
   - Heel Ups – 10 meters down and back.
→ Hill Sprint Warm-up:
   - 3–5 submaximal runs starting at 50% speed and adding 15%–20% each run.
→ Hill Sprints:
   - 2–3 max effort sprints of 5–15 seconds.
   - Rest as long as needed for full recovery between sprints—2–4 minutes on average.

Look for a hill with approximately a 5%–10% grade. It should not be so steep that you can't move quickly up it. The object of these sessions is not to leave feeling totally exhausted. They are just meant to help prep your body for flat ground sprinting in a lower impact way.

Note: If running/sprinting doesn't agree with you, you can perform sprints on a low impact machine like an elliptical or a bike.

PHASE IB: PREPARATORY NUTRITIONAL PROTOCOL

Continue following the nutritional strategies appropriate to optimizing your body composition. In Phase II we will stabilize your body weight and shift to a maintenance diet. For now, keep that scale moving in the right direction!

PHASE IB: PSYCHOLOGICAL AND SOCIAL/EMOTIONAL TRAINING

Now that you have learned how to meditate, identified ritualistic behaviors for your PPR, and are more aware of your emotional state during match play, it's time to integrate this information into a system.

Continue your daily meditation habit, but move beyond simply focusing on breathing and begin to utilize visualization techniques. Use the system outlined in the chapter on meditation to create a personalized PPR and start using it during practice matches.

Choose two more steps from the building confidence graphic and start working on incorporating them into your life. Experiment with the techniques described in the chapter on game day protocols and being working on controlling your arousal and emotional state during practice matches.

OFF-SEASON HOLISTIC PERIODIZATION MODEL

The following table provides an overview of the holistic periodization strategy for the off-season.

Training Phase >>	Preparatory/Off-Season (10–16 weeks)	
Domains	Anatomical Adaptation/ Endurance/ Hypertrophy (4–8 weeks)	Maximal Strength (6–8 weeks)
Energy Systems	Aerobic Endurance	Maintenance
Speed/ Agility	N/A	Introduction to Speed/ Agility
Strength	Muscular Endurance/ Hypertrophy/ Anatomical Adaptation	Maximal Strength
Psychological & Social/ Emotional	• Goal setting • Guided practice with psychological skills training • Identify ritualistic behaviors and flag for potential PPRs • Build confidence • Begin to build awareness of emotional state during match play	• Refine and adapt psychological skills training and begin to develop and practice skills under match conditions. • Continue building confidence
Nutrition	Tailored to move body toward optimal body composition	Tailored to move body toward optimal body composition

TAPER/TRANSITION WEEK (1 WEEK)

Once again, before transitioning to the next phase, we will take a week to reduce training volume and perform some testing for your main lifts.

Here's how to perform the taper and test week for this phase:

→ **Day One:** Eliminate this day and rest instead.

→ **Day Two:** Perform the workout as listed, but reduce each set count by one and take 10% off the load on the bar. Aim for the bottom end of each rep range.

→ **Day Three:** Perform a single AMRAP set of 3–6 reps for the squat and bench press. Deload all other exercises as described in Day Two.

→ **Day Four:** Perform a single AMRAP set of 3–6 reps for the trap bar deadlift. Deload all other exercises as described in Day Two.

Compare your new 1RMs to your previous ones and make sure you update your training percentages moving forward.

PHASE II: PRE-SEASON POWER AND AGILITY (6–8 WEEKS)

Now that we have worked our way across the strength-speed continuum, it's time to put that strength to use and focus on maximal power and agility. This is an important last step to take before the competition period because there is a demonstrated "lag time" between increasing strength and power and seeing those increases result in improved agility. [11] We will also use this period to stabilize your body weight so that you have time to fully adapt before serious competition begins.

PHASE II: RESISTANCE TRAINING PROTOCOL

In this phase, our focus shifts from maximal strength to developing maximum levels of power and speed. The overall volume and frequency of training will be reduced to allow for more recovery between sessions.

Day 1		
Order	Exercise	Sets x Reps
1A	Lateral Bound	4 x 5 (each side)
1B	Standing Front Rotary Scoop Toss	3 x 10 (each side)
2	Rear-foot Elevated Split Squat	3 x 4–6 (2–3 RIR)
3A	Bench Press	3 x 4–6 (2–3 RIR)
3B	DB Row	3 x 6–8 (2–3 RIR)

Day 2		
Order	Exercise	Sets x Reps
1A	Hang Power Clean (or Jump Squat)	3 x 5
1B	Rotational Med Ball Slams	3 x 5 (each side)
3A	Skater Squat	3 x 8–10 (1–2 RIR)
3B	Incline Dumbbell Press	3 x 10–12 (1–2 RIR)
3C	Chin-ups	3 x 10–12 (1–2 RIR)

Day 3		
Order	Exercise	Sets x Reps
1A	Broad Jump	4 x 5
1B	Standing Chest Throw	3 x 10
2A	Single-leg Straight-leg Deadlift[40]	3 x 6–8 (2–3 RIR)
2B	Push Press	3 x 4–6 (2–3 RIR)
4	Standing Transverse Chop	3 x 8–12

Schedule:

REST	Day 1	REST	Day 2	REST	Day 3	REST

TRAINING NOTES

You'll notice most of the speed/power focused movements now come first in each workout. This is because we are now aiming to prioritize these qualities and it's important to be fresh when training them. See each section below for specific guidelines on how to progress with your plyometric and ballistic movements this cycle.

WALL BALL THROWS PROGRESSION MODEL

Use the guidelines from the previous section to select the proper weight for your wall ball. For the first three weeks, perform each rep as if it were a single—focusing completely on technique and maximal force production with a slight pause between reps. Instead

---

40 If the form for this is too difficult, do not add load at first. Master with body weight or use one of the regressions from the video database available at peakperformancetabletennis.com/resources.

of increasing the weight of the ball or the number of reps performed, just try to throw harder each session.

After you have built up some skill and confidence with your throws, you can transition to a more continuous and rhythmic pattern where each rep leads right into the next. Again, rather than using a heavier ball or adding volume to progress, instead focus on force production. The sound of the ball hitting the wall can be a good auditory feedback mechanism for how forceful your throws are, so listen up!

Rest about two minutes between sets, or follow the "paired sets" protocol and rest around 30-60 seconds between alternating sets. You may autoregulate the rest periods as needed, but ensure you are fresh and recovered for each set.

PLYOMETRIC PROTOCOL

For the lateral bounds and the broad jump, your first focus should be on clean execution with a soft landing. Perform each rep as a "single" with a pause so you can learn to stick the landing in an athletic stance. You can rest a few seconds between reps if needed. Rest about two minutes between sets, or follow the "paired sets" protocol and rest around 60 seconds between alternating sets. Autoregulate the rest periods as needed to ensure you are fresh and recovered for each set.

Once you've mastered the form, you can increase the difficulty by attempting to increase the distance jumped. During the last 2-3 weeks of the training cycle, switch to a "multi-jump" method where you perform each rep one after the other with no break between reps.

HANG POWER CLEAN (OR JUMP SQUAT)

The hang power clean is a less technical variation of a hang clean, but as with any Olympic lift, it's very important to reach technical mastery before using a heavy weight. Make sure you work with a trainer and achieve proper form before adding a challenging weight to the bar. Once you've mastered the form, it can be progressed by adding weight to the bar.

If you don't have experience with Olympic lifting, you can use a weighted jump squat instead of the hang power clean. Use this formula[41] to figure out the proper weight:

[(Squat 1RM + body weight) x .4] – body weight = added load.

Squat jumps are less technical and are easier to learn than traditional Olympic lifts, but they still provide a great stimulus for power development. Much like your other jumps, start by performing each rep as a single. In the last two to three weeks of your training cycle, you may experiment with a more plyometric "multi-jump" protocol where each rep leads right into the next without pausing.

PHASE II: ENERGY SYSTEMS TRAINING PROTOCOL

In this pre-season phase of training, much of your focus will be spent working on agility drills, speed work, and specific technical and tactical drills directly related to areas of weakness in your table tennis game. This should be sufficient for most to maintain your base aerobic conditioning. If you feel like this is an area that is still lacking, you can perform a maintenance dose of one to two cardio

---

41   Once again, credit to Michael Boyle for the formula!

sessions per week, but be mindful of recovery as we will be adding additional agility and speed sessions.

PHASE II: SPEED TRAINING PROTOCOL

In this phase we've moved from 4 resistance training sessions a week to 3. This opens the door for us to dedicate a little more time working on speed and agility. During the last 2 weeks of the previous block, I had you introduce 2 sessions of hill sprints to help prepare your body for the speed sessions this block.

Continue with that same protocol for the first two weeks of this block as well.

For weeks 3–4, switch to the following protocol, performed on the off-days from your resistance training sessions.

SESSION 1: ACCELERATION FOCUS
→ General Warm-up:
  • Appx. 5–10 minutes light steady-state cardio (get warm).
  • Dynamic stretching/mobility as needed.
  • A-Marches—10 meters down and back.
  • High Knees with Foreleg Extension—10 meters down and back.
  • Heel Ups—10 meters down and back.
→ 1–2 40-meter build-ups: Begin jogging from a standing start and gradually build up speed until maximal speed is reached at 40 meters. Gradually slow the pace over the remaining 20 meters.
→ 3–5 10-meter sprints from a crouched start with 1 minute rest between sets.

→ 3–5 15-meter sprints from a falling start with 1.5 minutes rest between sets.

→ Cooldown.

SESSION 2: MAX VELOCITY FOCUS

→ General Warm-up:
   • Appx. 5–10 minutes light steady-state cardio (get warm).
   • Dynamic stretching/mobility as needed.
   • A-Marches—10 meters down and back.
   • High Knees with Foreleg Extension—10 meters down and back.
   • Heel Ups—10 meters down and back.

→ 1–2 40-meter build-ups: Begin jogging from a standing start and gradually build up speed until maximal speed is reached at 40 meters. Gradually slow the pace over the remaining 20 meters.

→ 2–4 flying 10s with 20-meter build-up and 3–5 minutes rest between sprints.

→ 2-4 flying 15s with 20-meter build-up and 3–5 minutes rest between sprints.

→ Cooldown.

Note: Always terminate a session when proper technique and/or max speed cannot be maintained, despite sufficient rest.

For weeks 5–6, perform the following:

SESSION 1: ACCELERATION FOCUS

→ General Warm-up:
   • Appx. 5–10 minutes light steady-state cardio (get warm).
   • Dynamic stretching/mobility as needed.

- A-Marches—10 meters down and back.
- High Knees with Foreleg Extension—10 meters down and back.
- Heel Ups—10 meters down and back.
→ 1–2 40-meter build-ups: Begin jogging from a standing start and gradually build up speed until maximal speed is reached at 40 meters. Gradually slow the pace over the remaining 20 meters.
→ 3–5 15-meter sprints from a crouched start with 1.5 minutes rest between sets.
→ 3–5 20-meter sprints from a falling start with 2 minutes rest between sets.
→ Cooldown.

SESSION 2: MAX VELOCITY FOCUS
→ General Warm-up:
- Appx. 5–10 minutes light steady-state cardio (get warm).
- Dynamic stretching/mobility as needed.
- A-Marches—10 meters down and back.
- High Knees with Foreleg Extension—10 meters down and back.
- Heel Ups—10 meters down and back.
→ 1–2 40-meter build-ups: Begin jogging from a standing start and gradually build up speed until maximal speed is reached at 40 meters. Gradually slow the pace over the remaining 20 meters.
→ 2–4 flying 15s with 20m build-up and 3–5 minutes rest between sprints.
→ 2–4 flying 20s with 30m build-up and 5–6 minutes rest between sprints.
→ Cooldown.

Note: Always terminate a session when proper technique and/or max speed cannot be maintained despite sufficient rest.

PHASE II: AGILITY TRAINING PROTOCOL

In this block, you can go from 1–2 agility sessions a week to 2–3, and move from 1–2 drills per session to 2–3 drills each session. These sessions should occur before your table tennis practice and be kept short and sweet—around 15–20 minutes including instruction time and rest periods. One way to make efficient use of your time is to intersperse serving practice during the rest periods in between drills.

In the following sections, I will list a variety of drills you can use to build multi-directional speed and agility. Since your sprinting sessions place a strong focus on linear acceleration, I recommend tailoring your agility sessions to place more of a focus on lateral movement and multi-directional speed. Pick two or three drills *total* each session and perform 3–5 minutes of work per drill. This time should include rest periods for recovery and coaching instruction. A "rep" for a given drill should stay somewhere in the 5–12 second range. Much longer than that is too difficult to maintain maximal intensity, focus, and speed.

I picked up many of these drills from legendary speed coach, Lee Taft. I've included a few basic descriptions of some of these drills to give you a rough idea of how to perform them, but I've purposefully avoided including a bunch of pictures or detailed descriptions because these drills are much better conveyed by *seeing* them in action. If a picture is worth a thousand words, a video is worth ten thousand. For access to a video library with all these drills, head to peakperformancetabletennis.com/resources.

ACTIVATION DRILLS

These are good priming drills to help you get a good feeling for the muscles that will be used during the session.

→ Bands around knees and do side walks
  • Stay level, stay low
  • Teaches propulsion forces
→ Agility ladder
  • 2–4 minutes various patterns
→ Bear crawl

LINEAR ACCELERATION DRILLS

In these drills you will be taking off in a forward direction.

Closed Drills:

→ Staggered stance take-offs
  • One knee on the ground
  • Load ankle, load hip, then take off
→ Resisted starts: (use a band for resistance)
→ Falling starts: posture drill to work on coordination
  • Feet square and together
  • Lean forward till you "fall" into the sprint
  • Must get arms and legs coordinated quickly

Open Drills:

→ Ball drops
  • Catch ball before it bounces twice
→ Partner chase

LATERAL ACCELERATION

In these drills you will be moving side to side. Remember to address both the right and the left!

Closed Drills:

→ Lateral shuffle
  • Shuffling left/right to a cone
→ Resisted lateral shuffle
  • Band around waist at first
  • Band around ribs can help stabilize shoulders and teach not to sway

Open Drills:

→ Reactionary shuffle
  • Coach is behind and says to shuffle left or right on clap
→ "Hot Feet" reactionary shuffle
  • Athlete keeps feet moving instead of planted
  • Coach stands in front and points left or right, athlete responds
  • Helps develop a better push off angle

RETREATING ACCELERATION

These drills help you learn how to move backward effectively.

Closed Drills:

→ Backpedal
  • "Nose over toes" staying low
  • Feet don't lift high, almost scraping ground
→ Band-resisted backpedal

→ "Quick Hips"
- A dissociation of the lower and upper body
- Quickly rotating hips and coming back into position with upper body staying oriented forward

→ Hip turn and "pop off"
- Quick hip turn and "pop off" as one action into a shuffle

Open Drills:

→ Hip turn and shuffle on clap
→ Hip turn ball catch
- Coach is far behind athlete
- Coach shouts "go" and athlete must turn, run, and catch ball before the second bounce

LINEAR CHANGE OF DIRECTION

Linear change of direction drills help you to learn how to effectively decelerate and *re*accelerate in the sagittal plane (forward and backward movements). As a chopper, this is something I pay special attention to because "in and out" footwork is especially important to help field drop shots from far off the table.

Closed Drills:

→ Shuttle run
- Run straight on toward a cone, plant your foot to turn and run back
- Ankle and hip joints should face the same direction and turn together

→ Decelerate to ready position
- Move forward quickly and decelerate into the ready position at the cone

Open Drills:

→ Reactive reverse
  • Athlete runs forward and must decelerate into ready position on coach's clap and then backpedal as quickly as possible
→ Partner mirroring
  • Run side by side with a partner and match movements as they stop and retreat
→ Red light/green light

LATERAL CHANGE OF DIRECTION

This is an area especially relevant for table tennis players. Being able to move quickly side-to-side is vitally important!

Closed Drills:

→ Low box "quick change" drill
  • Athlete starts with one foot up on a low box and rapidly hops laterally over the box and reaccelerates to get back to the starting position
  • You can use a band to add resistance
→ 5/5/5 Shuffle
  • Set up two cones five yards apart
  • Shuffle laterally from one cone to the other and back
→ Cone stack
  • Three cones on one side, one on the other
  • Race a partner to see who can bring back all three cones to the starting position first
→ Crossover
  • Upper body stays oriented forward, lower body runs laterally
  • If stride is short, use a band resistance to build power

Open Drills:

→ Partner mirroring
  • Face a partner and match his side-to-side movements as closely as possible
→ Ball toss and catch
  • Coach tosses balls to either side of you and you shuffle and catch before they drop
→ Ball toss and dodge
  • Coach tosses balls *at* you and you shuffle laterally to dodge

PHASE II: SAMPLE WEEKLY SCHEDULE

This training block has a lot of moving pieces, so I understand if it seems a little confusing to know how it all fits together. Here is a sample weekly schedule that shows one way everything could fit:

	Sun.	Mon.	Tues.	Wed.	Thurs.	Fri.	Sat.
A.M.	Rest	Resistance Training Day 1	Speed Session 1	Resistance Training Day 2	Speed Session 2	Resistance Training Day 3	Rest
P.M.	Rest	Agility Session 1 + Sport-Specific Practice	Sport-Specific Practice	Agility Session 2 + Sport-Specific Practice	Rest	Sport-Specific Practice	Agility Session 3 + Sport-Specific Practice

This may look like a lot, but it only comes to about five hours of physical training per week, as most sessions are fairly short. As an athlete, an investment period of one to three years dedicated to truly building up your physical capacity can result in *tremendous* physical changes. Once you've gained this extra strength, muscle, speed, and power, you can *maintain* those qualities on a much lower dose of volume and then go back to dedicating more time toward sport-specific practice. Invest early, and you can enjoy the dividends for the rest of your training career!

PHASE II: PRE-SEASON NUTRITIONAL PROTOCOL

Allow your body weight to stabilize within 1%–2% of your "fighting weight." This requires a shift toward maintenance calories and a focus on establishing enough regularity between meals to ensure you can maintain the body composition changes you made in the previous phases.

PHASE II: PSYCHOLOGICAL AND SOCIAL/EMOTIONAL SKILLS TRAINING

Here are some areas of focus during the pre-season:

→ Continue your daily meditation and visualization techniques.
→ Consider adding a daily gratitude journal to proactively improve your social and emotional well-being.
→ Work on the last two remaining steps from the building confidence graphic.
→ Use your PPR consistently during training and match play and experiment with implementing anti-choking techniques as well.

It is very important to have these skills and routines habituated before your competitive season starts. Now is the time to cement them into your game!

TAPER/TRANSITION WEEK (1 WEEK)

Before moving into your competition phase, we need to drop fatigue while *maintaining* the gains in power, speed, and agility that you've made during this phase. To achieve this, take one week to perform a taper:

→ **Resistance Training Sessions:** Reduce set count by *one* for each exercise and decrease the reps performed for each set of each exercise by *two*. Maintain the load on the bar and the intensity of effort for each movement.
→ **Agility Work:** Reduce sessions to 1–2 for the week and only perform 1–2 drills per session. Maintain speed and intensity of effort.
→ **Speed Work:** Cut volume by 50% for each session. Maintain speed and intensity of effort.

PHASE III: THE COMPETITION PERIOD (X WEEKS)

In the competition period, the primary objective of your physical training shifts from performance to maintenance. We will achieve this by slightly reducing the frequency of resistance training and keeping the intensity and volume moderate throughout the competitive season. This will ensure that you are fully recovered in between tournaments, and will minimize the risk of injury. By now, your body weight should be stabilized at an ideal point. Likewise, your psychological skills and emotional regulation protocols should also be well-rehearsed and battle-tested. The competition period is not the time to start changing things up. Trust the plan and focus on execution and refinement. The amount of time you should devote to drills/practice will depend on your competitive schedule. In general, practice should become even more specific to match play and should focus on shoring up weaknesses while maintaining your strengths as a player. Included below is a sample resistance training program which can be used during your competitive season to maintain your fitness.

PHASE III: RESISTANCE TRAINING PROTOCOL

A maintenance dose of training will be sufficient during your competitive season. Depending on your level, you may continue to make progress in the gym, but now is not the time to aggressively seek personal bests.

Day 1		
Order	Exercise	Sets x Reps
1A	Front Rotary Scoop Toss	3 x 5
1B	Lateral Bounds	3 x 5
2A	Rear-foot Elevated Split Squat	3 x 6–8 (2–3 RIR)
2B	Bench Press	3 x 6–8 (2–3 RIR)
2C	DB Row	3 x 6–8 (2–3 RIR)
3	Standing Transverse Chop	2 x 8–10 (2–3 RIR)

Day 2		
Order	Exercise	Sets x Reps
1A	Medicine Ball Slam	3 x 5 (each side)
1B	Band-Resisted Broad Jump	3 x 5
2A	Single-leg Straight-leg Deadlift	2 x 4–6 (2–3 RIR)
2B	Dumbbell Shoulder Press	2 x 10–12 (1–2 RIR)
2C	Pull-ups	2 x 10–12 (1–2 RIR)
3	Split Squat	2 x 10–12 (1–2 RIR)

Schedule:

Two sessions per week on nonconsecutive days. This can be reduced to one session during particularly busy times as this has been shown to be sufficient to maintain performance during the competitive season. [12]

PHASE III: ENERGY SYSTEMS, SPEED, AND AGILITY PROTOCOLS

Any cardiovascular conditioning should be moved to a maintenance dose schedule of 0–2 sessions per week, depending on the frequency of competitions played. Agility work can still be performed before sport-specific practice 1–2 times per week. For your speed sessions, try to maintain 1–2 sessions per week, but reduce training volume by appx. 30%–50%. The idea here is to maintain your current levels of fitness while maximizing recovery.

Pre-Season/Competitive Season Holistic Periodization Model

Training Phase	Pre-Season	Competitive Season
Focus	Power/Agility (6–8 weeks)	Maintenance/Recovery (*x* weeks)
Energy Systems	Power Endurance	Maintenance
Speed/Agility	Max Speed/Agility	Maintenance
Strength	Power/Specific Strength	Maintenance
Psychological & Social/Emotional	Maintain daily meditation and visualization techniques. Consider adding a daily gratitude journal. Continue building sports confidence. Use PPR consistently during training and match play and practice implementing anti-choking techniques.	Maintain psychological and emotional regulatory protocols. Minimize outside stressors to the extent possible and maximize rest and recovery.
Nutrition	Maintenance within +/- 1%–2% of ideal body weight	Maintenance within +/- 1%–2% of ideal body weight

PHASE IV: TRANSITION PERIOD (2—4 WEEKS)

After your competitive season ends, you should take a few weeks to relax a bit. Training should be low intensity, unstructured, and most importantly, FUN. This will give both your mind and body some much needed rest and will allow you to attack your next training block with increased focus and energy.

CONCLUDING THOUGHTS ON PERIODIZATION

What I have outlined above is only a rough model of what a holistic periodization model could look like for a table tennis player. There are many individual variables that could impact the optimal way to periodize training, so do not take what's written here as gospel. The main takeaway is that you should always have clear goals that you are working toward, and these goals need to fit together as part of a larger plan for improvement. This is the difference between *training* and merely exercising.

SECTION VI

PUTTING IT ALL TOGETHER

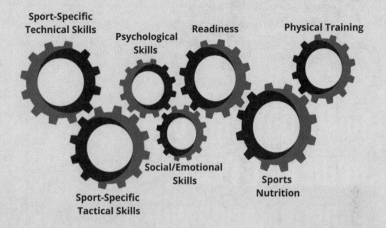

Sport-Specific Technical Skills

Psychological Skills

Readiness

Physical Training

Social/Emotional Skills

Sport-Specific Tactical Skills

Sports Nutrition

SECTION OVERVIEW

In this final section, I will provide some practical tips for what to do on the day of competition. I will also reveal some performance-enhancing strategies that have not yet been discussed in previous chapters. After that, I've included an "Expert Roundtable" chapter where I provide some exclusive insights from high-level players and coaches from around the world.

GAME DAY PROTOCOLS: ACHIEVING PEAK PERFORMANCE WHEN IT COUNTS

While much of this book is dedicated to training and nutritional strategies that prepare you in a general way for table tennis, this chapter provides specific recommendations to make sure you're performing your best on game day. I have included a list of some basic, big picture stuff as well as some more uncommon tips I've picked up from the literature regarding how to optimize performance, achieve that much coveted "flow state," and prevent choking.

STEP ONE: COME PREPARED

The first step required to achieve peak performance is coming prepared by following the holistic model of periodization outlined in this book. By following a phase-potentiated model that takes into account all the various domains covered in this book, you do 95% of the work required to perform your best. Don't expect any miracles on game day if you haven't put in the work beforehand!

That said, that last 5% can be the difference between coming out on top and losing by a narrow margin. On game day, you need to take an honest assessment of your physical, psychological, tactical, and emotional readiness and take action to address any issues. One of the key factors to take into consideration is covered in the next step.

WHAT'S IN YOUR BAG?

Part of coming prepared is making sure your table tennis bag is well stocked with all the items you need. Here's what I typically keep in my bag:

→ Racket (ideally with an identical backup one as well)
→ Extra balls
→ Rubber cleaner and sponge
→ Towels (for sweat and for the floor)
→ Fresh change of clothes (socks are especially clutch)
→ Water bottle
→ Snacks
→ Small thermos for ice
→ Notebook/pen
→ Lacrosse ball (for myofascial release)
→ Light resistance band
→ Supplements
→ Camera/tripod

STEP TWO: MANIPULATE AROUSAL TO ACHIEVE PEAK PERFORMANCE

For many males, learning to manipulate and control their arousal is a lifelong struggle. Fortunately, when talking about arousal in the arena of sports science, we are not talking about sexual arousal, but the physiological and psychological state of being alert and ready for action. To achieve peak performance, it is vital that one stays in the sweet spot of arousal levels. This is outlined by the Yerkes–Dodson law, which demonstrates that performance is poor at both low *and* high arousal levels; thus, to ensure peak performance, one must know how to both increase and decrease arousal levels during play so that one can stay within the ideal zone.

You can't force peak performance and the "flow state," but you can create the optimal environment for it to manifest. The training and preparation you undergo before the tournament is like building the infrastructure and wiring it up. Your arousal is the *electricity* that

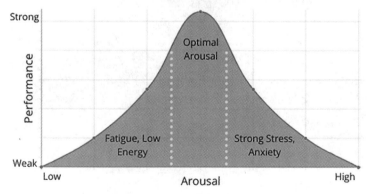

The Yerkes-Dodson Law

makes things come to life. Too little and you'll under-perform, too much and you'll fry the system.

Through past experience and training you should have a general idea of whether you are the type who generally needs to increase arousal or whether you typically need to *decrease* arousal. With this knowledge, you can take proactive steps to get yourself in the ballpark of your optimal levels. Then, as each match progresses, you can fine-tune and adjust as needed.

FUN FACT:

While we're on the subject of arousal...Ever wonder if there's any truth to the claim that having sex will negatively affect athleticism? Well, at least one study [1] suggests that it doesn't! In this study, they measured things such as grip strength, balance, reaction time, and anaerobic power and found them all to be unaffected by sexual intercourse within a 24-hour period.

STRATEGIES TO INCREASE AROUSAL

The most important thing you can do to increase your arousal and "readiness" for your first match is to show up well-rested, well-recovered, and well-fed, and then perform a thorough warm-up. Wake up the body and wake up the mind. Another way to increase arousal is to listen to some of your favorite high-energy music just before playing. There is research showing that this can have a measurable impact on performance by improving both motivation and arousal. [2–3] If you made a personal highlight reel, now is a good time to watch it. Having a friend or two around to serve as cheerleaders can also be extremely effective in keeping you amped-up emotionally.

Finally, using the strategic supplementation of caffeine + a few synergists can also help to increase arousal levels. Taking the "Looper" stack of caffeine + L-theanine + L-tyrosine is my preferred way of accomplishing this, and it really helps with achieving that "in the zone" feeling. Adding 2 mg of nicotine gum[42] on top of that can heighten arousal further and will work synergistically with the Looper stack.

STRATEGIES TO DECREASE AROUSAL

If you find yourself *too* amped-up, you may need to use strategies to bring your emotions under control. This could be before the match when you feel yourself getting a little shaky or your heart is pounding due to nerves, or *during* a match after your opponent gets a series of nets and edges and you feel your anger spiking out of control. Either way, it pays to have some methods of centering your emotions and reducing arousal.

BEFORE THE MATCH

One of the most important things you can do to calm your nerves on game day is to make sure you give yourself enough time to warm-up thoroughly and get your bearings at the location. Little things such as not knowing where the bathroom is, or not knowing which area you'll be playing in can contribute in sneaky ways to feeling overwhelmed. Feeling a little lost and/or out of sorts is *not* a good mental state right before playing!

So, arrive early. Make sure you know where the bathrooms are. Find the water fountains. Find the person in charge and make sure you know when and where you'll be playing and get set up. Once you've

---

42   Revisit the supplementation chapter for additional context and clarification regarding the use of nicotine for performance enhancement.

gotten settled, you can lean on the habits you've been practicing all along: perform a warm-up, meditate, listen to some calming music/ binaural beats, etc. One additional step you might take is developing a pre-game mantra that you can repeat to help get yourself in the right frame of mind. This one should be different from the short mantras you repeat to yourself during the game. For example, as a big sci-fi nerd, I will unironically recite the Bene Gesserit "Litany Against Fear" from Frank Herbert's *Dune*.[43]

I must not fear.

Fear is the mind-killer.

Fear is the little-death that brings total obliteration.

I will face my fear.

I will permit it to pass over me and through me.

And when it has gone past I will turn the inner eye to see its path.

Where the fear has gone there will be nothing. Only I will remain.

May be that's a little too "out there" for you. That's okay. Find something that resonates with *you*. A Bible verse, an ancient proverb, an inspiring quote from an athlete you admire, or even something you come up with yourself. The important thing is that you have something to lean on when you need it.

---

43   I did my senior thesis on *Dune* and consider it to be the greatest science fiction novel ever written.

DURING THE MATCH

During the match you will need to rely on your PPRs, positive mantras, and the deep-breathing techniques you've practiced during your meditation sessions to stay in the zone and regulate your emotional state. Remember, negative emotions slow you down! Replace negative self-talk with positive mantras and keep an eye on your breathing. Don't let it get too shallow.

An additional tip (which I picked up from Larry Hodges) is to choose a spot on a nearby wall that you can stare at to help you refocus after a mistake has been made in the game. Choose the spot before the beginning of the match and ensure it can be seen equally well regardless of which side of the table you're on. Use that spot as a cue to help you focus and begin your PPR rather than watching an "instant replay" of your mistake repeatedly in your head.

STEP THREE: CONTROL THE FLOW OF PLAY AND FIND YOUR WINNING MOMENTUM

In order to have both the time and the presence of mind to implement the strategies outlined here, you need to ensure you are taking steps to control the flow of play during a match. Research has demonstrated that taking a time-out in a negative momentum situation is an effective way to give yourself a window to recover psychologically, [4] but there are other ways to control the flow of play that you may be overlooking.

The Chinese National Team (CNT), for example, will calculate the "ball picking up" time of its top players and will identify a "winning rhythm" based on the patterns they find. In a rare video clip of the

CNT retrieved from an unlisted YouTube video, [5] the researchers for the CNT discovered that Ma Long tends to cut his ball picking-up time short in the games in which he loses. After analyzing many of his matches, the coaches found his best ball-picking time to be 31 seconds and his worst to be 17 seconds. Head coach, Li Xiaodong, noted the fluctuation in Ma Long's ball-picking time was too great and wanted him to control the flow of play better by staying closer to his winning rhythm—especially when he is falling behind in points.

The two things to take away from the above are that you should have an awareness of the pace at which you play your best, *and* you should aim for some level of consistency in maintaining that winning pace. Record your matches and take some data on your ball picking-up time. What patterns do you see? I'm not saying you should keep a running stopwatch on your wrist every match, but you should develop a sense of your ideal pacing through practice and work to maintain that during a match. Are you taking your towel breaks? If your opponent is serving, do you hold a hand up until you feel ready to receive? These are little details that can have a big impact if they are ignored!

Finally, make sure you are using your time between points productively by implementing your PPRs. Refer to the chapter on meditation for specific techniques to employ.

INTERESTING AND NOVEL PERFORMANCE BOOSTERS

In this section I will group together some easy-to-implement protocols that have some scientific support for acutely improving performance.

SLEEP INTERVENTIONS

Remember, as little as *one week* of sleep extension (adding roughly 2 hours to your habitual sleep time) can measurably improve energy levels and athletic performance. [6]

If you happen to be feeling especially tired and stressed out on game day—perhaps you slept poorly the night before because of nerves—taking a 30–45-minute nap can also acutely improve physical and cognitive performance. [7] Your priority should be getting as much sleep as possible in the week leading up to the tournament as this has the strongest evidence for improving performance, but using a strategic nap is a good back-up plan if that doesn't pan out. One of the potential drawbacks of napping is that it may negatively impact the subsequent night's sleep, but since we are interested in maximizing performance on a specific day, this is not a concern.

PRO TIP

caffeine + power nap = win.

I mentioned this tip previously in the sleep chapter, but it bears repeating. Because caffeine takes about 30 minutes to really start kicking in, if you take a short power nap immediately after drinking a caffeinated beverage, you can take advantage of that window to get some sleep in. The caffeine and the nap work synergistically, with the caffeine helping to eliminate that post-nap grogginess!

Finally, if your schedule allows it, building an extra day into your schedule as a buffer can help prevent things like jet lag and the *first-night effect* (see the "Sleep" chapter for more information) from negatively impacting your sleep and performance.

HEMISPHERE-SPECIFIC PRIMING

Is there anything more frustrating than choking and blowing an important match? If you're anything like me, this is an occurrence that is all too common. Fortunately, there are several science-based protocols you can implement to help reduce instances of choking: A 2017 systematic review of 47 studies found the most effective choking interventions to be PPRs, quiet eye training, left-hand contractions, and acclimatization training. [8] I've touched on PPRs, quiet eye training, and acclimatization training in other chapters. If you've done your due diligence, these are all things you should have practiced and rehearsed ahead of time. We have not, however, talked yet about left-hand contractions.

Left-hand contractions, or "hemisphere-specific priming," is a technique where you squeeze a soft ball in your left hand for 30 seconds (or simply clench your fist). Amazingly, this simple practice has been shown to stabilize or even improve performance while under pressure. The theory is that by squeezing the left hand, you potentiate activation of the *right* hemisphere of the brain. This is beneficial because a highly active right hemisphere of the brain is associated with improved motor performance.

Will this have a dramatic impact on your game? Probably not. But when used in conjunction with all the other techniques, it may make a small difference. Plus, how hard is it to squeeze on a soft ball or clench your fist for 30 seconds during a timeout or in between games? Might as well give it a shot!

NECK COOLING

There is some direct research on table tennis players [9] as well as more general research on aerobic and anaerobic exercise [10] that shows using an ice bag to cool your neck can lead to greater performance. In the study on table tennis players, they used an ice bag to cool the neck in between games for 1 minute and it resulted in significantly higher performance scores. One theory put forth by one of the authors is that the cooling effect seems to "trick" the brain into thinking the body is less fatigued than it really is.

The effect scaled with intensity, so if you are undergoing a particularly intense bout (or playing in hot/humid conditions), this protocol can be even more effective. The authors of this study recommend using this practice both during matches and during training, and I agree. Not only will the improved quality of practice lead to better match results, it also pays to experiment with the intervention first before trying it out during an important tournament. I typically bring a Ziplock bag with ice and keep it in a small, insulated thermos. It fits easily in my table tennis bag and the ice stays frozen for hours.

FOAM ROLLING

A 2019 meta-analysis [11] showed that post-exercise foam rolling can have a minor but *immediately beneficial* effect on recovery of speed and strength while reducing the perception of muscle pain. So, if you've got some downtime in between matches during a tournament, you might want to try foam rolling a bit to help you recover more quickly for your next game. Make sure you spend some time getting acquainted with foam rolling *before* you try this protocol, however. If you don't know what you're doing, foam rolling can actually cause some soreness if you're too heavy-handed with it!

CHAPTER SUMMARY:

→ It is essential to learn how to control and manipulate your level of arousal during important matches—both too much and too little arousal are problematic.

→ Supplementation, high-energy music, a good warm-up, and the emotional support of your teammates can be used to increase arousal.

→ Deep breathing, positive mantras, and PPRs can help decrease arousal if your emotions are running too high.

→ Control the flow of play! Be aware of your "ball picking-up time" and adjust it to optimal rates. Take your towel breaks. Don't let your opponent rush you.

→ Taking a time-out in a negative momentum situation is often a good idea.

→ Inserting some extra sleep around important matches may boost performance.

→ Hemisphere-specific priming has been shown to potentially stabilize performance while under pressure. This can be used in between points and/or during time-outs.

→ Neck cooling can acutely improve performance—particularly if you are prone to overheating.

→ Foam rolling after a tough match may help you recover a bit more quickly for the next one.

→ It may feel like catching lightning in a bottle, but achieving peak performance is well within your reach if you train hard, prepare well, and trust yourself!

EXPERT ROUNDTABLE

"For every expert, there is an equal and opposite expert."

—*Arthur C. Clarke*

As part of the researching phase for this book, I consumed dozens of interviews of current and former world-class players, read every scientific study on table tennis I could get my hands on, and consulted with some of the world's top trainers and sport scientists. I also created a questionnaire of my own that I sent out to a select group of coaches and players. My aim with this questionnaire was both to fill in some specific gaps in my own research, but also to get my finger on the pulse of current perspectives regarding some of the topics covered in this book. In this chapter, you will find the interview questions I sent along with the responses and some light commentary on my part.

The goal of this chapter is not to put any one person up on a pedestal. It's an opportunity to identify trends and commonalities between the answers given by these high performers. Success leaves clues, but you still need to piece those clues together in a coherent way for *you*.

LIST OF EXPERTS

LARRY HODGES

Larry Hodges is a man who needs no introduction, but I'll highlight a few of his accomplishments all the same. Larry is a USATT Hall of Fame member and 2018 Lifetime Achievement Award Winner. He has coached over 250 gold medalists at the US Junior Nationals and Junior Olympics, and he opened the first full-time training center in the United States, The Maryland Table Tennis Center. As a player, he has ranked as high as #18 in the United States and has achieved a 2292 USATT rating. He is most known, perhaps, for his prolific writing career with over 800 published coaching articles and eight instructional books.

YANGYANG JIA

Yangyang Jia was a Chinese National Second Level Athlete and is currently a Butterfly sponsored table tennis coach with a popular YouTube channel (yangyang TT). Her training videos break down techniques and mechanics of table tennis using simple explanations.

ELI BARATY

Eli Baraty is a former top ten English player and has played at the semi pro level in Germany, France, and Belgium. As a coach, he has helped produce over 20 players for England, including four England number one ranked players. He created the United Table Tennis Coaching Team and has a YouTube channel as well (eBaTT).

SETH PECH

Seth Pech has competed in international tournaments such as the Swedish Open, the Belgium Open, and the Finland Open. He has also had a few competitive wins in his time playing in the Swedish leagues. His highest USATT rating is 2494. His YouTube channel, "PechPong TT," is a hidden gem with lots of little-known tips and detailed match breakdowns. I highly recommend his "Tips No One Tells You" series.

MATT HETHERINGTON

Matt Hetherington is a former member of the New Zealand National Team and an ITTF Level 2 Coach. In 2017–2018, he became the New Zealand Open Doubles Champion. He currently works for JOOLA in the United States.

RICHARD MCAFEE

Richard McAfee was the Competition Manager for Table Tennis for the 1996 Atlanta Olympic Games. He was an inductee for the USA

Table Tennis "Hall of Fame," and he is the former US Table Tennis National Coaching Chairman. He is also the author of the popular book, *Table Tennis: Steps to Success*. He has trained more than 1,600 coaches and 4,500 athletes in over 30 countries.

JOEY COCHRAN

Joey Cochran is a five-time member of the United States team and a two-time U22 Men's Single Champion. His highest earned USATT rating is 2566. He has a growing YouTube channel called "Table Tennis Junkie" where he shares training tips and his competitive matches.

ALOIS ROSARIO

Alois Rosario is one of the creators of the informative YouTube channel, "Pingskills," and is a former Olympic and Paralympic coach for Australia. As a player, he has won two state men's singles titles and two national doubles titles.

SAMSON DUBINA

Samson Dubina is the top ranked player in Ohio and has been ranked within the top three in the country. He is a US National-Level Certified Coach and is the multi-time winner of the USATT Technology Coach of the Year award. He currently owns and operates the Samson Dubina Table Tennis Academy in Akron, Ohio.

QUESTIONS

Is there a particular change to your lifestyle (sleep, exercise, nutrition, etc.) that you've made in the past that seems to have had an outsized impact? If so, what was it?

Larry Hodges

I don't play well after a meal, so I made sure never to eat a full meal unless I had at least two hours afterwards to digest. That really meant 2.5 hours since I also needed to warm-up. If I had to play a lot of matches without a long break, I'd just snack continuously on granola bars, bananas, and similar items.

Yangyang Jia

Yes, sleep, exercise and nutrition are all very important. I usually sleep for 7–8 hours per day, so I will have energy to do daily tasks. I try to maintain regular exercise 40–60 minutes of cardio, and I train my abs four times per week. I am also really careful about the food I eat every day. All of that contributes to the healthy lifestyle.

Eli Baraty

I'm very much a believer in holistic methods: I focus on mindset, sleep, food, physical, and technical. If I had to pick one, it would be mindset—learning how to control the mind enables you to achieve what many think (even yourself) "is not possible" and makes it possible.

Seth Pech

Not any major changes. I would say it has been more a matter of reducing things that were not helping me optimize my performance, and then *increasing* the existing things that were. As I became older, I more easily found the things that were harming my performance—certain foods and sleeping habits—and I started mentally encouraging myself more. These are the things I started tweaking as well as a few others.

I will say that building my body while I was in Sweden was a very smart choice; it improved my power in my shots a great deal and gave me a lot more stability. It also helped me mentally because before I was always forcing my shots to get the power I wanted out of them. After working out though, I found I was able to hit the ball at my desired speed while only using 80% which let me focus on other aspects of my game. I think this has been the biggest change I made that had a good impact.

Matt Hetherington

Yes, I changed to an almost totally plant-based diet and everything has been amazing. I have more energy, spend less time bloating after meals, and am in much better health and physical shape.

Richard McAfee

Nutrition and exercise have always been key elements for me.

Joey Cochran

I love all food and my mom is an excellent cook, so I would eat whatever she made and a LOT of it. Consistency was key for me. I had a routine for practice and exercise that seemed to work so I stuck with it.

Alois Rosario

Weights program, Qigong, and sports psychology.

[Note from Kevin: Qigong (pronounced *chee*-gong) is a Chinese form of exercise that combines meditation and controlled breathing with various movement patterns and postures.]

Samson Dubina

I now give myself a two-hour window between when I wake up until the time of my workout. For example, if I'm going to work out at 9 a.m., I need to be up and walking around by 7 a.m. This helped me avoid many injuries in the last six years.

What are your "go to" foods on important tournament days? What do you snack on and drink between matches?

Larry Hodges

I always ate a big breakfast before a tournament, often pancakes, waffles, or French toast. I'd make sure to do it well before I had to play, meaning I sometimes had to get up extra early so I'd have at least two hours to digest before I had to warm-up. The rest of the day I mostly snacked on granola bars and bananas. If I had a long break (2.5 hours or more), then I'd eat a regular meal—spaghetti when possible!

Yangyang Jia

I usually don't eat a lot before tournaments, definitely no oily foods. I will have an energy drink or eat a banana—even though I don't like bananas. But those are good things to keep you energetic during the whole tournament.

Eli Baraty

As a coach I'm more relaxed about my food habits, but I do enforce healthy diets upon my players. This means shakes and smoothies full of organic and healthy nutrients, plenty of fruits and vegetables, and staying away from meat and milk products.

Seth Pech

To be honest, I don't exactly have a go to, I would say I typically leading up to a tournament like to get a lot of carbs in the form of rice, potatoes, and pastas. I also try to eat many fruits and vegetables leading up as I find these make me sharper overall. I try to eat some protein but I've never been a big meat eater. I like fish and beans to fill in those gaps. During tournaments, it ranges, sometimes I am very hungry and I go get a sub sandwich in between matches, and sometimes I just snack on nuts or small bits of carbs. I would say the one thing I cannot go without is my fruits and fruit juice during tournaments. I tend to have blood sugar drops after an intense game or match and the banana or apple really keeps me above water.

Matt Hetherington

Lots of water—more than most people think is enough. Nothing too heavy on the food front, just light small snacks like Clif bars, etc.

Richard McAfee

Water and slow digesting carbohydrates.

Joey Cochran

I like to eat a big breakfast and then munch on either carrots or bananas throughout the day while I compete.

Alois Rosario

Fruit buns.

Samson Dubina

Raw oats with fresh fruit and milk in the morning. Pasta with grilled chicken for lunch. Tons of healthy snacks between matches.

Do you regularly take any supplements? If so, what are they?

Larry Hodges

Just regular vitamins.

Yangyang Jia

Yes, some Vitamin D for bone support.

Eli Baraty

I take a multivitamin and biotin.

Seth Pech

I take a few supplements. I have worked with a doctor to help me keep my energy levels up. I take a spoon of pure Glutamine every day, as well as a multivitamin that has pretty much everything with an emphasis in iron. I take vitamin D daily as well as zinc and fish oil.

Matt Hetherington

Yes, I'm fortunate to be sponsored by Touchstone Essentials which is a vegan organic supplement company. I take organic vitamin D and also Wellspring which is a ginger/turmeric combo as well as super green juice shakes and green protein.

Richard McAfee

Multi-purpose vitamin and Vitamin D.

Joey Cochran

No.

Alois Rosario

No.

Samson Dubina

No.

What does a typical week of physical training look like for you during the off-season? Describe cardio, resistance training, mobility work, etc.

Larry Hodges

When I was in training, I did long distance running, sprints, jump rope, and lots of shadow practice. I also did pushups, sit-ups, and "bunny hops." When I got older, I did weight lifting. I should have done the weight lifting earlier.

Yangyang Jia

I don't train as much as before, but I was running for 5 miles every day to keep my physical condition when I was younger.

Eli Baraty

I don't compete anymore, but for me personally my cardio is playing table tennis, and I hit the gym three times a week—30 minutes, hard blast. For my players, we focus on fast-twitch training, endurance, and some strength training. This is all done according to their personal tournament schedules (off-season strength and endurance, etc.).

Seth Pech

The structure of my training varies depending on a few factors. If I am training a lot of table tennis, then the physical training outside of the hall is going to be less. When I am not training, I like to [do] a lot more physical preparation outside of table tennis—things like biking, swimming, frisbee, and badminton are a few examples. I try and stay away from running long distances because I don't think I have the proper technique to avoid damage to my knees and legs which is the most important part of the body in table tennis!

I try to stretch before and after practice always because I believe that is what will keep me going for longer in the future. I like to play other sports as much as I can. Something about playing other sports helps me gain stability in different areas and give me more body awareness when preforming table tennis strokes. Plus, playing other sports gives me a huge workout because it does not feel like a chore and I can play for longer and more frequently! When I go to the gym, I try to keep it simple and train all the different parts of the body. I don't want to over train one area. I have stayed away from maxing out training because I do not have the technique for that right now, and the last thing I need is an injury!

Matt Hetherington

Approximately 5 days a week of training: 3 days of cardio and weights on the days in between. Lot of focus on legs and core on weight days, and on speed and stamina on cardio days. I use resistance bands frequently also.

Richard McAfee

I am a 70-year-old coach, so most of my personal training revolves around maintaining mobility and balance.

Joey Cochran

There wasn't really ever an off-season. I trained a minimum of five times per week throughout the year and tried to compete in at least two tournaments per month. I did mostly cardio and interval training at the table and worked on my legs off the table by either running, biking, sprints, squats, sled pushes, or any other way I could find to build up my legs.

PEAK PERFORMANCE TABLE TENNIS

Alois Rosario

I jog four to five times per week and perform two strength and conditioning sessions.

Samson Dubina

Jogging with my kids pushing the triple jogging stroller. Also some occasional plyometrics.

The plastic balls play slower and spin a bit less. How do you think this will impact the training of current and future players? How has it impacted you?

Larry Hodges

Because it takes slightly more power to loop the ball with the same speed and spin as before, it slightly favors stronger players and those who do physical training, especially weight training.

However, the slower ball makes it easier to react to these power shots.

Yangyang Jia

Every sport has its certain rule, if you want to play it, you just need to follow the rule and try to adjust yourself to get used to it. It didn't really impact me a lot as I was training to adjust the change all the time. You just need more practice.

Eli Baraty

Slower? A little, yes. Less spin? No! It has the same spin amount but the spin reduces in rotation quicker than the celluloid balls. Reduced spin does have an effect! It means by the time the ball has reached your side it has less spin. What does this mean for training and coaching purpose?

It means we must focus on developing speed and power over spin.

Years prior, the main focus would be on high quality (energy) meaning plenty of spin. Spin is still a huge factor but it has gone down the pecking order due to the change in equipment.

As a coach, it has not impacted me but it's challenging for players who don't like change. I love change and I have always looked at innovation and different ways of learning and coaching. My players are not given or allowed to be comfortable at any given time. So, when the change came, all my players saw it as another day in Eli's unique training methods, meaning here's a new challenge.

Seth Pech

I think the ball change has put a lot more emphasis on physical training. Players are much more consistent now because of the reduction of speed and spin which means the game is more physical. I have enjoyed the impact because I have always enjoyed rallies and the physical side of the game.

Matt Hetherington

It won't impact them because most current upcoming and future players will not have the old ball to compare to. It did impact me for a while but I have adapted and adjusted now.

Richard McAfee

Table tennis, for some time, has been moving toward a more power sport with fewer styles of play. The plastic balls have accelerated movement in this direction. With less spin and the higher bounce of the plastic ball, attacking strokes now put the emphasis on forward movement with more direct (force) contact. With less spin, serve *returns* are now a bigger weapon than the serves themselves. Counter-attack play has become a more popular game strategy with half-long serves and returns often used to set up counter-attack tactics. The result of all of this is more physical training is now required with a focus on the lower body and power development.

Joey Cochran

The plastic ball dramatically impacted table tennis by reducing the spin. It's a lot easier to hit the ball flat and focus on power because the high spin balls aren't really a threat any more. My forehand has evolved quite a bit since the change. I used to add a lot more arc on it with lots of spin, but now it's easier and more effective to just power through the ball.

Alois Rosario

Not too much.

Samson Dubina

The new ball bounces higher and shorter, which really favors players close to the table using powerful shots. So, more explosive power is needed. I can see more exercises like the "Tornado Ball" being used in the future.

What are the biggest mistakes and myths you see in table tennis training? What are the biggest wastes of time?

Larry Hodges

One big mistake is players often wait too long before learning to loop, become ingrained as hitters, and so then have to undo bad habits. It's better to learn to loop as soon as you have a decent forehand and backhand.

Two other problems are related. Some players develop tricky serves, often deep, and rely on them so much they don't learn to attack effectively except against weak returns—and so they struggle against stronger players who, after seeing them a few times, return these serves more effectively, usually attacking them. The other extreme are players who develop mostly short serves that allow them to follow up with an attack, but don't develop any truly tricky serves (usually long serves), and so they don't get any "free" points. You need both types of serves. The higher the level, the more you need to rely on third-ball serves, but even at those levels, you can get a free point or two if you develop a tricky serve and use it sparingly.

Biggest wastes of time are players who only practice regular counter-looping, with both players off the table, topspin to topspin. In a match, the first counterloop is usually against an opponent's loop from close to the table, often against backspin—which comes out very differently, and so they aren't used to it. When they have trouble with it, what do they do? Most continue to practice regular counterlooping instead of starting the rally with one of them looping against backspin from close to the table.

[Note from Kevin: I feel personally attacked on this one. How dare he criticize my favorite drill!]

Yangyang Jia

I believe the biggest mistake is not being able to find your personal weakness and just following a general training exercise. That really is a waste of time. Because everyone has their different weaknesses and strengths, we all have to set our own plan and practice on our weaknesses.

Eli Baraty

Footwork myths: *"You don't need to move in table tennis!"*

Our sport is possibly the most technical sport on the planet and if our feet are not in the right place for a particular shot, the quality is reduced dramatically.

The biggest mistake and waste of time? Lack of eye knowledge.

95% of coaches try to correct players technically, and more often than not, it's a *visual* disability. We all use our eyes differently and perceive the world differently through our eyes. For example, all coaches tell their players to hit the ball in front of their body when playing a forehand topspin (early timing). Technically, that's correct but it also depends on which eye is stronger or predominantly used when the ball is approaching us.

For example, as a left-eye dominant person myself, I time the ball a little later on my forehand. That millisecond enables me to connect better with the ball. When I try to connect earlier, especially on a slow backspin ball, I do on occasion have an "air ball" because my weaker eye is being asked to work.

[Note from Kevin: Eli is left-handed.]

In simple terms, we must understand how our eyes work to give us the best possible development as individuals.

Here's a quick trick to find your dominant eye:

1. Hold your hands out in front of you and make a window with your thumbs and forefingers as if you were framing a shot.

2. Keeping both eyes open, find a distant object and center it within this "window."

3. Close your left eye.

4. If the object stays centered, you are *right eye* dominant.

5. If the object jumps out of center, your *left eye* is dominant.

My biggest gripe is when coaches coach in systems which are generic instead of tailoring the approach to the individual: Monkeys climb trees, fish swim, cheetahs run fast. We are all different and require specific, tailor-made systems, not generic systems. For me, that's the biggest mistake in table tennis.

Seth Pech

Training without purpose has to be the biggest one. From my experience as a coach and a player, if you are doing something that is well thought-out for *5 minutes*, it will be more valuable than doing something without an exact purpose for 10 hours or more. I have seen large improvements in my students and myself from being very specific. Also, being too "outcome oriented" is a problem. Sometimes I miss a shot but I performed the task perfectly. Something *else* went wrong which caused me to miss. I have learned to address that with full focus later. In the moment, I try not to get upset with missing, but instead be satisfied that I was able to do what I was aiming for in the first place. There are a hundred factors that go into landing a ball on the table and to get upset because you messed one of those up is crazy! Too many people get upset or discouraged from missing the table and should be more focused on something that they have control over and is tangible/doable!

Matt Hetherington

A common myth I see is that simply training a lot makes you good. Training with *purpose and intention* makes you good. Doing the same drills over and over are helpful but ultimately a waste of time. To improve, you need to be specific and have a plan and structure for your improvement.

Richard McAfee

In many countries, a big problem is a lack of understanding by athletes and coaches on how to practice effectively. There is often a lack of knowledge with how to plan effective lesson plans for teaching and training tactics and strategy and also how to plan training cycles to "peak" an athlete for major competitions.

[Note from Kevin: Bingo! Hence, this book!]

Joey Cochran

One of the biggest mistakes I find is that people tend to play way too many matches in training. There is a time and place for practice matches but a lot of people go directly into match play after warm-up.

Alois Rosario

Regular training drills for too long.

Samson Dubina

More practice! More practice! If you just keep making the same mistakes without any thought about it, you won't get to a high level. The "game changer" is getting good coaching and listening and applying what you learned.

What training/game-play mistakes are common, even at the Pro level?

Larry Hodges

The three biggest mistakes players make on tournament days are. . .

1.   Not arranging a practice partner in advance.

2.   Not warming-up serves.

3.   Not warming-up receives.

Yangyang Jia

Getting distracted sometimes during training or games. Everyone loses their focus sometimes, and it's hard to keep 100% focus during the whole game. We need to practice that too.

Eli Baraty

Receive of service.

Seth Pech

Too many elite players suffer from burnout. It happens to everyone and to find the line is very difficult. You can see when a player is really firing on all cylinders and one who just wants to go back to the room and sleep. Finding the balance between training and mental energy/motivation is something that is very individual. It's one's own quest to figure themselves out and what makes them play to the best of their ability.

Matt Hetherington

Players doing drills that they are comfortable with and avoiding drills they don't like doing or aren't good at.

Richard McAfee

Lack of adaptability to their opponent's tactics. This is often due to a lack of tactical training resulting in a player not having enough "tools" to make the needed adjustments in a match situation.

Joey Cochran

One of the biggest mistakes in table tennis is that people don't take advantage of the first attack when it's available. You always have to look to attack and go for it when it's there.

Alois Rosario

Serving long too often and flicking returns long.

Samson Dubina

Lack of discipline. Often they feel unmotivated to train hard and their discipline isn't good during the tournament—for example, going out drinking until 4 a.m. then playing the final of a Pro Tour the next day.

What are the biggest mistakes novices make when serving or practicing serving?

Larry Hodges

1. Rapid-fire serving instead of taking your time and making each serve a quality serve.

2. Lack of awareness of the ball's entire route, include where it bounces on both sides of the table.

3. Not accelerating into the ball for maximum spin.

Yangyang Jia

For beginners, they usually don't really know what kind of serve they did in the game, their serves lack purpose. A good serve is always matched with good planning. If I serve a side-topspin, mostly like I will be ready to attack on the following ball.

Eli Baraty

They don't break things down or they do the same movement over and over again and expect a different result. They try to emulate a cool service that they see pros doing and think like magic it should be quick and easy to learn!

Seth Pech

There are a couple. First and foremost, I think that when a beginner learns to serve, they need to learn how to touch the different sides of the ball as well as at different heights. If they can master that first, then serving different serves with different spins becomes A LOT easier. Secondly, I think that a lack of imagination and willingness to fail comes next. It's okay if you whiff the ball while trying to do your desired motion! Just go for it and you will learn a lot faster that way. My next tip is to "lose the table." You can learn to spin the ball and touch it correctly without the pressure of hitting it onto a table. I have practiced many new serve concepts on my living room floor!

Matt Hetherington

Again, not having intention. Service practice must be disciplined and not a mindless repetition activity. You have to focus on one element of a serve and engage in improving it by analyzing how it can get better. Repetition is only part of the process.

Richard McAfee

Not putting enough emphasis on spin production and control of the placement of the serve. Often a novice will "walk through" serve practice without putting the needed focus and effort in to improving each serve.

Joey Cochran

Novices tend to serve long way too much. Having a good short serve is crucial if you want to make it to the top level.

Alois Rosario

Too repetitive and without purpose.

Samson Dubina

They often focus on quantity (serving 60 balls/min) instead of quality.

Do you have a plan to help you get to your best-focused state? If so, what is it?

Larry Hodges

I always think back to my best matches, and get into that mental state. For me, I usually go back to a win over 2500+ Rey Domingo, where everything was so easy—the ball traveled in slow motion and I could do anything. It's purely mental.

Yangyang Jia

My only plan is to spend more time practicing.

Eli Baraty

Yes, of course I do! But if I tell you, I'd have to kill you (joking)!

I have a routine (and I stick to it religiously) that gives me the best chance to get into my zone more often than not.

Seth Pech

I have found that my focus is derived from my competitive nature. I used to think of that as a bad thing because I thought others would not enjoy practicing or training with me since I always wanted to dominate. But when I go to a tournament really wanting to win, I find myself playing much better because I am more willing to do the things that will win me points. I do basically anything that gets me feeling more competitive. Things like music, sleep, and watching things that inspire me. If you look at some of the most decorated athletes, you will find one common thread: they (and their peers) would say they are VERY competitive! Think Michael Jordan, Tiger Woods, Roger Federer, and Tom Brady—some most well-known athletes ever. The competitive switch has no "off mode." It's always on!

Matt Hetherington

Usually just breathe slowly and try and let go of any expectation or pressure.

Richard McAfee

As a coach, it is important that I give my athletes the mental tools they need and incorporate mental practice into the athlete's training sessions. While I give a variety of such tools to all my athletes, each athlete will reach into his/her "tool box" to select the tools that work best for them.

Joey Cochran

I like to watch my opponents play before my match with them so I have an idea of what to expect. I especially watch their serves to make sure I'm not surprised by anything during the match. I'll also create a game plan with my coach before the match to help me stay focused on what I need to do.

Alois Rosario

Good pre-game routine and good pre-point routines.

Samson Dubina

The Think Circle—see website.

[Note from Kevin: Here is a brief description taken from the article on his website[44]: "Between points, step back about 4–6 feet away from the table and draw an imaginary circle around yourself and collect your thoughts in your think circle." This can be a great addition to your personal PPR.]

What mental tools do you use under pressure?

Larry Hodges

I think about my best matches of the past against a player with a similar style, and get into that mental frame of mind. I also like to

---

44   https://samsondubina.com/coaching/think-circle

step back and just stare at something on the wall for ten seconds or so, to clear the mind. I also have a "go to" phrase that helps me play well—"Push yourself!" I'll say that over and over, especially as a match gets close. To me, "Push yourself!" means clear your mind and react instantly to everything.

Yangyang Jia

Every time I go through a tough time, I would tell myself two sentences: "Be tough, handling it!" and "All in, no regrets."

Eli Baraty

Breathing techniques, verbal and visual (in my mind) communication to myself, and physical triggers.

Seth Pech

I like to take pressure off by telling myself to do my best and to not worry about the outcome. When I have a big lead, I like to imagine that *I* am the one losing and have to make a comeback; this one helps me because I tend to go for crazy shots in an attempt to finish the game quickly when I'm ahead. If I am down, I try to build a comeback with my serves. Say the score is 8–4. I will think that if I can get both points with my serve and then one of theirs, I will be only two points down. Then I can get two more points with my serve and it's 9–9. I'm back in it!

This gives me a roadmap for the comeback. Instead of seeing a mountain of points that I have to win, I'm actually "allowed" to lose a few. Lastly I think it's really important to have a plan. If you can stick to the plan, you will win. This gets the job done when the pressure is really high and the game goes deep into the fifth. I say to myself or my students, "stick to the plan," and it helps give a thread to follow to the victory as opposed to being stranded in the middle of nowhere with nothing to guide you mentally.

Matt Hetherington

Towel breaks every six points. Control the pace of the game to stay focused, pressure your opponent more, or to calm yourself.

Richard McAfee

For me personally, breathing for relaxation and visualization.

Joey Cochran

I always try to have a plan. Everybody gets nervous but I find that if I focus on what I'm trying to do and the strategy of the match that the nerves go away.

Alois Rosario

Good pre-game routine and good pre-point routines.

Samson Dubina

The Think Circle.

If you were to train me for 12 weeks for a table tennis tournament and had a million dollars on the line, what would the training look like? What if I trained for 8 weeks?

Larry Hodges

It would depend on the player's fitness and technical level. But weight training would be huge, as would serve and receive. I'd focus on making the player's strengths overpowering (including practicing whatever it takes to get them into play), and either improve the weaknesses or find ways to avoid them in matches.

Yangyang Jia

Ha ha, interesting question. I think the first thing would be to define your problems and your goal at that tournament. Then set the plan to see what we can change only in those 12 or 8 weeks. Maybe I would focus more on the game strategies practice.

Eli Baraty

First analysis—I would vigorously analyse your game—in and out! Footwork, technical, mental, physical, lifestyle, and I would see how you function under pressure. I would speak to you about each element and we would collectively discuss a vision and plan to be implemented in the time frame we have.

We would work on our plan and deviate if need be. As the event came closer, we would start focusing on your strengths to develop confidence, physically and mentally. Throughout the whole time of working together, we would implement routines and rituals to enforce a culture and set a strong foundation.

Then we go enjoy the moment. The outcome is for us to experience as winners or learn by failure.

Seth Pech

If I were to train you for 12 weeks, I would do a lot of studying first. I think it's important to understand what a player has going for him and what he or she does not. Finding the strengths in one's game and then making that part of the game come out more by using serves and serve receives is the fastest way to improve. It's the best roadmap to reach your highest level. Not everyone is cut out to play like Ma Long, and trying to play like him will not give you the chance to reach your highest level. I think a coach has to have a special eye to see the hidden talents a player has or could be using. I can say that if we trained, we would expose you to a lot of tournament play and then review the footage. This is a way of not going too far off course, of finding what works and where we would need to go next.

Matt Hetherington

I would not focus on any techniques or make any changes. My best option would be to formulate a big focus on match play drills and practice matches and constantly evaluate performance. Tactics, mental game, and maintenance of technical and physical skills would be my process. With just 8 weeks you have to take the foundations that are already there and prepare them best for competition.

Richard McAfee

First thing would be to work with you to set goals for the tournament. I would then do a full evaluation of your current level to understand where we are starting from. Then I would work with you to set a list of objectives to accomplish within our training and preparation for the tournament. Based on this list of objectives and on the time available, I would prepare a written training cycle plan for the number of weeks. The plan would move you forward week by week to "peak" technically, tactically, psychologically, and physically on the day of the tournament. This is the overall process that is used to prepare an athlete for an event.

Joey Cochran

Twelve weeks isn't much time to prepare for a tournament with a million bucks on the line, but first we'd have to figure out what your strengths and weaknesses are. We'd also want to know who and what level your opponents are so we have an idea of what serves to practice and have a general idea of what to expect from your opponents. We'd probably work on mostly technical training while at the table and physical training away from the table. Table tennis is both highly technical and highly physical so you'll need both. However, with that short of a time to prepare I think it would be best to use most of your table time learning the techniques and strategies.

Alois Rosario

Lots of open drills with decision making.

Samson Dubina

Move to Ohio. I would coach you about 9 hours/day. . . 3 sessions of 3 hours each. Mainly on decision making skills and coaching you on match play against different players. Also, a huge theme would be serve return.

NEXT STEPS

"Great things are not done by impulse, but by a series of small things brought together; and great things are not something accidental, but must certainly be willed."

—*Van Gogh*

This book is a distillation of what I believe is the most relevant science for table tennis players looking to improve their performance. Whether you're a serious athlete looking to leave no stone unturned, or a coach looking for evidence-based guidelines for advising athletes, I hope this is a resource which you can return to many times. Table tennis is an amazing sport. I may not always agree with every decision the ITTF has made, but they certainly got one thing right: table tennis is for all, for LIFE.

TAKE YOUR GAME TO THE NEXT LEVEL!

For a needs-analysis and performance assessment, plus fully customized programming, and nutrition, you can apply for coaching or book a consultation at **https://peakperformancetabletennis.com/coaching**

RUN A TRAINING CAMP OR COACH A TEAM?

Don't let the physical and nutritional sides of table tennis be just an afterthought! Set your training camp apart by hiring a qualified professional to run targeted sessions for your players:

→ Advanced Sports Nutrition
→ Warm-Ups/Activation Drills
→ Strength Training Primer
→ Power Development
→ Speed and Agility Work
→ Recovery Tactics
→ Energy Systems Training
→ And More!

One of my primary passions is teaching and I love working with players hands-on. If you would like to book me to supplement a training camp, work with a team directly, or speak at an event, you can do so at the following address:

https://peakperformancetabletennis.com/contact

REFERENCES

A NEW ERA

1. Lee, M, Ozaki, H, & Goh, W. (2019). Speed and spin differences between the old celluloid versus new plastic table tennis balls and the effect on the kinematic responses of elite versus sub-elite players. *International Journal of Racket Sport Science,* 1: 26–36.

2. Kondrřic, M, Zagatto, A, & Sekulić, D. (2013). The Physiological Demands of Table Tennis: A Review. *Journal of Sports Science & Medicine*, 12(3): 362–370.

3. Kondric, Miran & Sekulic, Damir & Furjan-Mandić, Gordana. (2010). Substance Use and Misuse Among Slovenian Table Tennis Players. *Substance use & misuse*. 45. 543–53. 10.3109/10826080903452553.

4. Michael, M, (January 3, 2019). *A Day in the Life of a Pro Player*, *TableTennisDaily*. [Online video]. Available at https://youtu.be/rB-AYsb5e00. Accessed May 2021.

TAPPING INTO THE MATRIX:
IMPROVE YOUR TABLE TENNIS WITH RAPID LEARNING

1. Soderstrom, NC, & Bjork, RA. (2015). Learning Versus Performance: An Integrative Review. *Perspectives on Psychological Science*, 10(2): 176–199.

2. Adams, JA, & Reynolds, B. (1954). Effect of shift in distribution of practice conditions following interpolated rest. *Journal of Experimental Psychology*, 47(1): 32–36.

2a. Branscheidt, M., Kassavetis, P., Anaya, M., Rogers, D., Huang, H.D., Lindquist, M.A., & Celnik, P. (2019). Fatigue induces long-lasting detrimental changes in motor-skill learning. *eLife, 8, e40578.*

3. Shea, JB, & Morgan, RL, (1979). Contextual Interference Effects on the Acquisition, Retention, and Transfer of a Motor Skill. *Journal of Experimental Psychology: Human Learning and Memory*, 5(2): 179–87.

4. Ahmadvand, R, Kiani, S, & Shojae, M. (2016). The effect of mass & distributed practice on performance and learning of discrete simple and complex skills in volleyball. *Turkish Journal of Kinesiology*, 2(3): 49–55.

5. Safari, I, & Suherman, A, & Ali, M. (2017). The Effect of Exercise Method and Hand-Eye Coordination Towards the Accuracy of Forehand Topspin in Table Tennis. *IOP Conference Series: Materials Science and Engineering*, 180.

6. Ali, A, Fawver, B, Kim, J, Fairbrother, J, & Janelle, CM. (2012). Too much of a good thing: random practice scheduling and self-control of feedback lead to unique but not additive learning benefits. *Frontiers in Psychology*, 3: 503.

7. OOAK Forum Interview of Seo Hyowon. *OOAK Table Tennis Forum.* (2020). Available at https://ooakforum.com/viewtopic.php?f=56&t=23478 Accessed February 2020.

8. Landin, D, & Hebert, E, & Fairweather, M. (1993). The Effects of Variable Practice on the Performance of a Basketball Skill. *Research Quarterly for Exercise and Sport*, 64: 232–237.

9. Green, DP, Whitehead, J, & Sugden, DA. (1995). Practice Variability and Transfer of a Racket Skill. *Perceptual and Motor Skills*, 81(3 Part 2): 1275–1281.

10. North, JS, Bezodis, NE, Murphy, CP, Runswick, OR, Pocock, C, & Roca, A. (2019). The effect of consistent and varied follow-through practice schedules on learning a table tennis backhand. *Journal of Sports Sciences*, 37:6: 613–620.

11. Smith, S, Glenberg, A, & Bjork, R. (1978). Environmental Context and Human Memory. *Memory & Cognition*, 6: 342–353.

12. Smith, S, & Rothkopf, E. (1984). Contextual Enrichment and Distribution of Practice in the Classroom. *Cognition and Instruction*, 1(3):341–358.

13. Liao, C, & Masters, R. (2001). Analogy learning: A means to implicit motor learning. *Journal of Sports Sciences*, 19(5): 307–319.

14. Valeh, F, Saberi, A, & Noghondar, F. (2020). The comparison of Linear and Nonlinear pedagogy on the learning of table tennis forehand stroke. *International Journal of Physical Education, Sports and Health*, 7: 106–111.

15. Turi, Z, Bjørkedal, E, Gunkel, L, Antal, A, Paulus, W, & Mittner, M. (2018). Evidence for Cognitive Placebo and Nocebo Effects in Healthy Individuals. *Scientific Reports*, 8(1): 17443.

16. Gröpel, P, & Mesagno, C. (2019) Choking interventions in sports: A systematic review. *International Review of Sport and Exercise Psychology*, 12:1: 176–201.

17. Sekiya, H, & Tanaka, Y. (2019). Movement Modifications Related to Psychological Pressure in a Table Tennis Forehand Task. *Perceptual and Motor Skills*, 126(1): 143–156.

18. Ruud JR, Hartigh, D, & Gernigon, C. (2018) Time-out! How psychological momentum builds up and breaks down in table tennis, *Journal of Sports Sciences*, 36(23): 2732–2737.

19. Liu, W, Zhou, C, Ji, L, & Watson, JC. (2012). The Effect of Goal Setting Difficulty on Serving Success in Table Tennis and the Mediating Mechanism of Self-regulation. *Journal of Human Kinetics*, 33: 173–185.

20. Chiara, M, Cavedon, V, Corte, S, & Agostini, T. (2017) The effects of two different correction strategies on the snatch technique in weightlifting. *Journal of Sports Sciences*, 35(5): 476–483.

21. Fogel, S, Ray, L, Binnie, L, & Owen, A. (2015). How to become an expert: A new perspective on the role of sleep in the mastery of procedural skills. *Neurobiology of Learning and Memory*, 125: 236–248.

22. Mednick, S, Nakayama, K, & Stickgold, R. (2003). Sleep-dependent learning: a nap is as good as a night. *Nature Neuroscience*, 6: 697–698.

23. Carrier, C, & Titus, A. (1979). The effects of notetaking: A review of studies. *Contemporary Educational Psychology*, 4(4): 299–314.

24. Mangen A, Velay JL. (2011). Digitizing Literacy: Reflections on the Haptics of Writing. In Zadeh, MH, (Ed.) *Advances in Haptics*. Intech. 2011.

25. Mueller, PA, & Oppenheimer, D M. (2014). The Pen Is Mightier Than the Keyboard: Advantages of Longhand Over Laptop Note Taking. *Psychological Science*, 25(6): 1159–1168.

26. Garcia-Argibay M, Santed MA, Reales JM. (2019), Efficacy of binaural auditory beats in cognition, anxiety, and pain perception: a meta-analysis. *Psychological Research*, 83(2):357–372.

MASTERING THE MENTAL GAME

1. Elferink-Gemser, MT, Faber, IR, Visscher, C, Hung, TM, de Vries, SJ, & Nijhuis-Van der Sanden, M. (2018). Higher-level cognitive functions in Dutch elite and sub-elite table tennis players. *PloS one*, 13(11): e0206151.

2. You, Y, Ma, Y, Ji, Z, Meng, F, Li, A, & Zhang, C. (2018). Unconscious response inhibition differences between table tennis athletes and non-athletes. *PeerJ Life and Environment*, 6: e5548

3. Chang-Yong, C, Chen, I, Chen, L, Huang, C, & Hung, T. (2011). Sources of psychological states related to peak performance in elite table tennis players. *International Journal of Table Tennis Sciences*, 7, 86–90

4. Cece, V, Guillet-Descas, E, & Martinent, G. (2020). Mental training program in racket sports: A systematic review. *International Journal of Racket Sports Science*, 2(1): 55–71.

5. Chen, I, Chang, C, Hung, C, Chen, L, & Hung, T. (2010). Investigation of Underlying Psychological Factors in Elite Table Tennis Players. *International Journal of Table Tennis Sciences*, 6, 48–50

6. Pascoe, Michaela & Thompson, David & Jenkins, Zoe & Ski, Chantal. (2017). Mindfulness mediates the physiological markers of stress: Systematic review and meta-analysis. *Journal of Psychiatric Research*. 95. 10.1016/j.jpsychires.2017.08.004.

7. Gong, Hong & Ni, Chen-Xu & Liu, Yun-Zi & Zhang, yi & Su, Wen-Jun & Lian, Yong-Jie & Peng, Wei & Chun, Jiang. (2016). Mindfulness meditation for insomnia: A meta-analysis of randomized controlled trials. *Journal of Psychosomatic Research*. 89.

8. Barnes, S.W., Brown, K., Krusemark, E., Campbell, W., & Rogge, R. (2007). The role of mindfulness in romantic relationship satisfaction and responses to relationship stress. *Journal of marital and family therapy*, 33, 482–500.

9. Hilton L, Hempel S, Ewing BA, Apaydin E, Xenakis L, Newberry S, Colaiaco B, Maher AR, Shanman RM, Sorbero ME, Maglione MA. (2017). Mindfulness Meditation for Chronic Pain: Systematic Review and Meta-analysis. *Annals of Behavioral Medicine*, 51(2): 199–213.

10. Carrière, K., Khoury, B., Günak, M. M., and Knäuper, B. (2018) Mindfulness-based interventions for weight loss: a systematic review and meta-analysis. *Obesity Reviews*, 19: 164– 177.

11. Bühlmayer, L, Birrer, D, Röthlin, P, Faude, O, & Donath, L. (2017). Effects of Mindfulness Practice on Performance-Relevant

Parameters and Performance Outcomes in Sports: A Meta-Analytical Review. *Sports Medicine*, 47(11):2309–2321.

12. Kachanathu, S, Verma, S, & Khanna, G. (2011). The effect of mindfulness meditation on HPA axis in reducing pre competition stress to improve performance of elite shooters. *National Journal of Integrated Research in Medicine.* 2: 15–21.

13. Rooks, J, Morrison, A, Goolsarran, M, Rogers, S, & Jha, A. (2017). "We Are Talking About Practice": The Influence of Mindfulness vs. Relaxation Training on Athletes' Attention and Well-Being over High-Demand Intervals. *Journal of Cognitive Enhancement*, 1(2): 141–153.

14. Rivera, O., Quintana, M., & Rincón, M. E. (2014). Effects of mindfulness on sport, exercise and physical activity : A systematic review. *Online Open Science in Mindfulness*, 77, 1–7.

15. Kaufman, K, Glass, C, & Arnkoff, D. (2009). Evaluation of Mindful Sport Performance Enhancement (MSPE): A New Approach to Promote Flow in Athletes. *Journal of Clinical Sport Psychology*, 3(4): 334–356.

16. Noetel, M, Ciarrochi, J, Van Zanden, B, & Lonsdale, C. (2019). Mindfulness and acceptance approaches to sporting performance enhancement: a systematic review. *International Review of Sport and Exercise Psychology*, 12(1): 139–175.

17. Moran, A. (1996). *The Psychology of Concentration in Sport Performers: A Cognitive Analysis.* (1st edn), London, UK: Taylor & Francis.

18. Gröpel, P, & Mesagno, C. (2019). Choking interventions in sports: A systematic review. *International Review of Sport and Exercise Psychology*, 12(1): 176–201.

19. Brown, Richard & Gerbarg, Patricia. (2009). Yoga Breathing, Meditation, and Longevity. *Annals of the New York Academy of Sciences*. 1172. 54–62.

20. Lejeune, M., Decker, C., & Sanchez, X. (1994). Mental Rehearsal in Table Tennis Performance. *Perceptual and Motor Skills*, *79*(1), 627–641.

21. Adeyeye, M., Edward, H., Kehinde, A., & Afolabi, F. (2013). Effects of Mental-Skills Training On the Performance of Table- Tennis Players of National Institute for Sport, Lagos. *IOSR Journal of Research & Method in Education, 3*, 22–27.

SOCIAL AND EMOTIONAL SKILLS

1. Luberto, C, Shinday, N, Song, R, Philpotts, L, Park, E, Fricchione, G, & Yeh, G. (2017). A Systematic Review and Meta-analysis of the Effects of Meditation on Empathy, Compassion, and Prosocial Behaviors. *Mindfulness*, 9(3): 708–724.

2. Beaumont, C, Maynard, I, & Butt, J. (2014). Effective Ways to Develop and Maintain Robust Sport-Confidence: Strategies Advocated by Sport Psychology Consultants. *Journal of Applied Sport Psychology*. 27: 1–18.

3. Bayley, W, (March, 22 2019). *A day in the life of a Pro Player* [Table Tennis Daily]. [Video File]. Available at https://youtu.be/_abCOx8LHng Accessed May 2021.

4. Hays, K, Thomas, O, Butt, J, & Maynard, I. (2010). The Development of Confidence Profiling for Sport. *The Sport Psychologist.* 24: 373–392.

5. Flora, S. (2000). Praise's magic reinforcement ratio: Five to one gets the job done. *The Behavior Analyst Today.* 1: 64–69.

6. Weinberg, E, Butt, J, & Culp, B. (2011) Coaches' views of mental toughness and how it is built. *International Journal of Sport and Exercise Psychology*, Vol 9(2): 156–172.

7. Cuddy, AJC, Schultz, SJ, Fosse, NE. (2018). P-Curving a More Comprehensive Body of Research on Postural Feedback Reveals Clear Evidential Value for Power-Posing Effects: Reply to Simmons and Simonsohn (2017). *Psychological Science,* Vol 29(4): 656–666.

8. Aarts, H, & Custers, R. (2012). Unconscious Goal Pursuit: Nonconscious Goal Regulation and Motivation. *The Oxford Handbook of Human Motivation.* 10.1093/ oxfordhb/9780195399820.013.0014.

9. Lyu, W, & Zhang, L. (2020). Effect of Unconscious Goal Priming on Athletes' Self-Confidence. *Journal of Science in Sport and Exercise*, Vol 2: 120–131.

10. Blanchfield, A, Hardy, J, & Marcora, S. (2014). Non-conscious visual cues related to affect and action alter perception of effort and endurance performance. *Frontiers in Human Neuroscience, 8: 967.*

11. Karremans, J, Stroebe, W, & Claus, J. (2006). Beyond Vicary's fantasies: The impact of subliminal priming and brand choice. *Journal of Experimental Social Psychology*, Vol 42(6): 792–798.

12. Walton, C, Baranoff, J, Gilbert, P, & Kirby, J. (2020). Self-compassion, social rank, and psychological distress in athletes of varying competitive levels. *Psychology of Sport and Exercise*, Vol 50: 101733.

13. Noteboom, J, Fleshner, M, & Enoka, R. (2001). Activation of the arousal response can impair performance on a simple motor task. *Journal of Applied Physiology*, Vol 91: 821–31.

14. Li, X, Zhang, G, Zhou, C, & Wang, X. (2019). Negative emotional state slows down movement speed: behavioral and neural evidence. *Peerj Brain and Cognition*, 7: e7591.

15. Liu, YC, Wang, MY, & Hsu, CY. (2018). Competition Field Perceptions of Table-tennis Athletes and their Performance. *Journal of Human Kinetics*, Vol 61: 241–247.

16. Steffgen, G. (2017). Anger Management – Evaluation of a Cognitive-Behavioral Training Program for Table Tennis Players. *Journal of Human Kinetics*, Vol 55: 65–73.

17. Boll, T, (October, 9 2020). *Mental Strength.* [Video File]. Available at https://youtu.be/V-a1WOtYsZA Accessed May 2021.

THE MOTIVATION MYTH: ACHIEVING SUCCESS THROUGH HABITS, GOAL SETTING, SYSTEMS, AND STRUCTURE

1. Galla, BM, & Duckworth, AL. (2015). More than resisting temptation: Beneficial habits mediate the relationship between self-control and positive life outcomes. *Journal of Personality and Social Psychology*, Vol 109(3): 508–525.

ERF

2. Carter, E, Kofler, L, Forster, D, & Mccullough, M. (2015). A Series of Meta-Analytic Tests of the Depletion Effect: Self-Control Does Not Seem to Rely on a Limited Resource. *Journal of Experimental Psychology. General,* Vol 144(4): 796–815.

3. Job, V, Walton, G, Bernecker, K, & Dweck, C. (2013). Beliefs about willpower determine the impact of glucose on self-control. *Proceedings of the National Academy of Sciences*, Vol 110(37): 14837–14842.

4. Hershfield, HE, Goldstein, DG, Sharpe, WF, Fox, J, Yeykelis, L, Carstensen, LL, & Bailenson, JN. (2011). Increasing Saving Behavior Through Age-Progressed Renderings of the Future Self. *Journal of Marketing Research*, Vol 48: S23–S37.

5. Stadler, G, Oettingen, G, & Gollwitzer, P. (2009). Physical Activity in Women. *American Journal of Preventive Medicine*, Vol36(1): 29–34.

6. Leary, MR, Tate, EB, Adams, CE, Allen, AB, & Hancock, J. (2007). Self-compassion and reactions to unpleasant self-relevant events: The implications of treating oneself kindly. *Journal of Personality and Social Psychology*, Vol 92(5): 887–904.

7. Breines, JG, & Chen, S. (2012). Self-Compassion Increases Self-Improvement Motivation. *Personality and Social Psychology Bulletin*, Vol 38(9): 1133–1143.

SLEEP: THE DARK HORSE OF PERFORMANCE ENHANCERS

1. Consensus Conference Panel: Watson, NF, Badr, MS, Belenky, G, Bliwise, DL, Buxton, OM, Buysse, D, Dinges, DF, Gangwisch,

J, Grandner, MA, Kushida, C, Malhotra, RK, Martin, JL, Patel, SR, Quan, SF, & Tasali, E. (2015). Joint Consensus Statement of the American Academy of Sleep Medicine and Sleep Research Society on the Recommended Amount of Sleep for a Healthy Adult: Methodology and Discussion. *Journal of clinical sleep medicine*, Vol 11(8): 931–952.

2. Mah, CD, Mah, KE, Kezirian, EJ, & Dement, WC. (2011). The effects of sleep extension on the athletic performance of collegiate basketball players. *Sleep*, Vol 34(7): 943–950.

3. Schwartz, J, & Simon, R. (2015). Sleep extension improves serving accuracy: A study with college varsity tennis players. *Physiology & Behavior*, Vol 151: 541–544.

4. Kirschen, G, Jones, J, & Hale, L. (2018). The Impact of Sleep Duration on Performance Among Competitive Athletes : A Systematic Literature Review. *Clinical Journal of Sport Medicine*, Vol 30(5):1.

5. Patrick, Y, Lee, A, Raha, O, Pillai, K, Gupta, S, Sethi, S, Mukeshimana, F, Gerard, L, Moghal, MU, Saleh, SN, Smith, SF, Morrell, MJ, & Moss, J. (2017). Effects of sleep deprivation on cognitive and physical performance in university students. *Sleep and Biological Rhythms*, Vol 15(3): 217–225.

6. Uehli, K, Mehta, A, Miedinger, D, Hug, K, Schindler, C, Holsboer-Trachsler, E, Leuppi, JD, & Künzli, N. (2014). Sleep problems and work injuries: A systematic review and meta-analysis. *Sleep Medicine Reviews*, Vol 18(1): 61–73.

7. Milewski, M, Skaggs, D, Bishop, G, Pace, J, Ibrahim, D, Wren, T, & Barzdukas, A. (2014). Chronic Lack of Sleep is Associated

With Increased Sports Injuries in Adolescent Athletes. *Journal of Pediatric Orthopedics*. Vol 34(2): 129–133.

8. Wang, Y, Guo, Z, Zhang, F. Zhang, Y, Wang, S-S, & Zhao, Y. (2017). Sleep problems and injury risk among juveniles: A systematic review and meta-analysis of observational studies. *Scientific Reports*, Vol 7: 9813.

9. Dattilo, M, Antunes, H, Medeiros, A, Mônico Neto, M, Souza, H, Tufik, S, & de Mello, M. (2011). Sleep and muscle recovery: Endocrinological and molecular basis for a new and promising hypothesis. *Medical Hypotheses*, Vol 77(2): 220–222.

10. Grandner, MA. (2018). The Cost of Sleep Lost: Implications for Health, Performance, and the Bottom Line. *American Journal of Health Promotion*, Vol 32(7): 1629–1634.

11. Kang, JH, & Chen, SC. (2009). Effects of an irregular bedtime schedule on sleep quality, daytime sleepiness, and fatigue among university students in Taiwan. *BMC Public Health*, Vol 9, 248.

12. Drake, C, Roehrs, T, Shambroom, J, & Roth, T. (2013). Caffeine Effects on Sleep Taken 0, 3, or 6 Hours before Going to Bed. *Journal of Clinical Sleep Medicine*. Vol 9: 1195–200.

13. Ebrahim, I, Shapiro, C, Williams, A, & Fenwick, P. (2013). Alcohol and Sleep I: Effects on Normal Sleep. *Alcoholism: Clinical and Experimental Research*, Vol 37(4): 539–549.

14. Horne, J, & Reid, A. (1985). Night-time sleep EEG changes following body heating in a warm bath. *Electroencephalography and Clinical Neurophysiology*, Vol 60(2): 154–157.

15. Haghayegh, S, Khoshnevis, S, Smolensky, M, Diller, K, & Castriotta, R. (2019). Before-bedtime passive body heating by warm shower or bath to improve sleep: A systematic review and meta-analysis. *Sleep Medicine Reviews*, Vol 46: 124–135.

16. Tamaki, M, Bang, JW, Watanabe, T, & Sasaki, Y. (2016). Night Watch in One Brain Hemisphere during Sleep Associated with the First-Night Effect in Humans. *Current Biology*, Vol 26(9): 1190–1194.

17. Li, T, Jiang, S, Han, M, Yang, Z, Lv, J, & Deng, C. Reiter, RJ, & Yang, Y. (2019). Exogenous melatonin as a treatment for secondary sleep disorders: A systematic review and meta-analysis. *Frontiers in Neuroendocrinology*, 52: 22–28.

18. Harrison, Y, & Horne, JA. (2000). Sleep Loss and Temporal Memory. *The Quarterly Journal of Experimental Psychology*, Vol 53(1): 271–279.

19. Banks, S, Van Dongen, HP, Maislin, G, & Dinges, DF. (2010). Neurobehavioral dynamics following chronic sleep restriction: dose-response effects of one night for recovery. *Sleep*, Vol 33(8): 1013–1026.

20. Belenky, G, Wesensten, N, Thorne, D, Thomas, M, Sing, H, & Redmond, D. Russo, MB, & Balkin, TJ. (2003). Patterns of performance degradation and restoration during sleep restriction and subsequent recovery: a sleep dose-response study. *Journal of Sleep Research*, Vol 12(1): 1–12.

21. Arnal, PJ, Sauvet, F, Leger, D, van Beers, P, Bayon, V, Bougard, C, Rabat, A, Millet, GY, & Chennaoui, M. (2015). Benefits of Sleep

Extension on Sustained Attention and Sleep Pressure Before and During Total Sleep Deprivation and Recovery. *Sleep*, Vol 38(12): 1935–1943.

22. Rupp, TL, Wesensten, NJ, Bliese, PD, & Balkin, TJ. (2009). Banking sleep: realization of benefits during subsequent sleep restriction and recovery. *Sleep*, Vol 32(3): 311–321.

23. Facer-Childs, E, Middleton, B, Skene, D, & Bagshaw, A. (2019). Resetting the late timing of 'night owls' has a positive impact on mental health and performance. *Sleep Medicine*, Vol 60: 236–247.

24. Milner, C., & Cote, K. (2009). Benefits of napping in healthy adults: impact of nap length, time of day, age, and experience with napping. *Journal of Sleep Research*, Vol 18(2): 272–281.

25. Herxheimer A, Petrie KJ. (2002). Melatonin for the prevention and treatment of jet lag. *Cochrane Database of Systematic Reviews*, 2: CD001520.

BECOMING BULLETPROOF: INJURY PREVENTION, ADVANCED RECOVERY TACTICS, AND DEALING WITH SICKNESS

1. Mann, J, Bryant, K, Johnstone, B, Ivey, P, & Sayers, S. (2016). Effect of Physical and Academic Stress on Illness and Injury in Division 1 College Football Players. *Journal of Strength and Conditioning Research*, Vol 30(1): 20–25.

2. Gabbett, TJ. (2016). The training-injury prevention paradox: should athletes be training smarter and harder? *British Journal of Sports Medicine*, Vol 50(5): 273–280.

3. Shimazaki, T, de Almeida, E, Vanderlei, FM, de Aguiar Cintra Filho, D, & Vanderlei, LCM, Pastre, CM, & Bastos, FN. (2012). Exploration of risk factors for sports injuries in athletes of table tennis. *Fisioterapia e Pesquisa.* Vol 19: 158–164.

4. Nazem, TG, & Ackerman, KE. (2012). The female athlete triad. *Sports Health,* Vol 4(4): 302–311.

5. Thacker, S, Gilchrist, J, Stroup, D, & Kimsey, C. (2004). The Impact of Stretching on Sports Injury Risk: A Systematic Review of the Literature. *Medicine & Science in Sports & Exercise,* Vol 36(3): 371–378.

6. Shrier, I. (1999). Stretching before exercise does not reduce the risk of local muscle injury: a critical review of the clinical and basic science literature. *Clinical Journal of Sport Medicine: Official Journal of the Canadian Academy of Sport Medicine,* Vol 9(4): 221–227.

7. Fradkin, A, Zazryn, T, & Smoliga, J. (2010). Effects of Warming-up on Physical Performance: A Systematic Review With Meta-analysis. *Journal of Strength and Conditioning Research,* Vol 24(1): 140–148.

8. Hsu, F, Tsai, K, Lee, C, Chang, W, & Chang, N. (2020). Effects of Dynamic Stretching Combined With Static Stretching, Foam Rolling, or Vibration Rolling as a Warm-Up Exercise on Athletic Performance in Elite Table Tennis Players. *Journal of Sport Rehabilitation,* 1–8.

9. Ebadi, L. & Günay, M. (2018). Analysing of the types of injuries observed in table tennis players according to the some variables.

IOSR Journal of Sports and Physical Education, Volume 5, Issue 4, 21-26.

10. Kay, A, & Blazevich, A. (2012). Effect of Acute Static Stretch on Maximal Muscle Performance. *Medicine & Science in Sports & Exercise*, Vol 44(1): 154–164.

11. Simic, L, Sarabon, N, & Markovic, G. (2012). Does pre-exercise static stretching inhibit maximal muscular performance? A meta-analytical review. *Scandinavian Journal of Medicine & Science in Sports*, Vol 23(2): 131–148.

12. Taylor, K, Sheppard, J, Lee, H, & Plummer, N. (2009). Negative effect of static stretching restored when combined with a sport specific warm-up component. *Journal of Science and Medicine in Sport*, Vol 12(6): 657–661.

13. *Kreanga*k, K, (November, 1 2019) *A Day in The Life With All Time Great Kalinikos Kreanga! TableTennisDaily*. [Video File]. Available at https://youtu.be/dlkbcpuiS-w Accessed May 2021.

14. Laursen JB, Andersen TE, & Andersen LB. (2018). Strength training as superior, dose-dependent and safe prevention of acute and overuse sports injuries: a systematic review, qualitative analysis and meta-analysis. *British Journal of Sports Medicine*, Vol 52: 1557–1563.

15. Laursen JB, Bertelsen DM, & Andersen LB. (2014). The effectiveness of exercise interventions to prevent sports injuries: a systematic review and meta-analysis of randomised controlled trials. *British Journal of Sports Medicine*, Vol 48: 871–877.

16. Suchomel, T, Nimphius, S, & Stone, M. (2016). The Importance of Muscular Strength in Athletic Performance. *Sports Medicine.* Vol 46(10): 1419–1449.

17. Farup, J, Rahbek, S, Vendelbo, M, Matzon, A, Hindhede, J, & Bejder, A, Ringgard, S, & Vissing, K. (2013). Whey protein hydrolysate augments tendon and muscle hypertrophy independent of resistance exercise contraction mode. *Scandinavian Journal of Medicine and Science in Sports,* Vol 24(5): 788–798.

18. Gelberman, R. (1985). Flexor tendon physiology: tendon nutrition and cellular activity in injury and repair. *Instructional Course Lectures.* Vol 34: 351–60.

19. Schoenfeld, B, Peterson, M, Ogborn, D, Contreras, B, & Sonmez, G. (2015). Effects of Low- vs. High-Load Resistance Training on Muscle Strength and Hypertrophy in Well-Trained Men. *Journal of Strength and Conditioning Research,* Vol 29(10): 2954–2963.

20. Schoenfeld, B, Ratamess, N, Peterson, M, Contreras, B, Sonmez, G, & Alvar, B. (2014). Effects of Different Volume-Equated Resistance Training Loading Strategies on Muscular Adaptations in Well-Trained Men. *Journal of Strength and Conditioning Research,* Vol 28(10): 2909–2918.

21. Nakajima, T, Kurano, M, Iida, H, Takano, H, Oonuma, H, & Morita, T, Meguro, K, Sato, Y, & Nagata, T. (2006). Use and safety of KAATSU training: Results of a national survey. *International Journal of KAATSU Training Research,* Vol 2(1): 5–13.

22. Beaven, C, Cook, C, Kilduff, L, Drawer, S, & Gill, N. (2012). Intermittent lower-limb occlusion enhances recovery after

strenuous exercise. *Applied physiology, nutrition, and metabolism*. Vol 37(6): 1132–1139.

23. Shaw, G, Lee-Barthel, A, Ross, ML, Wang, B, & Baar, K. (2017). Vitamin C-enriched gelatin supplementation before intermittent activity augments collagen synthesis. *The American Journal of Clinical Nutrition*, Vol 105(1): 136–143.

24. Clark, KL, Sebastianelli, W, Flechsenhar, KR, Aukermann, DF, Meza, F, Millard,RL, Deitch, JR, Sherbondy, PS, & Albert, A. (2008) 24-Week study on the use of collagen hydrolysate as a dietary supplement in athletes with activity-related joint pain, *Current Medical Research and Opinion*, Vol 24(5): 1485–1496.

25. Ristow, M, Zarse, K, Oberbach, A, Klöting, N, Birringer, M, Kiehntopf, M, Stumvoll, M, Kahn, CR, & Blüher, M. (2009). Antioxidants prevent health-promoting effects of physical exercise in humans. *Proceedings of the National Academy of Sciences of the United States of America*, Vol 106(21): 8665–8670.

26. Dupuy, O, Douzi, W, Theurot, D, Bosquet, L, & Dugué, B. (2018). An Evidence-Based Approach for Choosing Post-exercise Recovery Techniques to Reduce Markers of Muscle Damage, Soreness, Fatigue, and Inflammation: A Systematic Review With Meta-Analysis. *Frontiers in Physiology*, 9.

27. Brown, F, Gissane, C, Howatson, G, van Someren, K, Pedlar, C, & Hill, J. (2017). Compression Garments and Recovery from Exercise: A Meta-Analysis. *Sports Medicine*, Vol 47(11), 2245–2267.

28. Peake, JM, Roberts, LA, Figueiredo, VC, Egner, I. Krog, S, Aas, SN, Suzuki, K, Markworth, JF, Coombes, JS, Cameron-Smith, D, & Raastad, T. (2017). The effects of cold water immersion and active recovery on inflammation and cell stress responses in human skeletal muscle after resistance exercise. *The Journal of Physiology*, Vol 595(3): 695–711.

29. Quinlan, R, & Hill, J. (2020). The Efficacy of Tart Cherry Juice in Aiding Recovery After Intermittent Exercise. *International Journal of Sports Physiology and Performance*, Vol 15(3): 368–374.

30. Ortega, D, López, A, Amaya, H, & Berral de la Rosa, F. (2020). Tart cherry and pomegranate supplementations enhance recovery from exercise-induced muscle damage: a systematic review. *Biology of Sport*, Vol 38(1): 97–111.

31. Leite, C, Profeta, V, Chaves, S, Benine, R, Bottaro, M, & Ferreira-Júnior, J. (2019). Does exercise-induced muscle damage impair subsequent motor skill learning? *Human Movement Science*, Vol 67: 102504.

32. Kaptchuk, T, Friedlander, E, Kelley, J, Sanchez, M, Kokkotou, E, & Singer, JP, Kowalczykowski, M, Miller,FG, Kirsch, I, Lembo, AJ. (2010). Placebos without Deception: A Randomized Controlled Trial in Irritable Bowel Syndrome. *Plos one*, Vol 5(12): e15591.

33. Ariel, G., Saville, W. (1972). Anabolic steroids: the physiological effects of placebos. *Medicine and Science in Sports*, 4: 124–26.

34. Lilja, M & Mandić, M, Apró, W, Melin, M, Olsson, K, Rosenborg, S, Gustafsson, T, & Lundberg, T. (2017). High-doses of anti-inflammatory drugs compromise muscle strength and

hypertrophic adaptations to resistance training in young adults. *Acta Physiologica*. 222.

35. Roberts, L, Raastad, T, Markworth, J, Figueiredo, V, Egner, I, & Shield, A, Cameron-Smith, D, Coombes, JS, & Peake, JM. (2015). Post-exercise cold water immersion attenuates acute anabolic signalling and long-term adaptations in muscle to strength training. *The Journal of Physiology*, Vol 593(18): 4285–4301.

36. Cirer-Sastre, R, Beltrán-Garrido, JV, & Corbi, F. (2017). Contralateral Effects After Unilateral Strength Training: A Meta-Analysis Comparing Training Loads. *Journal of Sports Science & Medicine*, Vol 16(2): 180–186.

37. Haaland, D, Sabljic, T, Baribeau, D, Mukovozov, I, & Hart, L. (2008). Is Regular Exercise a Friend or Foe of the Aging Immune System? A Systematic Review. *Clinical Journal of Sport Medicine*, Vol 18(6): 539–548.

38. Spence, L, Brown, W, Pyne, D, Nissen, M, Sloots, T, & McCcormack, J, Locke, AS, & Fricker, PA. (2007). Incidence, Etiology, and Symptomatology of Upper Respiratory Illness in Elite Athletes. *Medicine & Science in Sports & Exercise*, Vol 39(4): 577–586.

39. Nantz, M, Rowe, C, Muller, C, Creasy, R, Stanilka, J, & Percival, S. (2012). Supplementation with aged garlic extract improves both NK and γ⊠-T cell function and reduces the severity of cold and flu symptoms: A randomized, double-blind, placebo-controlled nutrition intervention. *Clinical Nutrition*, Vol 31(3): 337–344.

40. Josling, P. (2001). Preventing the common cold with a garlic supplement: A double-blind, placebo-controlled survey. *Advances in Therapy*. Vol 18: 189–93.

41. Hemilä H, & Chalker E. (2013) Vitamin C for preventing and treating the common cold. *Cochrane Database of Systematic Reviews*, 1: CD000980.

42. Autier, P, Mullie, P, Macacu, A, Dragomir, M, Boniol, M, Coppens, K, Pizot, C, & Boniol, M. (2017). Effect of vitamin D supplementation on non-skeletal disorders: a systematic review of meta-analyses and randomised trials. *The Lancet Diabetes and Endocrinology*, Vol 5(12): 986–1004.

43. Prasad, AS, Beck, FWJ, Bao, B, Fitzgerald, JT, Snell, DC, Steinberg, JD, Cardozo, LC. (2007). Zinc supplementation decreases incidence of infections in the elderly: effect of zinc on generation of cytokines and oxidative stress. *The American Journal of Clinical Nutrition*, Vol 85(3): 837–844.

44. Szabo, G, & Saha, B. (2015). Alcohol's Effect on Host Defense. *Alcohol Research: Current Reviews*, Vol 37(2): 159–170.

45. Möller, G, da Cunha Goulart, M, Nicoletto, B, Alves, F, & Schneider, C. (2019). Supplementation of Probiotics and Its Effects on Physically Active Individuals and Athletes: Systematic Review. *International Journal of Sport Nutrition and Exercise Metabolism*, Vol 29(5): 481–492.

46. *Can you boost your flu shot with prebiotics and probiotics?* (2020). Examine.com. Accessed February 20, 2020, from

https://examine.com/nutrition/boost-flu-prebiotics-and-probiotics/

47. Singh M, & Das RR. (2013). Zinc for the common cold. *Cochrane Database of Systematic Reviews,* 6: CD001364.

48. Lizogub, V, Riley, D, & Heger, M. (2007). Efficacy of a Pelargonium Sidoides Preparation in Patients With the Common Cold: A Randomized, Double Blind, Placebo-Controlled Clinical Trial. *Explore,* Vol 3(6): 573–584.

49. Agbabiaka, T, Guo, R, & Ernst, E. (2008). Pelargonium sidoides for acute bronchitis: A systematic review and meta-analysis. *Phytomedicine,* Vol 15(5): 378–385.

50. *Pelargonium sidoides.* (2020). Examine.com. Accessed January 8, 2021, from https://examine.com/supplements/pelargonium-sidoides/

51. Hopkins, Alan. (2003). Chicken soup cure may not be a myth. *The Nurse practitioner.* Vol 28(6): 16.

52. Rennard, B, Ertl, R, Gossman, G, Robbins, R, & Rennard, S. (2000). Chicken Soup Inhibits Neutrophil Chemotaxis In Vitro. *Chest,* Vol 118(4): 1150–1157.

LEVEL ONE: ENERGY BALANCE, CALORIC INTAKE, AND RATE OF WEIGHT CHANGE

1. Swinton, P, Lloyd, R, Keogh, J, Agouris, I, & Stewart, A. (2014). Regression Models of Sprint, Vertical Jump, and Change of

Direction Performance. *Journal of Strength and Conditioning Research*, Vol 28(7): 1839–1848.

2. Logue, D, Madigan, SM, Delahunt, E, Heinen, M, McDonnell, SJ, & Corish, CA. (2018). Low Energy Availability in Athletes: A Review of Prevalence, Dietary Patterns, Physiological Health, and Sports Performance. *Sports Medicine*, Vol 48: 73–96.

3. Márquez S, Molinero O. Energy availability, menstrual dysfunction and bone health in sports; an overview of the female athlete triad. *Nutr Hosp*. 2013 Jul-Aug;28(4):1010-7.

4. Pilis, K, Stec, K, Pilis, A, Mroczek, A, Michalski, C, & Pilis, W. (2019). Body composition and nutrition of female athletes. *Roczniki Państwowego Zakładu Higieny*. Vol 70: 243–251.

5. Leibel, RL, Hirsch, J, Appel, BE, Checani, GC. (1992). Energy intake required to maintain body weight is not affected by wide variation in diet composition. *The American Journal of Clinical Nutrition*, Vol 55(2): 350–355.

6. Sacks FM, Bray GA, Carey VJ, Smith SR, Ryan DH, Anton SD, McManus K, Champagne CM, Bishop LM, Laranjo N, Leboff MS, Rood JC, de Jonge L, Greenway FL, Loria CM, Obarzanek E, Williamson DA. 2009). Comparison of weight-loss diets with different compositions of fat, protein, and carbohydrates. *N Engl J Med*. 2009 Feb 26;360(9):859-73.

7. A Golay, AF Allaz, Y, Morel, de Tonnac, N, Tankova, S, & Reaven, G. (1996). Similar weight loss with low- or high-carbohydrate diets. *The American Journal of Clinical Nutrition*, Vol 63(2): 174–178.

8. Schoeller, DA, & Buchholz, AC. (2005). Energetics of Obesity and Weight Control: Does Diet Composition Matter? *Journal of the American Dietetic Association*, Vol 105(5): Supplement 24–28.

9. Kinsell, LW, Gunning, B, Michaels, GC, Richardson, J, Cox, SE, & Lemon, C. (1964). Calories do count. *Metabolism*, Vol 13(3): 195–204.

10. Howell, S, & Kones, R. (2017). "Calories in, calories out" and macronutrient intake: the hope, hype, and science of calories. *American Journal of Physiology-Endocrinology and Metabolism*, Vol 313(5): E608–E612.

11. Gardner CD, Trepanowski JF, Del Gobbo LC, Hauser ME, Rigdon J, Ioannidis JPA, Desai M, King AC. (2018). Effect of Low-Fat vs Low-Carbohydrate Diet on 12-Month Weight Loss in Overweight Adults and the Association With Genotype Pattern or Insulin Secretion: The DIETFITS Randomized Clinical Trial. *JAMA*. Vol 319(7): 667–679. doi:10.1001/jama.2018.0245

12. Lichtman SW, Pisarska K, Berman ER, Pestone M, Dowling H, Offenbacher E, Weisel H, Heshka S, Matthews DE, Heymsfield SB. (1992). Discrepancy between self-reported and actual caloric intake and exercise in obese subjects. *N Engl J Med*. 1992 Dec 31; 327(27):1893-8.

13. Champagne, CM, Bray, GA, Kurtz, AA, Bressan Resende Monteiro, J, Tucker, E, Volaufova, J, & Delany, JP. (2002). Energy Intake and Energy Expenditure: A Controlled Study Comparing Dietitians and Non-dietitians. *Journal of the American Dietetic Association*, Vol 102(10): 1428–1432.

14. Donahoo WT, Levine JA, Melanson EL. (2004). Variability in energy expenditure and its components. Curr Opin Clin Nutr Metab Care. 2004 Nov;7(6):599-605.

15. Levine, J, Eberhardt, NL, Jensen, MD. (1999). Role of Nonexercise Activity Thermogenesis in Resistance to Fat Gain in Humans. *Science*, Vol: 283(5399): 212–214.

16. Helms, ER, Aragon, AA. & Fitschen, PJ. (2014). Evidence-based recommendations for natural bodybuilding contest preparation: nutrition and supplementation. *Journal of the International Society of Sports Nutrition*, 11: 20.

LEVEL TWO: MACRONUTRIENT AND FIBER INTAKE

1. Palascha, A, van Kleef, E, van Trijp, HCM. (2015). How does thinking in Black and White terms relate to eating behavior and weight regain? *Journal of Health Psychology*. Vol 20(5): 638–648.

2. Stewart, T, Williamson, D, & White, M. (2002). Rigid vs. flexible dieting: Association with eating disorder symptoms in nonobese women. *Appetite*. 38: 39–44.

3. Ismaeel, A, Weems, S, & Willoughby, DS. (2018). A Comparison of the Nutrient Intakes of Macronutrient-Based Dieting and Strict Dieting Bodybuilders. *International Journal of Sport Nutrition and Exercise Metabolism*, Vol 28(5): 502–508.

4. Fryar, Cheryl & Kruszon-Moran, Deanna & Gu, Qiuping & Ogden, Cynthia. (2018). Mean Body Weight, Height, Waist

Circumference, and Body Mass Index Among Adults: United States, 1999-2000 Through 2015-2016. *National Health Statistics Reports*. 2018.

5. *Intake of calories and selected nutrients for the United States population, 1999-2000.* (2003). Stacks.cdc.gov. Accessed February 18, 2020, from https://stacks.cdc.gov/view/cdc/57227

6. Morton RW, Murphy KT, McKellar SR, Schoenfeld BJ, Henselmans M, Helms E, Aragon AA, Devries MC, Banfield L, Krieger JW, Phillips SM. (2018). A systematic review, meta-analysis and meta-regression of the effect of protein supplementation on resistance training-induced gains in muscle mass and strength in healthy adults. *British Journal of Sports Medicine,* 52: 376–384.

7. Lemon, PWR. (2000) Beyond the Zone: Protein Needs of Active Individuals. *Journal of the American College of Nutrition*, 513S-521S.

8. Paddon-Jones, D, Westman, E, Mattes, RD, Wolfe,RR, Astrup, A, & Westerterp-Plantenga, M. (2008). Protein, weight management, and satiety. *The American Journal of Clinical Nutrition*, Vol 87(5): 1558S–1561S,

9. Longland, TM, Oikawa, SY, Mitchell, CJ, Devries, MC, & Phillips, SM. (2016). Higher compared with lower dietary protein during an energy deficit combined with intense exercise promotes greater lean mass gain and fat mass loss: a randomized trial. *The American Journal of Clinical Nutrition*, Vol 103(3): 738–746.,

10. Antonio, J, Ellerbroek, A, Silver, T, Vargas, L, Tamayo, A, Buehn, R, & Peacock, C. (2016). A High Protein Diet Has No Harmful

Effects: A One-Year Crossover Study in Resistance-Trained Males. *Journal of Nutrition and Metabolism*, 9104792.

11. Kumar, V, Selby, A, Rankin, D, Patel, R, Atherton, P, & Hildebrandt, W, Williams, J, Smith, K, Seynnes, O, Hiscock, N, & Rennieet, M J. (2009). Age-related differences in the dose-response relationship of muscle protein synthesis to resistance exercise in young and old men. *The Journal of Physiology*, Vol 587(1): 211–217.

12. Brennan, J, Keerati-u-rai, M, Yin, H, Daoust, J, Nonnotte, E, & Quinquis, L, St-Denis, T, & Bolster, DR. (2019). Differential Responses of Blood Essential Amino Acid Levels Following Ingestion of High-Quality Plant-Based Protein Blends Compared to Whey Protein—A Double-Blind Randomized, Cross-Over, Clinical Trial. *Nutrients*, Vol 11(12): 2987.

13. Devries, MC, Sithamparapillai, A, Scott Brimble, K, Banfield, L, Morton, RW, & Phillips, SM. (2018). Changes in Kidney Function Do Not Differ between Healthy Adults Consuming Higher- Compared with Lower- or Normal-Protein Diets: A Systematic Review and Meta-Analysis. *The Journal of Nutrition*, Vol 148(11): 1760–1775.

14. Pham NM, Mizoue T, Tanaka K, Tsuji I, Tamakoshi A, Matsuo K, Wakai K, Nagata C, Inoue M, Tsugane S, Sasazuki S. (2014). Meat Consumption and Colorectal Cancer Risk: An Evaluation Based on a Systematic Review of Epidemiologic Evidence Among the Japanese Population. *Japanese Journal of Clinical Oncology*, Vol 44(7): 641–650.

15. Durko, L, & Malecka-Panas, E. (2014). Lifestyle Modifications and Colorectal Cancer. *Current Colorectal Cancer Reports,* Vol 10: 45–54.

16. Johnston BC, Zeraatkar D, Han MA, Vernooij RWM, Valli C, El Dib R, Marshall C, Stover PJ, Fairweather-Taitt S, Wójcik G, Bhatia F, de Souza R, Brotons C, Meerpohl JJ, Patel CJ, Djulbegovic B, Alonso-Coello P, Bala MM, Guyatt GH. (2019). Unprocessed Red Meat and Processed Meat Consumption: Dietary Guideline Recommendations From the Nutritional Recommendations (NutriRECS) Consortium. *Annals of Internal Medicine*, 171: 756–764.

17. Wan, Y., Wang, F., Yuan, J., Li, J., Jiang, D., Zhang, J., Li, H., Wang, R., Tang, J., Huang, T., Zheng, J., Sinclair, A., Mann, J., & Li, D. (2019). Effects of dietary fat on gut microbiota and faecal metabolites, and their relationship with cardiometabolic risk factors: a 6-month randomised controlled-feeding trial. *Gut, 68*, 1417–1429.

18. Schwingshackl, L, & Hoffmann, G. (2014). Monounsaturated fatty acids, olive oil and health status: a systematic review and meta-analysis of cohort studies. *Lipids in Health and Disease*, 13: 154.

19. Mahmassani, HA, Avendano, EE, Raman, G, & Johnson, EJ. (2018). Avocado consumption and risk factors for heart disease: a systematic review and meta-analysis. *The American Journal of Clinical Nutrition*, Vol 107(4): 523–536.

20. Crestani, Dhiego & Bonin, Érick & Barbieri, Ricardo & Zagatto, Alessandro & Higino, Wonder & Milioni, Fabio. (2017). Chronic supplementation of omega-3 can improve body composition and maximal strength, but does not change the resistance to neuromuscular fatigue. *Sport Sciences for Health*, 13: 259–265.

21. Tachtsis, B, Camera, D, & Lacham-Kaplan, O. (2018). Potential Roles of n-3 PUFAs during Skeletal Muscle Growth and Regeneration. *Nutrients*, Vol 10(3): 309.

22. Mocking, R, Harmsen, I, Assies, J, Koeter, MWJ, Ruhé, HG, & Schene, AH. (2016). Meta-analysis and meta-regression of omega-3 polyunsaturated fatty acid supplementation for major depressive disorder. *Translational Psychiatry*, 6: e756.

23. Maki, K, Palacios, O, Bell, M, & Toth, P. (2017). Use of supplemental long-chain omega-3 fatty acids and risk for cardiac death: An updated meta-analysis and review of research gaps. *Journal of Clinical Lipidology*, Vol 11(5): 1152–1160.e2.

24. Miller, PE, Van Elswyk, M, Alexander, DD. (2014). Long-Chain Omega-3 Fatty Acids Eicosapentaenoic Acid and Docosahexaenoic Acid and Blood Pressure: A Meta-Analysis of Randomized Controlled Trials. *American Journal of Hypertension*, Vol 27(7): 885–896.

25. Du, S, Jin, J, Fang, W, & Su, Q. (2015). Does Fish Oil Have an Anti-Obesity Effect in Overweight/Obese Adults? A Meta-Analysis of Randomized Controlled Trials. *PloS one*, Vol 10(11): e0142652.

26. Calder, PC. (2017). Omega-3 fatty acids and inflammatory processes: from molecules to man. *Biochemical Society Transactions*, Vol 45(5): 1105–1115.

27. Siri-Tarino, PW, Sun, Q, Hu, FB, & Krauss, RM. (2010). Meta-analysis of prospective cohort studies evaluating the association of saturated fat with cardiovascular disease. *The American Journal of Clinical Nutrition*, Vol 91(3): 535–546.

28. Chowdhury, R., Warnakula, S., Kunutsor, S., Crowe, F., Ward, H.A., Johnson, L., Franco, O.H., Butterworth, A.S., Forouhi, N.G., Thompson, S.G., Khaw, K.T., Mozaffarian, D., Danesh, J.,

Di Angelantonio, E. (2014). Association of Dietary, Circulating, and Supplement Fatty Acids With Coronary Risk: A Systematic Review and Meta-analysis. *Annals of Internal Medicine*, 160: 398–406.

29. Lecerf, JM, & de Lorgeril M. (2011). Dietary cholesterol: from physiology to cardiovascular risk. *The British Journal of Nutrition*, 106: 6–14.

30. Riechman, SE, Andrews, RD, MacLean, DA, & Sheather, S, (2007). Statins and Dietary and Serum Cholesterol Are Associated With Increased Lean Mass Following Resistance Training. *The Journals of Gerontology: Series A*, Vol 62(10): 1164–1171.

31. Lee, CW, Lee, TV, Chen, VSW, Bui, S, & Riechman, SE. (2011). Dietary Cholesterol Affects Skeletal Muscle Protein Synthesis Following Acute Resistance Exercise. *The FASEB Journal*, 25:1_ supplement, lb563–lb563.

32. van Vliet, S, Shy, EL, Abou Sawan, S, Beals, JW, West, DWD, Skinner, SK, Ulanov, AV, Li, Z, Paluska, SA, Parsons, CM, Moore, DR, & Burd, NA. (2017). Consumption of whole eggs promotes greater stimulation of postexercise muscle protein synthesis than consumption of isonitrogenous amounts of egg whites in young men, *The American Journal of Clinical Nutrition*, Vol 106(6): 1401–1412.

33. Downs, SM, Thow, AM, & Leeder, SR. (2013). The effectiveness of policies for reducing dietary trans fat: a systematic review of the evidence. *Bulletin of the World Health Organization*, Vol 91(4): 262–9H.

34. Escobar, KA, Morales, J, & Vandusseldorp, TA. (2016). The Effect of a Moderately Low and High Carbohydrate Intake on Crossfit Performance. *International Journal of Exercise Science*, Vol 9(3): 460–470.

35. Burke, LM., Ross, ML, Garvican-Lewis, LA, Welvaert, M, Heikura, IA, Forbes, SG, Mirtschin, JG, Cato, LE, Strobel, N, Sharma, AP, & Hawley, JA. (2017). Low carbohydrate, high fat diet impairs exercise economy and negates the performance benefit from intensified training in elite race walkers. *The Journal of Physiology*, Vol 595(9): 2785–2807.

36. Stepto, NK, Carey, AL, Staudacher, HM, Cummings, NiK, Burke, LM, & Hawley, JA. (2002). Effect of short-term fat adaptation on high-intensity. *Medicine & Science in Sports & Exercise*. Vol 34(3): 449–455.

37. Walberg, J, Leidy, M, Sturgill, D, Hinkle, D, Ritchey, S, & Sebolt, D. (1988). Macronutrient Content of a Hypoenergy Diet Affects Nitrogen Retention and Muscle Function in Weight Lifters. *International Journal of Sports Medicine*, 9: 261–6.

38. Horswill CA, Hickner, RC, Scott, JR, Costill, DL, & Gould, D. (1990). Weight loss, dietary carbohydrate modifications, and high intensity, physical performance. *Medicine & Science in Sports & Exercise*, Vol 22(4): 470–476.

39. Helge, JW, Richter, EA, & Kiens, B. (1996). Interaction of training and diet on metabolism and endurance during exercise in man. *The Journal of Physiology*, 492.

40. Cholewa, J, Newmire, D, & Zanchi, N. (2019). Carbohydrate restriction: Friend or foe of resistance-based exercise performance? *Nutrition*, 60, 136–146.

41. Zeevi D, Korem T, Zmora N, Israeli D, Rothschild D, Weinberger A, Ben-Yacov O, Lador D, Avnit-Sagi T, Lotan-Pompan M, Suez J, Mahdi JA, Matot E, Malka G, Kosower N, Rein M, Zilberman-Schapira G, Dohnalová L, Pevsner-Fischer M, Bikovsky R, Halpern Z, Elinav E, Segal E. (2015). Personalized Nutrition by Prediction of Glycemic Responses. Cell, Vol 163(5): 1079–1094.

42. Wang, X, Ouyang, Y, Liu, J, Zhu, M, Zhao, G, Bao, W, & Hu, F. (2014). Fruit and vegetable consumption and mortality from all causes, cardiovascular disease, and cancer: systematic review and dose-response meta-analysis of prospective cohort studies. *The BMJ*, 349: g4490–g4490.

43. Zong, G. Gao, A. Hu, F. & Sun, Q. (2016). Whole Grain Intake and Mortality From All Causes, Cardiovascular Disease, and Cancer. *Circulation*, Vol 133(24): 2370–2380.

44. Hajihashemi, P, & Haghighatdoost, F. (2019) Effects of Whole-Grain Consumption on Selected Biomarkers of Systematic Inflammation: A Systematic Review and Meta-analysis of Randomized Controlled Trials. *Journal of the American College of Nutrition*, Vol 38(3): 275–285.

45. Hajihashemi, P, Azadbakht, L, Hashemipor, M, Kelishadi, R, & Esmaillzadeh, A. (2014), Whole-grain intake favorably affects markers of systemic inflammation in obese children: A randomized controlled crossover clinical trial. *Molecular Nutrition and Food Research*, Vol 58(6): 1301–1308.

46. Katcher, HI, Legro, RS, Kunselman, AR, Gillies, LJ, Demers, LM, Bagshaw, DM, & Kris-Etherton, PM. (2008). The effects of a whole grain–enriched hypocaloric diet on cardiovascular disease risk factors in men and women with metabolic syndrome. *The American Journal of Clinical Nutrition*, Vol 87(1): 79–90.

47. Rippe JM, & Angelopoulos TJ. (2016). Sugars, obesity, and cardiovascular disease: results from recent randomized control trials. *European Journal of Nutrition,* Vol 55(Suppl 2):45–53.

48. Veronese, N, Solmi, M, Caruso, MG, Giannelli, G, Osella, AR, Evangelou, E, Maggi, S, Fontana, L, Stubbs, B, & Tzoulaki, I. (2018). Dietary fiber and health outcomes: an umbrella review of systematic reviews and meta-analyses. *The American Journal of Clinical Nutrition*, Vol 107(3): 436–444.

LEVEL THREE: MICRONUTRIENT AND WATER INTAKE

1. Forrest, K, & Stuhldreher, W. (2011). Prevalence and correlates of vitamin D deficiency in US adults. *Nutrition Research*, Vol 31(1): 48–54.

2. Frank, K, Patel, K, Lopez, G, & Willis, B. (2021). Vitamin D Supplement - Health Benefits, Dosage, Side Effects. *Vitamin D Research Analysis.* Available at https://examine.com/supplements/vitamin-d/. Accessed May 2021.

3. Economos, CD, Bortz, SS, & Nelson, ME. (1993). Nutritional Practices of Elite Athletes. *Sports Medicine,* 16: 381–399.

4. Butchko, Harriett & Stargel, W & Comer, C & Mayhew, Dale & Benninger, Christian & Blackburn, George & de Sonneville, Leo & Geha, Raif & Hertelendy, Zsolt & Koestner, Adalbert & Leon, Arthur & Liepa, George & Mcmartin, Kenneth & Mendenhall, Charles & Munro, Ian & Novotny, Edward & Renwick, Andrew & Schiffman, Susan & Schomer, Donald & Trefz, Friedrich. (2002). Aspartame: Review of Safety. *Regulatory Toxicology and Pharmacology*, Vol 35(2): S1–S93.

5. *Alcohol and Cancer Risk Fact Sheet. (2020)*. Available at https://www.cancer.gov/about-cancer/causes-prevention/risk/alcohol/alcohol-fact-sheet#r1 Accessed April 29, 2020.

6. Toews, I, Lohner, S, Küllenberg de Gaudry, D, Sommer, H, & Meerpohl, J. (2019). Association between intake of non-sugar sweeteners and health outcomes: systematic review and meta-analyses of randomised and non-randomised controlled trials and observational studies. *The BMJ*, 364: k4718.

7. Sathyapalan, T, Thatcher, NJ, Hammersley, R, Rigby, AS, Courts, FL, Pechlivanis, A, Gooderham, NJ, Holmes, E, le Roux, CW, & Atkin, SL. (2015). Aspartame sensitivity? A double blind randomised crossover study. *PloS one*, Vol 10(3): e0116212.

8. Smith-Spangler, Crystal & Brandeau, Margaret & Hunter, Grace & Bavinger, J & Pearson, Maren & Eschbach, Paul & Sundaram, Vandana & Liu, Hau & Schirmer, Patricia & Stave, Christopher & Olkin, Ingram & Bravata, Dena. (2012). Are Organic Foods Safer or Healthier Than Conventional Alternatives? *Annals of Internal Medicine*, Vol 157(5): 348.

9. Cressey, P, Vannoort, R, & Malcolm, C. (2009) Pesticide residues in conventionally grown and organic New Zealand produce. *Food Additives & Contaminants: Part B*, Vol 2(1): 21–26.

10. *Pesticide Residue Monitoring Program Reports and Data. (2020).* Available at https://www.fda.gov/food/pesticides/pesticide-residue-monitoring-program-reports-and-data Accessed April 30, 2020.

11. Searchinger, T, Wirsenius, S, Beringer, T, & Dumas, P. (2018). Assessing the efficiency of changes in land use for mitigating climate change. *Nature*, Vol 564(7735): 249–253.

12. Pellegrino, E, Bedini, S, Nuti, M, Ercoli, L. (2018). Impact of genetically engineered maize on agronomic, environmental and toxicological traits: a meta-analysis of 21 years of field data. *Scientific Reports*, 8: 3113.

13. Klein, A, & Kiat, H. (2014). Detox diets for toxin elimination and weight management: a critical review of the evidence. *Journal of Human Nutrition and Dietetics*, Vol 28(6): 675–686.

14. Thorning, T, Raben, A, Tholstrup, T, Soedamah-Muthu, S, Givens, I, & Astrup, A. (2016). Milk and dairy products: good or bad for human health? An assessment of the totality of scientific evidence. *Food & Nutrition Research*, Vol 60(1): 32527.

15. Shaukat, Aasma & Levitt, Michael & Taylor, Brent & Macdonald, Roderick & Shamliyan, Tatyana & Kane, Robert & Wilt, Timothy. (2010). Systematic Review: Effective Management Strategies for Lactose Intolerance. *Annals of Internal Medicine*, 152: 797–803.

16. Hungin APS, Mitchell CR, Whorwell P, Mulligan C, Cole O, Agréus L, Fracasso P, Lionis C, Mendive J, Philippart de Foy JM, Seifert B, Wensaas KA, Winchester C, de Wit N. (2018). Systematic review: probiotics in the management of lower gastrointestinal symptoms - an updated evidence-based international consensus. *Alimentary Pharmacology & Therapeutics*, Vol 47(8): 1054–1070.

17. Suez J, Zmora N, Zilberman-Schapira G, Mor U, Dori-Bachash M, Bashiardes S, Zur M, Regev-Lehavi D, Ben-Zeev Brik R, Federici S, Horn M, Cohen Y, Moor AE, Zeevi D, Korem T, Kotler E, Harmelin A, Itzkovitz S, Maharshak N, Shibolet O, Pevsner-Fischer M, Shapiro H, Sharon I, Halpern Z, Segal E, Elinav E. (2018). Post-Antibiotic Gut Mucosal Microbiome Reconstitution Is Impaired by Probiotics and Improved by Autologous FMT. *Cell*, Vol 174(6): 1406–1423.e16.

18. Graudal, N, Jürgens, G, Baslund, B, & Alderman, MH. (2014). Compared With Usual Sodium Intake, Low- and Excessive-Sodium Diets Are Associated With Increased Mortality: A Meta-Analysis. *American Journal of Hypertension*, Vol 27(9): 1129–1137.

19. Krikorian, R, Shidler, M, Nash, T, Kalt, W, Vinqvist-Tymchuk, M, Shukitt-Hale, B, & Joseph, J. (2010). Blueberry Supplementation Improves Memory in Older Adults†. *Journal of Agricultural and Food Chemistry*, Vol 58(7): 3996–4000.

20. Morris, M, Wang, Y, Barnes, L, Bennett, D, Dawson-Hughes, B, & Booth, S. (2017). Nutrients and bioactives in green leafy vegetables and cognitive decline. *Neurology*, Vol 90(3): e214–e222.

21. Amen, D, Harris, W, Kidd, P, Meysami, S, & Raji, C. (2017). Quantitative Erythrocyte Omega-3 EPA Plus DHA Levels are

Related to Higher Regional Cerebral Blood Flow on Brain SPECT. *Journal of Alzheimer's Disease: JAD*. Vol 58(4): 1189–1199.

22. Nehlig, A. (2013). The neuroprotective effects of cocoa flavanol and its influence on cognitive performance. *British Journal of Clinical Pharmacology*, Vol 75(3): 716–27.

23. Chang, D, Song, D, Zhang, J, Shang, Y, Ge, Q, & Wang, Z. (2018). Caffeine Caused a Widespread Increase of Resting Brain Entropy. *Scientific Reports*, Vol 8(1): 2700.

24. Porcelli, S, Pugliese, L, Rejc, E, Pavei, G, Bonato, M, Montorsi, M, La Torre, A, Rasica, L, & Marzorati, M. (2016). Effects of a Short-Term High-Nitrate Diet on Exercise Performance. *Nutrients*, Vol 8(9): 534.

25. Gao, X, Zhang, H, Guo, X, Li, K, Li, S, & Li, D. (2019). Effect of Betaine on Reducing Body Fat—A Systematic Review and Meta-Analysis of Randomized Controlled Trials. *Nutrients*, Vol 11(10): 2480.

25a. Trexler, Eric. (2020). Beetroot juice enhances bench press power and strength endurance. *Monthly Applications in Strength Sports, Vol 4, Issue 3. p.* 88-89.

26. Murray, B. (2007) Hydration and Physical Performance. *Journal of the American College of Nutrition*, 26 (5 suppl): 542S-548S.

27. Frank, K, Patel, K, Lopez, G, & Willis, B. (2019). *Green Tea Catechins Research Analysis.* Available at https://examine.com/supplements/green-tea-catechins/ Accessed February 19, 2020.

LEVEL FOUR: NUTRIENT TIMING AND MEAL FREQUENCY

1. Venne, WP, & Westerterp, KR. (1991). Influence of the feeding frequency on nutrient utilization in man: consequences for energy metabolism. *European Journal of Clinical Nutrition*, Vol 45(3): 161–169.

2. Smeets, A, & Westerterp-Plantenga, M. (2008). Acute effects on metabolism and appetite profile of one meal difference in the lower range of meal frequency. *British Journal of Nutrition*, Vol 99(6): 1316–1321.

3. Schübel, R, Nattenmüller, J, Sookthai, D, Nonnenmacher, T, Graf, ME, Riedl, L, Schlett,Cl, von Stackelberg, O, Johnson, T, Nabers, D, Kirsten, R, Kratz, M, Kauczor, H-U, Ulrich, CM, Kaaks, R, & Kühn, T. (2018). Effects of intermittent and continuous calorie restriction on body weight and metabolism over 50 wk: a randomized controlled trial. *The American Journal of Clinical Nutrition*, Vol 108(5): 933–945.

4. Capaldo, B., Gastaldelli, A., Antoniello, S., Auletta, M., Pardo, F., Ciociaro, D., Guida, R., Ferrannini, E., & Saccá, L. (1999). Splanchnic and leg substrate exchange after ingestion of a natural mixed meal in humans. *Diabetes, 48 5*, 958-66.

5. Phillips, SM, & Van Loon, LJC. (2011). Dietary protein for athletes: From requirements to optimum adaptation. *Journal of Sports Sciences*, 29(Suppl 1): S29–S38.

6. Atherton, PJ. (2013). Is There an Optimal Time for Warfighters to Supplement with Protein? *The Journal of Nutrition*, Vol 143(11): 1848S–1851S.

7.   Brown, AW, Bohan Brown, MM, & Allison, DB. (2013). Belief beyond the evidence: using the proposed effect of breakfast on obesity to show 2 practices that distort scientific evidence. *The American Journal of Clinical Nutrition*, Vol 98(5): 1298–1308.

8.   Facer-Childs, E, Middleton, B, Skene, D, & Bagshaw, A. (2019). Resetting the late timing of 'night owls' has a positive impact on mental health and performance. *Sleep Medicine*, 60: 236–247.

9.   Richter, J, Herzog, N, Janka, S, Baumann, T, Kistenmacher, A, & Oltmanns, KM. (2020). Twice as High Diet-Induced Thermogenesis After Breakfast vs Dinner On High-Calorie as Well as Low-Calorie Meals. *The Journal of Clinical Endocrinology & Metabolism*, Vol 105(3): e211–e221.

10. Sensi, S, & Capani, F. (1987). Chronobiological Aspects of Weight Loss in Obesity: Effects of Different Meal Timing Regimens. *Chronobiology International*, Vol 4(2): 251–261.

11. Al-Hourani, H, & Manar, A. (2007). Body composition, nutrient intake and physical activity patterns in young women during Ramadan. *Singapore Medical Journal*. 48: 906–10.

12. Aragon, A, & Schoenfeld, BJ. (2013). Nutrient timing revisited: is there a post-exercise anabolic window? *Journal of the International Society of Sports Nutrition*, Vol 10: 5

13. Schoenfeld, BJ, & Aragon, AA. (2018). How much protein can the body use in a single meal for muscle-building? Implications for daily protein distribution. *Journal of the International Society of Sports Nutrition*, 15: 10.

14. Ayotte, D, Jr, & Corcoran, MP. (2018). Individualized hydration plans improve performance outcomes for collegiate athletes engaging in in-season training. *Journal of the International Society of Sports Nutrition*, Vol 15(1): 27.

15. Ochiană, N, Dobosiş Ş, Apostu, P. (2017). The effect of glucose supplements on exercise capacity in table tennis players. *The 15th ITTF Sports Science Congress Dusseldorf Germany.*

16. Baker, LB, Rollo, I, Stein, KW, & Jeukendrup, AE. (2015). Acute Effects of Carbohydrate Supplementation on Intermittent Sports Performance. *Nutrients*, Vol 7(7): 5733–5763.

17. Bottoms, L, Sinclair, J, Taylor, K, Polman, R, & Fewtrell, D. (2011). The effects of carbohydrate ingestion on the badminton serve after fatiguing exercise. *Journal of Sports Sciences.* 30: 285–293.

18. Murray, B, & Rosenbloom, C. (2018). Fundamentals of glycogen metabolism for coaches and athletes. *Nutrition Reviews*, Vol 76(4): 243–259.

19. Fuchs, C, Gonzalez, J, & Loon, L. (2019). Fructose co-ingestion to increase carbohydrate availability in athletes. *The Journal of Physiology*, Vol 597(14): 3549–3560.

20. Leidy, HJ, Armstrong, CL, Tang, M, Mattes, RD, & Campbell, WW. (2010). The influence of higher protein intake and greater eating frequency on appetite control in overweight and obese men. *Obesity*, Vol 18(9): 1725–1732.

LEVEL FIVE: SUPPLEMENTATION

1. Kondrič, M, Sekulic, D, & Mandic, GF. (2010) Substance Use and Misuse Among Slovenian Table Tennis Players. *Substance Use & Misuse*, Vol 45(4): 543–553.

2. Lanhers, C., Pereira, B., Naughton, G., Trousselard, M., Lesage, F., & Dutheil, F. (2015). Creatine Supplementation and Lower Limb Strength Performance: A Systematic Review and Meta-Analyses. *Sports Medicine, 45*, 1285-1294.

3. Lanhers, C., Pereira, B., Naughton, G., Trousselard, M., Lesage, F., & Dutheil, F. (2016). Creatine Supplementation and Upper Limb Strength Performance: A Systematic Review and Meta-Analysis. *Sports Medicine, 47*, 163-173.

4. Branch, J. (2003). Effect of Creatine Supplementation on Body Composition and Performance: A Meta-analysis. *International Journal of Sport Nutrition and Exercise Metabolism*, Vol 13(2): 198–226.

5. Avgerinos, KI, Spyrou, N, Bougioukas, KI, & Kapogiannis, D. (2018). Effects of creatine supplementation on cognitive function of healthy individuals: A systematic review of randomized controlled trials. *Experimental Gerontology*, 108: 166–173.

6. Grgic, J., Trexler, E., Lazinica, B., & Pedisic, Z. (2018). Effects of caffeine intake on muscle strength and power: a systematic review and meta-analysis. *Journal of the International Society of Sports Nutrition*, 15: 11.

7. Southward, K, Rutherfurd-Markwick, KJ, & Ali, A. (2018). The Effect of Acute Caffeine Ingestion on Endurance Performance: A Systematic Review and Meta–Analysis. *Sports Medicine*, 48: 1913–1928.

8. McLellan, T, Caldwell, J, & Lieberman, H. (2016). A review of caffeine's effects on cognitive, physical and occupational performance. *Neuroscience & Biobehavioral Reviews*, 71: 294–312.

9. Zaknich, D, Dawson, B, Wallman, K, & Henry, G. (2011). Effect of Caffeine on Reactive Agility Time When Fresh and Fatigued. *Medicine and Science in Sports and Exercise.* 43: 1523–1530.

10. Adan, A, & Serra-Grabulosa, J. (2010). Effects of caffeine and glucose, alone and combined, on cognitive performance. *Human Psychopharmacology: Clinical and Experimental*, Vol 25(4): 310–317.

11. Grosso, G, Godoś, J, Galvano, F, & Giovannucci, E. (2017). Coffee, Caffeine, and Health Outcomes: An Umbrella Review. *Annual Review of Nutrition.* 37: 131–156.

12. Domínguez, R, Cuenca, E, Maté-Muñoz, J, García-Fernández, P, Serra-Paya, N, & Estevan, M., Herreros, P.V., & Garnacho-Castano, M. 2017). Effects of Beetroot Juice Supplementation on Cardiorespiratory Endurance in Athletes. A Systematic Review. *Nutrients*, Vol 9(1): 43.

13. Williams TD, Martin MP, Mintz JA, Rogers RR, & Ballmann CG. (2020). Effect of Acute Beetroot Juice Supplementation on

Bench Press Power, Velocity, and Repetition Volume. *Journal of Strength and Conditioning Research*. Vol 34(4): 924–928.

14. Hobson, RM, Saunders, B, Ball, G, Harris, RC, & Sale, C. (2012). Effects of β-alanine supplementation on exercise performance: a meta-analysis. *Amino Acids,* Vol 43(1): 25–37.

14a. Rezende, N., Swinton, P., de Oliveira, L., da Silva, R., da Eira Silva, V., & Nemezio, K., Yamaguchi, G., Guilherme Giannini, A., Gualano, B., Saunders, B., Dolan, E. (2020). The Muscle Carnosine Response to Beta-Alanine Supplementation: A Systematic Review With Bayesian Individual and Aggregate Data E-Max Model and Meta-Analysis. *Frontiers In Physiology, 11.* doi: 10.3389/fphys.2020.00913

15. Trexler, E., Persky, A., Ryan, E.D., Schwartz, T., Stoner, L., & Smith-Ryan, A. (2019). Acute Effects of Citrulline Supplementation on High-Intensity Strength and Power Performance: A Systematic Review and Meta-Analysis. *Sports Medicine, 49,* 707-718.

16. Leung, A, LaMar, A, He, X, Braverman, L, & Pearce, E. (2011). Iodine Status and Thyroid Function of Boston-Area Vegetarians and Vegans. *The Journal of Clinical Endocrinology and Metabolism,* Vol 96(8): E1303–E1307.

17. Mednick, SC, Cai, DJ, Kanady, J, & Drummond, SP. (2008). Comparing the benefits of caffeine, naps and placebo on verbal, motor and perceptual memory. *Behavioural Brain Research*, Vol 193(1): 79–86.

18. Le Mansec, Y, Pageaux, B, Nordez, A, Dorel, S, & Jubeau, M. (2017). Mental fatigue alters the speed and the accuracy of

the ball in table tennis. *Journal of Sports Sciences*. Vol 36(23): 2751–2759.

19. Owen, GN, Parnell, H, De Bruin, EA, & Rycroft, JA. (2008). The combined effects of L-theanine and caffeine on cognitive performance and mood. *Nutritional Neuroscience*, Vol 11(4): 193–198.

20. Giesbrecht, T, Rycroft, JA, Rowson, MJ, & De Bruin, EA. (2010). The combination of L-theanine and caffeine improves cognitive performance and increases subjective alertness. *Nutritional Neuroscience*, Vol 13(6): 283–290.

21. Banderet, L, & Lieberman, H. (1989). Treatment with tyrosine, a neurotransmitter precursor, reduces environmental stress in humans. *Brain Research Bulletin*, Vol 22(4): 759–762.

22. Shurtleff, D, Thomas, J, Schrot, J, Kowalski, K, & Harford, R. (1994). Tyrosine reverses a cold-induced working memory deficit in humans. *Pharmacology Biochemistry and Behavior*, Vol 47(4): 935–941.

23. Jongkees, B, Hommel, B, Kühn, S, & Colzato, L. (2015). Effect of tyrosine supplementation on clinical and healthy populations under stress or cognitive demands—A review. *Journal of Psychiatric Research*, 70: 50–57.

24. Zaragoza, J., Tinsley, G., Urbina, S.L., Villa, K., Santos, E.N., Juaneza, A., Tinnin, M., Davidson, C., Mitmesser, S., Zhang, Z., & Taylor, L. (2019). Effects of acute caffeine, theanine and tyrosine supplementation on mental and physical performance in

athletes. *Journal of the International Society of Sports Nutrition,* 16: 56.

24a. Mündel, T. (2017). Nicotine: Sporting Friend or Foe? A Review of Athlete Use, Performance Consequences and Other Considerations. *Sports medicine (Auckland, N.Z.),* *47*(12), 2497–2506.

25. Heishman, SJ, Kleykamp, BA, & Singleton, EG. (2010). Meta-analysis of the acute effects of nicotine and smoking on human performance. *Psychopharmacology,* Vol 210(4): 453–469.

26. Lee, PN, & Fariss, MW. (2017). A systematic review of possible serious adverse health effects of nicotine replacement therapy. *Archives of Toxicology,* Vol 91(4): 1565–1594.

27. Frank, K, Patel, K, Lopez, G, & Willis, B. (2019). *Nicotine Research Analysis.,* Available at https://examine.com/supplements/nicotine/ Accessed February 19, 2020.

28. Morgan, K, Johnson, AJ, & Miles, C. (2014). Chewing gum moderates the vigilance decrement. *British Journal of Psychology,* 105: 214–225.

29. Johnson, Aj, Muneem, M, & Miles, C. (2013). Chewing gum benefits sustained attention in the absence of task degradation. *Nutritional Neuroscience,* Vol 16(4): 153–159.

30. Hirano, Y, & Onozuka, M. (2015). Chewing and attention: a positive effect on sustained attention. *BioMed Research International,* 367026.

PUTTING IT ALL TOGETHER: PRACTICAL IMPLEMENTATION, DIETARY HEURISTICS, AND SAMPLE MEAL PLANS

1. Westenhoefer, J., von Falck, B., Stellfeldt, A., Fintelmann, S. (2004). Behavioural correlates of successful weight reduction over 3 y. Results from the Lean Habits Study. *Int J Obes* 28, 334–335.

2. Leidy, H, Tang, M, Armstrong, C, Martin, C, & Campbell, W. (2010). The Effects of Consuming Frequent, Higher Protein Meals on Appetite and Satiety During Weight Loss in Overweight/Obese Men. *Obesity*, Vol 19(4): 818–824.

3. Mytton, O, Nnoaham, K, Eyles, H, Scarborough, P, & Mhurchu, CN. (2014). Systematic review and meta-analysis of the effect of increased vegetable and fruit consumption on body weight and energy intake. *BMC Public Health*, 14: 886.

4. Daniels, M, & Popkin, B. (2010). Impact of water intake on energy intake and weight status: a systematic review. *Nutrition Reviews*, Vol 68(9): 505–521.

PHYSICAL TRAINING: MYTHS, MISTAKES, AND GENERAL GUIDELINES

1. Davies, T, Orr, R, Halaki, M, Hacket, D. (2016). Effect of Training Leading to Repetition Failure on Muscular Strength: A Systematic Review and Meta-Analysis. *Sports Medicine*, 46, 487–502.

2. Santanielo, N, Nóbrega, S, Scarpelli, M, Alvarez, I, Otoboni, G, & Pintanel, L., Libardi, C. (2020). Effect of resistance training to muscle failure vs non-failure on strength, hypertrophy and

muscle architecture in trained individuals. *Biology of Sport*, Vol 37(4): 333–341.

3. Carroll, KM, Bazyler, CD, Bernards, JR, Taber, CB, Stuart, CA, DeWeese, BH, Sato, K, & Stone, MH. (2019). Skeletal Muscle Fiber Adaptations Following Resistance Training Using Repetition Maximums or Relative Intensity. *Sports (Basel)*. Vol 11(7): 169.

4. Lacerda, LT, Marra-Lopes, RO, Diniz, RCR, Lima, FV, Rodrigues, SA, Martins-Costa, HC, Bemben, MG, & Chagas, MH. (2020). Is Performing Repetitions to Failure Less Important Than Volume for Muscle Hypertrophy and Strength? *Journal of Strength and Conditioning Research*. Vol 34(5): 1237–1248.

5. Sousa CA. (2018). *Assessment of Accuracy of Intra-set Rating of Perceived Exertion in the Squat, Bench Press, and Deadlift*. (Doctoral dissertation, Florida Atlantic University). August 2018.

6. Nuckols, G. (2018). *Training Frequency for Strength Development: What the Data Say. Stronger by Science*. Available at https://www.strongerbyscience.com/training-frequency/ Accessed February 21, 2020.

7. Nuckols, G. (2020). *Training Frequency for Muscle Growth: What the Data Say. Stronger by Science*. Available at https://www.strongerbyscience.com/frequency-muscle/ Accessed February 21, 2020.

8. Henselmans, M, & Schoenfeld, BJ. (2014). The Effect of Inter-Set Rest Intervals on Resistance Exercise-Induced Muscle Hypertrophy. *Sports Medicine*, 44: 1635–1643.

9. Michaelson, J , Brilla, L, Suprak, D, Mclaughlin, W, & Dahlquist, D. (2019). Effects of Two Different Recovery Postures during High-Intensity Interval Training. *Translational Journal of the ACSM*, Vol 4(4): 23–27.

10. González-Badillo, JJ, Rodríguez-Rosell, D, Sánchez-Medina, L, Gorostiaga, EM, & Pareja-Blanco, F. (2014). Maximal intended velocity training induces greater gains in bench press performance than deliberately slower half-velocity training, *European Journal of Sport Science*, Vol 1498): 772–781.

11. Ralston, GW, Kilgore, L, Wyatt, FB, & Baker, JS. (2017). The Effect of Weekly Set Volume on Strength Gain: A Meta-Analysis. *Sports Medicine*, Vol 47(12): 2585–2601.

12. Androulakis-Korakakis P, Fisher JP, Steele J. (2020). The Minimum Effective Training Dose Required to Increase 1RM Strength in Resistance-Trained Men: A Systematic Review and Meta-Analysis. *Sports Medicine*, Vol 50(4): 751–765.

13. Schoenfeld BJ, Peterson MD, Ogborn D, Contreras B, & Sonmez GT. (2015). Effects of Low- vs. High-Load Resistance Training on Muscle Strength and Hypertrophy in Well-Trained Men. *Journal of Strength and Conditioning Research*, Vol 29(10): 2954–2963.

14. Schoenfeld BJ, Ratamess NA, Peterson MD, Contreras B, Sonmez GT, & Alvar BA. (2014). Effects of different volume-equated resistance training loading strategies on muscular adaptations in well-trained men. *Journal of Strength and Conditioning Research*. Vol 28(10): 2909–2918.

15. Schoenfeld BJ, Ogborn D, & Krieger JW. (2017). Dose-response relationship between weekly resistance training volume and increases in muscle mass: A systematic review and meta-analysis. *Journal of Sports Science*. Vol 35(11): 1073–1082.

16. Schoenfeld BJ, & Grgic J. (2020). Effects of range of motion on muscle development during resistance training interventions: A systematic review. *SAGE Open Medicine*. 8: 2050312120901559.

17. Medeiros, D, & Lima, C. (2017). Influence of chronic stretching on muscle performance: Systematic review. *Human Movement Science*, 54: 220–229.

18. Serpell, B, Young, W, & Ford, M. (2011). Are the Perceptual and Decision-Making Components of Agility Trainable? A Preliminary Investigation. *Journal of Strength and Conditioning Research*, Vol 25(5): 1240–1248.

19. Zouhal, Hassane & Abderrahman, Abderraouf & Dupont, Gregory & Truptin, Pablo & Bris, Régis & Postec, Erwan & Zouita, s & Brughelli, Matt & Granacher, Urs & Bideau, Benoit. (2019). Effects of Neuromuscular Training on Agility Performance in Elite Soccer Players. *Frontiers in Physiology*: 10.

20. Lloyd, R, Read, P, Oliver, J., Meyers, R, Nimphius, S, & Jeffreys, I. (2013). Considerations for the Development of Agility During Childhood and Adolescence. *Strength and Conditioning Journal*. 35: 2–11.

21. Keogh, JWL, & Winwood, PW. (2017). The Epidemiology of Injuries Across the Weight-Training Sports. *Sports Medicine*, 47: 479–501.

22. Sofiene, K, Hermassi, S, Safa, K, & Passelergue, P. (2016). Effect of an Integrated Resistance Program Based Weightlifting Exercises on Improving Physical Performance of Young Table Elite's Tennis Players. *Advances in Physical Education*. 06: 364–377.

23. Paz-Franco, A, Rey, E, & Barcala-Furelos, R. (2017). Effects of 3 Different Resistance Training Frequencies on Jump, Sprint, and Repeated Sprint Ability Performances in Professional Futsal Players. *Journal of Strength and Conditioning Research*, Vol 31(12): 3343–3350.

24. Draganidis, D, Chatzinikolaou, A, Jamurtas, AZ, Barbero, JC, Tsoukas, D, Spyridon, A, Theodorou, Margonis, K, Michailidis, Y, Avloniti, A, Theodorou, A, Kambas, A, & Fatouros, I. (2013) The time-frame of acute resistance exercise effects on football skill performance: The impact of exercise intensity. *Journal of Sports Sciences*, Vol 31(7): 714–722.

25. Barber-Westin, S, Hermeto, A, & Noyes, F. (2010). A Six-Week Neuromuscular Training Program for Competitive Junior Tennis Players. *Journal of Strength and Conditioning Research*, Vol 24(9): 2372–2382.

26. Kondrič, M, Zagatto, AM, & Sekulić, D. (2013). The physiological demands of table tennis: a review. *Journal of Sports Science & Medicine*, Vol 12(3): 362–370.

27. Damas, F, Phillips, SM, Libardi, CA, Vechin, FC, Lixandrão, ME, Jannig, PR, Costa, LA, Bacurau, AV, Snijders, T, Parise, G, Tricoli, V, Roschel, H, & Ugrinowitsch, C. (2016). Resistance training-induced changes in integrated myofibrillar protein synthesis are

related to hypertrophy only after attenuation of muscle damage. *The Journal of Physiology*, Vol 594(18): 5209–5222.

28. Androulakis-Korakakis P, Fisher JP, & Steele J. (2020). The Minimum Effective Training Dose Required to Increase 1RM Strength in Resistance-Trained Men: A Systematic Review and Meta-Analysis. *Sports Medicine*, Vol 50(4): 751–765.

29. Chanavirut, R, Udompanich, N, Udom, P, Yonglitthipagon, P, Donpunha, W, Nakmareong, S, & Yamauchi, J. (2017). The effects of strengthening exercises for wrist flexors and extensors on muscle strength and counter-stroke performance in amateur table tennis players. *Journal of Bodywork and Movement Therapies*, Vol 21(4): 1033–1036.

30. Ryu Seung Min, (December, 19 2019). [박PD]. *[Eng] Most important in table tennis.* [Online video]. Available at https://youtu.be/k4_mWWJkfAU. Accessed May 2021.

31. Southard, D, & Groomer, L. (2003). Warm-up with Baseball Bats of Varying Moments of Inertia: Effect on Bat Velocity and Swing Pattern, *Research Quarterly for Exercise and Sport*, Vol 74(3): 270–276.

32. Otsuji, Tamiki & Abe, Masafu & Kinoshita, Hiroshita. (2002). After-Effects of Using a Weighted Bat on Subsequent Swing Velocity and Batters' Perceptions of Swing Velocity and Heaviness. *Perceptual and motor skills:* 94. 119-26.

33. Bompa, TO. (1999). *Periodization Training for Sports.* Champaign, IL: Human Kinetics.

34. Iino, Y & Kojima, T. (2009). Kinematics of table tennis topspin forehands: effects of performance level and ball spin. *Journal of Sports Sciences*, Vol 27(12): 1311–1321

35. Szymanski, D, & Szymanski, J, Bradford, T, Schade, R, & Pascoe, D. (2007). Effect of Twelve Weeks of Medicine Ball Training on High School Baseball Players. *Journal of Strength and Conditioning Research, Vol* 21(3): 894–901.

36. Jones, BH, & Knapik, JJ. (1999). Physical Training and Exercise-Related Injuries. *Sports Medicine*, 27, 111–125.

37. Santos, E., Rhea, M., Simão, R., Dias, I., Salles, B.F., Novaes, J., Leite, T., Blair, J., & Bunker, D. (2010). Influence of Moderately Intense Strength Training on Flexibility in Sedentary Young Women. *Journal of Strength and Conditioning Research, 24,* 3144-3149.

HOLISTIC PERIODIZATION MODEL FOR TABLE TENNIS: AN ANNUAL PLAN

1. Kondrič, M, Zagatto, AM, & Sekulić, D. (2013). The physiological demands of table tennis: a review. *Journal of Sports Science & Medicine*, Vol 12(3): 362–370.

2. Katsikadelis, Michail & Theophilos, Pilianidis & Mantzouranis, Nikolaos & Fatouros, Ioannis & Aggeloussis, Nikolaos. (2014). Heart rate variability of young table tennis players with the use of the Multiball training. *Journal Biology of Exercise*, 10. 25-35.

3. Zagatto, A, Leite, J, Papoti, M, & Beneke, R. (2016). Energetics of Table Tennis and Table Tennis–Specific Exercise Testing. *International Journal of Sports Physiology and Performance*, Vol 11(8): 1012–1017.

4. Tomiya, S, Kikuchi, N, & Nakazato, K. (2017). Moderate Intensity Cycling Exercise after Upper Extremity Resistance Training Interferes Response to Muscle Hypertrophy but Not Strength Gains. *Journal of Sports Science & Medicine*, Vol 16(3): 391–395.

5. Sabag, A, Najafi, A, Michael, S, Esgin, T, Halaki, M, & Hackett, D. (2018). The compatibility of concurrent high intensity interval training and resistance training for muscular strength and hypertrophy: a systematic review and meta-analysis, *Journal of Sports Sciences*, Vol 36(21): 2472–2483.

6. Robineau, J, Babault, N, Piscione, J, Lacome, M, & Bigard, A. (2016). Specific Training Effects of Concurrent Aerobic and Strength Exercises Depend on Recovery Duration. *Journal of Strength and Conditioning Research*, Vol 30(3): 672–683.

7. Jiménez-Reyes, P, Samozino, P, Brughelli, M, & Morin, J. (2017). Effectiveness of an Individualized Training Based on Force-Velocity Profiling during Jumping. *Frontiers in Physiology*, 7:677.

8. Xin, X, (February, 8 2012). *A day with World No. 1 - STIGA star Xu Xin*, (STIGA Table Tennis). [Video File]. Available at https://youtu.be/k5P25njgcYA Accessed May 2021.

9. Maia, M, Willardson, J, Paz, G, & Miranda, H. (2014). Effects of Different Rest Intervals Between Antagonist Paired Sets

on Repetition Performance and Muscle Activation. *Journal of Strength and Conditioning Research*, Vol 28(9): 2529–2535.

10. Tsoukos, A, Veligekas, P, Brown, L, Terzis, G, & Bogdanis, G. (2018). Delayed Effects of a Low-Volume, Power-Type Resistance Exercise Session on Explosive Performance. *Journal of Strength and Conditioning Research*, Vol 32(3):643–650.

11. Joyce, D, & Lewindon, D. (2014). *High-Performance Training for Sports*. Champaign, IL: Human Kinetics.

12. Rønnestad, B, Nymark, B, & Raastad, T. (2011). Effects of In-Season Strength Maintenance Training Frequency in Professional Soccer Players. *Journal of Strength and Conditioning Research*, Vol 25(10): 2653–2660.

GAME DAY PROTOCOLS: ACHIEVING PEAK PERFORMANCE WHEN IT COUNTS

1. Zavorsky, GS, & Newton, WL. (2018). Effects of sexual activity on several measures of physical performance in young adult males. *The Journal of Sports Medicine and Physical Fitness*, Vol 59(7): 1102–1109.

2. Ballmann, C, McCullum, M, Rogers, R, Marshall, M, & Williams, T. (2018). Effects of Preferred vs. Nonpreferred Music on Resistance Exercise Performance. *Journal of Strength and Conditioning Research*, Online Ahead of Print.

3. Karow, M. C., Rogers, R. R., Pederson, J. A., Williams, T. D., Marshall, M. R., & Ballmann, C. G. (2020). Effects of Preferred

and Nonpreferred Warm-Up Music on Exercise Performance. Perceptual and Motor Skills, 127(5), 912–924.

4. Ruud JR, Hartigh, D, & Gernigon, C. (2018). Time-out! How psychological momentum builds up and breaks down in table tennis. *Journal of Sports Sciences*, Vol 36(23): 2732–2737.

5. Jenwen, MJ. (May, 4 2015). *體育人間/ 國家隊的秘密 [Sports World: Secrets of the National Team] 2015.05.04 (低清版) [Low definition version]*. [Video File]. Available at https://youtu.be/oeJsyKJtQAk Accessed May 2021.

6. Schwartz, J, & Simon, R. (2015). Sleep extension improves serving accuracy: A study with college varsity tennis players. *Physiology & Behavior*, 151: 541–544.

7. Hsouna, H, Boukhris, O, Abdessalem, R, Trabelsi, K, Ammar, A, Shephard, R, & Chtourou, H. (2019). Effect of different nap opportunity durations on short-term maximal performance, attention, feelings, muscle soreness, fatigue, stress and sleep. *Physiology & Behavior*, 211: 112673.

8. Gröpel, P, & Mesagno, C. (2019). Choking interventions in sports: A systematic review, *International Review of Sport and Exercise Psychology*, Vol 12(1): 176–201.

9. Desai, T, & Bottoms, L. (2017). Neck Cooling Improves Table Tennis Performance amongst Young National Level Players. *Sports*, Vol 5(1): 19.

10. Douzi, W, Dugué, B, Vinches, L, Al Sayed, C, Hallé, S, Bosquet, L, & Dupuy, O. (2019). Cooling during exercise enhances

performances, but the cooled body areas matter: A systematic review with meta-analyses. *Scandinavian Journal of Medicine & Science in Sports*, Vol 29(11): 1660–1676.

11. Wiewelhove, T, Döweling, A, Schneider, C, Hottenrott, L, Meyer, T, & Kellmann, M, Pfeiffer, M, & Ferrauti, A. (2019). A Meta-Analysis of the Effects of Foam Rolling on Performance and Recovery. *Frontiers in Physiology*, 10:376.

ABOUT THE AUTHOR

Kevin Finn is a strength and conditioning specialist, a certified speed and agility coach, and the owner and creator of Peak Performance Table Tennis. As a sports performance consultant with a master's degree in education, he specializes in breaking down complex information and arming people with the  knowledge and tools necessary to transform their physiques and take their performance to the next level.

Kevin's love for table tennis began in high school and never left. As a player, he specializes in playing defensively, losing frequently, and spending inordinate amounts of time researching and tweaking his setup. He can be found frequenting the online table tennis forums under the moniker, Joo Se Kev.

CREDITS

Cover design: Hannah Park

Interior design: Anja Elsen

Layout: DiTech Publishing Services, www.ditechpubs.com

Cover photo: picture alliance/dpa | Swen Pförtner

Cover illustration: © AdobeStock

Interior graphics: © AdobeStock

Interior figures: Courtesy of Kevin Finn, unless otherwise noted

Managing editor: Elizabeth Evans

Copyeditor: Sarah Tomblin, www.sarahtomblinediting.com